The Future of Chinese Capitalism: Choices and Chances

D1256737

The Future of Chinese Capitalism: Choices and Chances

Gordon Redding and Michael A. Witt

OXFORD
UNIVERSITY PRESS

OXFORD
UNIVERSITY PRESS

Great Clarendon Street, Oxford OX2 6DP

Oxford University Press is a department of the University of Oxford.
It furthers the University's objective of excellence in research, scholarship,
and education by publishing worldwide in

Oxford New York

Auckland Cape Town Dar es Salaam Hong Kong Karachi
Kuala Lumpur Madrid Melbourne Mexico City Nairobi
New Delhi Shanghai Taipei Toronto

With offices in

Argentina Austria Brazil Chile Czech Republic France Greece
Guatemala Hungary Italy Japan Poland Portugal Singapore
South Korea Switzerland Thailand Turkey Ukraine Vietnam

Oxford is a registered trademark of Oxford University Press
in the UK and in certain other countries

Published in the United States
by Oxford University Press Inc., New York

© Gordon Redding and Michael A. Witt, 2007

The moral rights of the authors have been asserted
Database right Oxford University Press (maker)

First published 2007
First published in paperback 2010

All rights reserved. No part of this publication may be reproduced,
stored in a retrieval system, or transmitted, in any form or by any means,
without the prior permission in writing of Oxford University Press,
or as expressly permitted by law, or under terms agreed with the appropriate
reprographics rights organization. Enquiries concerning reproduction
outside the scope of the above should be sent to the Rights Department,
Oxford University Press, at the address above

You must not circulate this book in any other binding or cover
and you must impose the same condition on any acquirer

British Library Cataloguing in Publication Data

Data available

Library of Congress Cataloging in Publication Data

Redding, S. G.
   The future of Chinese capitalism / Gordon Redding and Michael A. Witt.
      p.   cm.
   Includes bibliographical references and index.
   ISBN 978-0-19-921813-4
   1. Capitalism–China.   2. China–Economic policy.   I. Witt, Michael A.
II. Title.
   HC427.95.R44   2007
   330.12'20951–dc22   2007028208

Typeset by SPI Publisher Services, Pondicherry, India
Printed in Great Britain
on acid-free paper by
Biddles Ltd., King's Lynn, Norfolk

ISBN 978-0-19-921813-4
      978-0-19-957587-9 (Pbk.)

Contents

Preface and Acknowledgments   vi
List of Tables and Figures   viii

1. Another Miracle?   1
2. Describing Business Systems   13
3. Escape from History?   36
4. The Legacies of History   51
5. The Regional Ethnic Chinese in Business   61
6. The State-owned Enterprises   81
7. From Collectives to Local Corporates   103
8. The Private Sector   123
9. Introduction to the Comparative Chapters   147
10. United States   153
11. Japan   168
12. Germany   182
13. South Korea   196
14. The Future of Chinese Capitalism   210

Appendix   235
Bibliography   241
Index   255

Preface and Acknowledgments

Our objective in this book is to attempt an answer to the question of what kind of economic system—and more specifically, what kind of capitalism—is likely to emerge in the People's Republic of China. Capitalism comes in different varieties, historically grown and shaped by societal forces, and China's will be no exception in this regard. Along with this variety comes specialization in certain types of industries, as evident in varying patterns of comparative advantage across the advanced industrialized nations. What comparative advantages will China develop as its economy grows and matures? The answer will emerge only over time, but its implications will be profound—not only for business inside and outside China, but also for policy-makers as well as scholars in fields such as international business, strategy, political science, sociology, and economics.

We consequently decided to hazard an informed guess—well aware that making predictions is a very difficult thing indeed. In doing so, we draw on knowledge acquired during the more than forty-five years we have, taken together, been following developments in China and East Asia, twenty-four of which living in Hong Kong, five in Singapore, and more than two on the Mainland. Our general approach—that of 'comparative business systems', an emerging field of research also known as 'varieties of capitalism' or 'coevolution'—is inspired by friends and mentors at a number of places, including Peter Hall at Harvard, Arie Y. Lewin at the Fuqua School at Duke, and Richard Whitley at Manchester.

The style of this book may strike our academic readership as unusual. While this is in essence an academic book, aimed to make a contribution to our understanding of the likely evolution of the Chinese business system, we have endeavored to keep the book as accessible as possible to a wider audience, including business people and policy-makers with an interest in China. We have sought to avoid academic jargon to the extent possible, and we apologize in advance if there remain some sections requiring hard thinking. In the interest of focus and legibility, we have also deviated from the convention of citing a large number of sources in the text or in extensive footnotes that can take up much of the page. We keep footnotes intentionally sparse, and the text mostly uninterrupted by citations. Instead, we provide at the end of each chapter a set of main references appropriate for most readers. For specialists with more detailed interest, we include a fuller list of pertinent references at the end of the book.

Like most books, this work owes its existence not only to us, but also to the generous help and contributions extended to us by a number of individuals and organizations. Conversations over time with many people have helped to shape our arguments, and in particular we would like to express our gratitude to Regina Abrami, Bob Baylis, Peter Berger, Michael Bond, Max Boisot, Derong Chen, Philip Chen, Stan Cheung, John Child, Peter Cundill, Ken DeWoskin, Clinton Dines, Doug Guthrie, Yasheng Huang, Barbara Krug, Raymond Lum, Roderick MacFarquhar, Marshall Meyer, Dwight Perkins, Elizabeth Perry, Peter Redding, Victor Shih, Edward Steinfeld, Lily Tsai, Anne Tsui, Wang Zhong Ming, and Richard Whitley. Emilio Manso-Salinas and Ming Zeng conducted a number of interviews with senior executives for us in China and Hong Kong, and their help is acknowledged with much gratitude. Likewise, we would like to thank Ted Chan and Cheong Kheong Tan for their invaluable research assistance. Special thanks are due to Nathalie Gonord for technical help in preparing diagrams and for other support.

We are also very grateful for the organizational support we have received in preparing the manuscript for this book. Profound thanks go especially to the Lee Foundation of Singapore, which generously provided funding of the senior executive interviews undertaken for this project. We are also grateful for support from Erasmus University, Harvard University, the University of Hong Kong, Xiamen University, and Zhejiang University, but particularly we have been supported by INSEAD and the INSEAD Euro-Asia and Comparative Research Centre. Gordon Redding further expresses his thanks to The International Forum for over ten years of joint China explorations, and specifically the exploratory zeal of Michael Alexander and Nan Doyal. The stimulus provided in the two China workshops of the INSEAD/Wharton Alliance was most valuable. We are most grateful for all this help, but we acknowledge our own responsibility for the final product.

Last, but not least, we would like to thank our families. This project would not have been possible without their patient support.

Fontainebleau, April 11, 2007
Gordon Redding
Michael A. Witt

List of Tables and Figures

Tables

5.1. Ethnically Chinese-owned 'Dragon Multinationals' from the
UNCTAD list of top 50 MNEs from developing countries   72

Figures

2.1. The elements of a business system   20

2.2. Development ideals, institutions, and organizational responses   27

6.1. The Chinese state-owned enterprise sector as a complex adaptive
system   85

7.1. Trends in the value of production per worker by enterprise type 106

7.2. Changes in types of organization by ownership in the Chinese
economy   107

7.3. The Chinese local corporate sector seen as a complex adaptive system   109

8.1. The private sector of the Chinese economy seen as a complex
adaptive system   126

8.2. Mainland Chinese comparative advantage by industries, 2003   144

10.1. Key aspects of the US business system   154

10.2. US comparative advantage by industries, 2003   163

11.1. Key aspects of the Japanese business system   169

11.2. Japanese comparative advantage by industries, 2003   178

12.1. Key aspects of the German business system   183

12.2. German comparative advantage by industries, 2003   192

13.1. Key aspects of the South Korean business system   197

13.2. South Korean comparative advantage by industries, 2003 205

1

Another Miracle?

In the last half-century we have witnessed a historically large share of miracles in the field of economic progress. From the wreckage of war there emerged the German miracle in the 1950s and 1960s. Already under way from the 1950s onward, the Japanese miracle became the focus of public attention from the mid-1970s through the 1980s—the period of Western bewitchment by 'Japanese management'. In close pursuit of Japan as the lead 'flying goose' were the East Asian 'dragons' with their own miracles, the Korean of which fell apart in 1997 and has now been reconstituted. It might be argued that the 1990s for the United States were close to miraculous in the creation of wealth, seemingly stimulated by the nebulous and still little understood economic logics of the information technology revolution. A perspective on that is visible in the fact that US GDP has now reached twenty times the level of Russia.

Now we have indications of an economic miracle in China. A cynic would conclude that we may need to be quick to catch this one. A more sober analyst might ponder its size and its evolution and—given the amount of slack to be taken up there—its potential longevity, perhaps reaching an optimistic appraisal. Whatever the viewpoint, any appraisal of the 'China miracle' needs to be informed. It is necessary to understand the surroundings of the complex question: How will China modernize? This book attempts to contribute to such understanding.

China has in the past century been through three massive transformations, with chaotic intervening periods between the first, second, and third. The first was the 1911 overthrow of the Manchu dynasty and is associated with Sun Yat-sen. This led to decades of civil war and was disturbed deeply by World War II. The second was the Communist revolution associated with Mao Zedong, and normally dated from 1949. It led to the world's largest collectivized state, but also to the inanities of the Great Leap Forward, and the insanities of the Cultural Revolution. The third transformation, less seemingly epoch-making in its pronouncement, but perhaps even more of a revolution in practice than the two others, is associated with Deng Xiaoping. It began in 1978, and its progress was marked by a series of brave statements: 'Poverty is not socialism'; 'To be rich is glorious'; 'It does not matter whether the cat is black or white, so long as it catches mice'; 'We will cross the river by groping for stones'. Deng's radical break with dogma was a commonsense acknowledgment of core human instincts—the ownership of property, self-responsibility, and competing for status—and its subsequent momentum has only accelerated. China's vibrant private sector now accounts for about two-thirds of the economy, and is set to continue advancing its domain, leading the charge of Chinese industry into world markets. The scale of this third transformation is breathtaking.

And yet, in those world markets, few consumers could identify a Chinese brand of anything. The labels say 'Made in China', in small lettering, on cameras, toys, electrical goods, clothing, underwear, computers, etc.; the shelves of Wal-Mart, Macy's, Selfridges, Karstadt, and Galeries Lafayettes are packed with goods from China bearing supposedly reassuring Italian or French names, or global brands like Canon and Hewlett Packard. Complex machines, such as automobiles or computers, are full of electric motors, parts of carburetors, memory chips, disc readers, of Chinese origin, not acknowledged in the Japanese, German, or US brand names. This revolution, this trend to become the workshop of the world, is unusual for its unobtrusiveness. Such power needs to be understood, and so too its implications for industry, especially in manufacturing where it is most potent, and where World Trade Organization (WTO) stimulus will see it grow.

The Chinese private-sector revolution, especially as it has picked up speed since the 1990s, is also introducing a new feature on the demand side. A huge new market is growing as the Chinese people, having 'stood up' in 1949, now turn their attention to *catching up* on the thirty lost years which that form of standing up cost them. There is a deep and powerful urge to make up for lost time, to consume, to compete, to achieve, and to find security from the turbulence they have seen as inevitably their lot. For thirty years they acted out the roles demanded of them. Now they are choosing to behave according to their own instincts. One of the deepest Chinese instincts is to engage in business and to do it independently. This is now in full flow.

In longer-term historical perspective, China has for centuries been attempting to deal with the shifting currents of national success and failure, looking backward to the time between a thousand and five hundred years ago, when it could justifiably claim to be the world's greatest civilization. This was an era during which Chinese mastery of the most advanced technologies of the time provided them with a lofty independence, and a clear and justified sense of superiority to other nations. This was Marco Polo's land of wonders. They could put a million-strong army in the field and provide it with explosive weapons at a time when England would wage war with 20,000 soldiers and longbows. They had the printing of books and widespread reading, when in Europe a truly rich individual might possess half a dozen handwritten volumes. They were so advanced in navigation and the calculation of both latitude and longitude that they seem to have made voyages of world discovery seventy years before Columbus and Vasco da Gama, and three centuries before John Harrison's chronometer would give the West the handling of longitude. Zheng He's oceangoing ships of the fifteenth century included more than sixty that were 385- to 440-feet long,[1] when Columbus's flagship was 70 feet.

This dominance would be challenged. Another miracle, that of Europe's bursting out from its supercharged space, between the fifteenth and nineteenth centuries, driven by—among other things—the mastery of science on the basis of rational enquiry, the political Enlightenment, and the connecting of technical invention to commerce, would succeed in moving China aside. China is too large ever to have been irrelevant but, by the nineteenth century, it was left as a backwater, in any case seeking isolation, protecting itself from invasion, but above all else remaining under the tight control of a central government and thus premodern.

The current agenda in China, in both economics and politics, is the entry of the world's largest society to the modern world for the first time. The essential difficulty, in that context, is the dismantling of central power and its replacement with other forms of stable order. Such a transformation, and on such a scale, is a challenge of formidable dimensions. There lurks always the possibility that it may not succeed.

Being modern is in essence having a society in which the problem of mistrust has been solved sufficiently well to allow most people to take the risk of transacting business (at least potentially) with most other people,

[1] Dreyer 2007.

even if they are strangers. This means escaping from the limitations of trusting only those you know, or who are recommended by friends, and moving into the realm of being able to transact with anybody within reason. The result is an exponential increase in the total volume of business that a single individual can initiate and handle, and which, given a mass of interacting people, can drive national wealth upwards to previously unheard-of heights. In Japan and the West this was achieved over a long period by the accumulation of reliable laws, institutions, stable forms of government, and the development of associations outside state control in what is commonly called 'civil society'.

The kind of institutions which the West built over the centuries, and which made exchange easier and more reliable, are visible in the world of commerce. Here, the rules for everyday transactions such as borrowing, lending, making payments, taking out insurance, keeping trustworthy and understandable accounts, employing agents, all crystallized out in the experimental social structures of the mediaeval and Renaissance worlds, in places such as Augsburg, Florence, Paris, Bruges, London, and the Hanseatic and Mediterranean ports. Many of these systems owe much to the interplay between major civilizations, and they were not always Western monopolies in their origins. Accounting and mathematics use Arabic numerals, for instance. The use of the zero has an Indian beginning. The great European trading centers were points of exchange and cross-fertilization, and the absence of such crossroads in China would eventually weaken its capacity to understand the outside world, and to connect with the fast-moving technological advances of that world.

By the nineteenth century, when national legislation began to fix the European patterns into commercial law, most of the structures for modern capitalism were already available. Accounting, banking, insurance, securities, and trading methods were all exhibiting the traces of evolutionary processes going back centuries. A key aspect of their transformation into the institutions of the present day was the fact that most of them were the preserve of freestanding bodies whose interest lay in protecting the rules of a trade or profession. Examples would be societies or guilds, of bankers or accountants, and the networks of the insurance industry that began in Lloyds coffee house in London much earlier. They were all bodies that found their justification in setting and maintaining rules for conduct. When those rules were kept, the economy benefited from the stability and predictability that resulted. Members of such bodies also were able to achieve status and security in exchange for the benefits they delivered.

The example of Japan shows that modernity is not a Western prerogative. While Japan was almost completely cut off from trade with the rest of the world for most of the Tokugawa era (1603–1868), domestic commerce flourished and in some respects even surpassed developments in the rapidly modernizing West. For example, the world's first trading of futures, on rice, occurred in Osaka. A key element in the prosperity of the time was the emergent merchant class. In line with Confucian thought, the Japanese government of the time viewed trading and commerce as putting profit and self-interest above virtue and the public good. Competition was closely circumscribed, as government officials were concerned about a possible threat to social harmony (*wa*). Violations of any of the manifold government rules, or any action that could be interpreted as challenge to the ruling samurai or the social order they put in place, found severe punishment, often execution.

The crucial question for the merchants of the time was thus how to thrive and justify their existence in a system that essentially viewed them as parasites. A number of responses emerged. One was the use of guilds as a means of collective enforcement of proper conduct. Guild members normally lived in close proximity, enabling them to watch over one another. Similar to their European counterparts, the guilds controlled quality and prices; pooled resources in storage and shipping; set wage levels; outlawed advertising and the luring away of customers; collectively punished dishonesty by members or suppliers; and in emergencies provided loans to one another. Among the sanctions available for breach of guild rules was the forcible closure of the offending member's business.

Internal codes of ethics supplemented external enforcement of proper conduct by the guilds. The most important objective for merchants of the time was the survival of the 'house,' that is, the maintenance of the family business as a going concern. Allowing the decay of the house's fortunes, or even its closure by the government or the guild, meant bringing disgrace and dishonor not only on oneself, but more importantly on one's ancestors. The intention behind house rules was to inculcate internal values conducive to long-term prosperity. Assiduously observed, the house rules stressed, among others, the importance of honesty as a basis of long-term prosperity. In the words of Hirschmeier and Yui (1981: 40, partially quoting one of the house rules), 'Even a blind man, a child or an ignorant peasant' should be able to buy without being cheated.

Arguably, this spirit of honesty, and thus potential for anonymous exchange, continues to permeate Japanese business to this day. That is not to say that there are no crooks or opportunists; but there is a general understanding that this type of behavior is deplorable rather than a sign of shrewdness in business, and that it should and will be sanctioned by society.

The evolution of the modern West, and by a different but parallel trajectory that of Japan, point to a set of questions that pose challenges for China as it modernizes. The most important of these pertains, as already stated, to the establishment of horizontal order. More specifically:

> *Question 1.* How does the society build stable, widespread horizontal order of a kind that fosters efficient exchange between economic units across the society? On what basis does trust work and how?

Connected to, and interdependent with, this first issue are questions concerning legitimate **purpose, authority, and innovation** in society. Specifically:

> *Question 2.* How does the society make a tight set of connections between the purposes (for economic action) seen as legitimate by most people, and the rationally organized pursuit of those purposes?

> *Question 3.* How does authority in the society come to work effectively to channel the behavior of people in work? Where does legitimate, motivating authority come from?

> *Question 4.* How does innovation become part of the behavior in the economy, and with it the flexibility of the system and the organizations within it?

Not only the Western advanced industrialized nations, but also Japan and South Korea, have found answers to these questions, though to different extents and in different ways. How and to what extent China may find its own answers is one of the key issues we seek to address in this book, because until they are dealt with, no amount of gyrating around with other issues will produce annual wealth of $30,000 per capita.

Understanding Business and Its Context

The regeneration of China begins with the political will to change, and three features of the context have promoted this. First, the collapse of Communism as a viable ideology has been virtually complete, even though there may be many remnants of the power it accumulated. Second, the pressure on the Chinese government to feed, provide with livelihoods, and keep from staging a revolution, 1.3 billion people concentrates the mind on what works best. Third, what works best, in terms of those challenges and on the present evidence, is market-driven capitalism.

This does not prescribe what *kind* of market-driven capitalism should be developed—and an important second theme of this book is that there are several kinds—but it does channel the direction of movement away from more state-controlled alternatives. Two forces already heavily constrain the choice, and they are referred to among researchers as *path dependence* and *embeddedness*. Path dependence means that systems of economic organization get shaped by earlier formative influences and tend to perpetuate the responses they have learned. Embeddedness implies that they also exist in a societal context, and their evolution, as it works itself out today, is connected with that context. The societal context and the system of business evolve together and remain permanently interwoven. These influences mean that choice is severely constrained both by history and by the present. It is the understanding of these forces that will lead to a better appreciation of the options available, and also of the outcomes and future effects of such interactions.

We explain the way we propose for viewing this continuing evolution in Chapter 2, but a note of introduction to the core idea is appropriate here. The boundary of a nation-state normally encompasses a distinct language, often a specific religion, or an ethnic identity, and it usually contains legal structures, educational processes, and many rules for the conduct of life that are specific to that country, for instance, commercial law and taxation. These add up to a distinct context within which a business system evolves, and also a shared history presenting a legacy of experience and ideals. It is only necessary to go from the United States to Mexico, from Germany to Italy, or from Japan to China, to feel the sense of these contrasts, and to see them present in behavior.

The 'rules of the game' in doing business—which in their totality make up a system of ways of doing things, or a 'business system'—reflect such distinct contexts. As later chapters will make clear, to work in a Japanese factory is very different from doing so in a Chinese factory; being out of work in Germany is very different from being out of work in the United States, in terms of how society treats you; and chairing a board in Korea is very different from chairing a board in the United States. It is possible to examine these and other contrasts systematically and in doing so to create a sense of how the differences have emerged.

This is done by seeing the business system as embedded in the fabric of institutions in the society, and that fabric in turn shaped by the society's culture. The total, seen in terms of these three layers of mutually interacting features, is affected by external influences that can be taken into account. So, in brief, culture shapes (and is shaped by) institutions, which in turn shape (and are shaped by) the way business is conducted. The process is a continuous flow of influences, with everything connected together. Each society produces its own solution, in line with its own ideals and historical experience.

The introduction of the notion of 'ideals' brings out a further key feature of this book. That is its examination of the reasons why senior executives act as they do, not in a micro sense covering the specifics of behavior, but in a macro sense, looking at their views on why firms exist. What is economic behavior intended to achieve and how is sense made of that? What is it all about?

It turns out that in real life, the standard business school answer—'to maximize shareholder value'—applies almost exclusively to one context only, the Anglo-Saxon one. We report the finding of substantial differences in this rationale across societies generally. If the purposes of economic action are different, it is then not surprising to discover, as we also show, that the business systems themselves vary greatly. This adds further complexity to the issues of change and evolutionary options. Such boardroom mentalities, as well as being largely unresearched, are also both hidden from view, and silently potent.

Models for China's Evolution

The evolution of China's economy is not then a matter of entirely free choice. As well as the forces of history suggested earlier, there are also the circumstances of the present day. Among these, there are three that stand out. The first is negative: it is now clear what does *not* work, and that is state domination of economic life. The second is positive: it is now clear what *can* work, from the experience of the ethnic Chinese in East and Southeast Asia, from Hong Kong, and from China's own test beds along the coast in the special economic zones (SEZs). Third, the evolution of world trade presents certain growth options, and especially certain paths of access to markets, to capital, and to technology.

The failure of state-controlled industry, following the Soviet model, is now so apparent that it needs little analysis. The absence of the discipline of markets and competition, and the inability of central planning to cope with the immense complexity of China, led organizations toward the buildup of huge inefficiencies. Factory space grew to about twice the amount the market could logically sustain. The wish of the state—that welfare responsibility should be discharged through the state-owned enterprises, and in a more decentralized manner through the 'collectives', added to the burden. Ideas such as 'profit', efficient return on assets, and response to market demand were excluded. A typical attitude was reported in Doug Guthrie's study of eighty such enterprises; when, irritated by his questions, a CEO eventually banged the desk and shouted 'I don't do profit'. She then explained her duties to the workforce and its thousands of dependants.[2]

A model that works was waiting in the wings. Chinese capitalism was alive and well in the countries around the South China Sea, and had accumulated a set of advantages of the kind China needed when the return exodus began. Over fifty million ethnic Chinese live around the borders of the South China Sea, mainly now descendents of refugees from China over the last century and a half. They took themselves out of poverty to become the dominant economic elite of the region. The *Nanyang huaqiao* (the ethnic Chinese 'sojourners' of the Southern Ocean) had developed skills in organization, connections into world markets, the acquisition of technology, large volumes of capital, and an understanding of environments where political power still counts in the economy. They have one extra characteristic: they share a wish to see China restored to its former glory, a feature commonly associated also, in individual cases, with a strong sentimental attachment to the ancestral home area.

The form of capitalism with which the ethnic Chinese entrepreneurs had come to dominate the economies of East and Southeast Asia in the second half of the twentieth century, was family business, or at least personally owned and dominated business. We will refer to it as 'private business'. It took a number of forms, but with clear common denominators. Small and medium enterprise (SME) was the most common form, usually based on family ownership or partnership, and this type came to dominate fields such as retailing, distribution, professional services, small-scale manufacturing, and entertainment. In manufacturing, their instinctive skills for networking allowed them to transcend the scale limitations and

<hr>

[2] Guthrie 1999.

to build industrial competence via the integration of separately owned units in components supply, subassembly, and assembly. By this means they came to dominate, quietly and unobtrusively, the world's use of original equipment manufacturing (OEM) methods in a wide range of industries, without facing the growth dilemmas of large-scale enterprise.

They also produced larger versions of the family business form, in the shape of closely held conglomerates, a form we shall come to refer to as 'clan conglomerates,' to reflect the typical dominance of extended family in both ownership and control. Typically also this form would be subject to the domination of strategy making by a single powerful individual, often a founder or his immediate successor. The preferred fields of such enterprises reflect a *rentier* perspective. For instance they dominate the region in banking and property development, and they have strong positions in many countries in key infrastructure domains such as power, telecommunications, transport, hotels, and container ports. They are also major actors in forestry and agribusiness. Given their size and sophistication, such enterprises are often also partners with Western or Japanese multinationals in the opening of new fields, especially where technology needs to be built into the set of competences. The great hidden strength of this conglomerate form of regional enterprise is its mastery of the art of co-opting political support, a key aspect of the building of unassailable barriers to entry. Such skill is likely to remain crucial in the context of China for a long time to come, and decades of experience in its practice outside give them a head start against other contenders for the opportunities that China now presents.

Much less likely to 'fit' the Chinese context are other major forms of capitalism, as represented by the United States, Japan, Germany, and South Korea. While China must feel the temptation to copy 'best practices' piecemeal from these (and other) nations, path dependence is likely to get in the way more often than not. Most of the key patterns that give these systems their distinct flavors and institutional comparative advantages are incompatible with the existing context in China, which raises the question of how well foreign institutional imports will work. This is true particularly for the cases of Germany and Japan, but also that of the United States. Perhaps the least unrealistic model to emulate for China is the South Korean one, though even this is likely to be a long shot.

While the business model of the Regional Ethnic Chinese is well suited especially for SMEs, one thing that it does not produce is modern multinational enterprises (MNEs). Since MNEs are perceived to represent one way for Chinese business to create and capture higher levels of value added than is possible for its SMEs, China has been looking for alternative routes to building its own breed of MNEs. In particular, it has placed a large bet on select state-owned enterprises (SOEs), hoping to reform them into modern multinational enterprises capable of entering the Fortune 500. As we will elaborate, the chances of success are low at best. The reason, in a nutshell, is that the structure of Chinese society is likely to prevent the emergence of firms capable of handling the levels of complexity associated with modern MNEs, at world standards of efficiency.

Outline of This Book

In Chapter 2, we lay out the analytical framework that forms the basis for most of the rest of this book. As mentioned, this model incorporates culture, the institutions surrounding the firm, and the rules of coordination within and among businesses. It further calls attention to the characteristics of the state, key historical events, and external influences. We divide the latter into the *material*, covering such tangible forces as price and technology, and the *ideational*, covering the arrival of ideas such as consumerism or democracy.

Chapters 3 through 8 apply this framework to the Chinese context. Chapters 3 and 4 introduce the fundamentals of Chinese history and culture as well as its institutions and order. Chapter 5 examines the impact of the Regional Ethnic Chinese on business in present-day China. Chapters 6 through 8 then analyze the shape of the three major business systems present in China today, which are the SOE sector, the local corporate sector, and the private sector.

We subsequently change tack and explore alternative systems of capitalism, with the objective of using a comparative perspective to generate additional insights into China and its possible trajectory. Chapter 9 lays out the rationale for doing so. Chapters 10 through 13 then offer brief analyses of the business systems of the United States, Japan, Germany, and South Korea. We identify key themes in these business systems, how they are linked to comparative advantage of their industries, and how these themes may apply to the context of China.

Chapter 14 concludes the book. We revisit the four questions posed earlier in this chapter and discuss the implications of our answers for the future evolution of Chinese capitalism. We propose a set of concrete implications for business, especially from the perspective of entering the

Chinese market, sourcing from it, partnering with Chinese firms, and crafting strategic responses to China's status as the workshop of the world, and we discuss the possibility of a Chinese threat to today's modern MNEs. We further spell out the implications of this book for academic research on China and on understanding economies and businesses in general. We conclude with a brief discussion of other major issues China will have to contend with on its path to further economic development.

Key References

Dreyer, Edward L. 2007. *Zheng He: China and the Oceans in the Early Ming Dynasty 1404–1433*. London: Longman.

Guthrie, Douglas. 1999. *Dragon in a Three-Piece Suit: The Emergence of Capitalism in China*. Princeton, NJ: Princeton University Press.

Hirschmeier, Johannes, and Tsunehiko Yui. 1981. *The Development of Japanese Business, 1600–1980*, 2nd edn. London: Allen & Unwin.

Redding, Gordon. 1990. *The Spirit of Chinese Capitalism*. Berlin: W. de Gruyter.

2

Describing Business Systems

To make the world of business come to life, people should be able to exchange things of value, and to leave enough parts of the total value with members of the system to keep them satisfied. The things exchanged might be work for money, goods for money, money for goods, money for money, loyalty for welfare, services for money, or information for favors; the list goes on. In many ways the basic activities, conditions, and challenges are standard and universal across all societies: there need to be agreed measures of quantity, quality, and payment; there need to be ways of underwriting risk; reputation has value; information is crucial; a sense of surrounding order helps. So certain aspects are visible almost everywhere, where economies are active: people are either employees, employers, or free agents; the prices of things are known and discussed and markets form; 'firms' exist in one form or another; demand goes up and down; things change; participants in the system come and go. It looks the same everywhere. Money makes the world go round.

But it is not really the same everywhere. Four things cause differences. The first is that in some societies, either specific people or groups of people with a common interest distort the distribution of the surpluses to their own benefit. In northern Europe, the interest group of labor has—through the political system—arranged to receive a higher than (inter-national) average portion of industrial value-added. In the United States, a similar but opposite distortion has, in recent years, allocated a higher-than-average portion of benefits to its finance sector and board members. In Korea, the *chaebol* founders were permitted by government policy to build colossal family fortunes as a reward for economic performance. A new industrial elite now has a grip on Russian industry and wealth. These distinct features have their origins in the ways their societies deal with their own evolution towards a desirable future. Each response reflects societal conditions and history.

The second cause of differences is the role of government. The variety of governmental systems is immense and complex to describe. But one feature especially is of note in affecting the conduct of business: does the government get involved in planning and orchestrating the economy, and does it share in the risk-taking associated with investment? A continuum of formulae exists, from the deliberately noninterventionist case of the United States and the United Kingdom—where if you go bankrupt it is your problem, and where the market rules over industrial policy—to the opposite in a planned economy such as that of Singapore, where government intervention and risk-sharing are both high. At various points in between are economies like that of Germany, Japan, and Sweden, where close cooperation is maintained between business and government and with all interested parties such as unions, banks, and so on.

When government is involved, it usually brings with it certain overrides like taxation, licensing, regulations, investment policies, and controls over capital access to affect the choices of the players themselves. An extension of this is its international aspect, when deals between governments might well add further conditions, such as tariff barriers, specific market access, or compliance needs.

The third cause of societal differences in how economies get to be organized, is the stage of development of the society, represented most simply in its wealth per capita. What a society is capable of doing is clearly going to be very different between a case where the system can command access to $40,000 per capita, and one where only $4,000 is available, or even in some cases $400. But it is not simply a difference in quantity of wealth that is at issue. Nor is it just a matter of how long a country has been 'developed'—although both factors play a part. It is more a matter of the particular trajectory of development, which allowed the society to transform itself from poverty to wealth. *How* did it evolve? (We leave aside here, for the moment, the question of how long has it been trying, and the deeper underlying question of whether it has been trying at all.) A society's trajectory usually is more a series of twists and turns than a smooth progression, and at each of these junctures it might take one of several paths. There is often a large element of chance, as when in 1617 the Ming emperor took the decision to abolish the Chinese government salt monopoly. Instead of having government salt certificates usable in the same way as paper currency, from then on the rights to trade in salt were allocated to merchants in a system of imperial patronage. To get these rights, merchants had to make donations—the equivalent of taxes. But these were arbitrary, and from then on large enterprises operated in a patron–client relationship with government, a feature still visible in the nineteenth and twentieth centuries, although no longer based in the salt trade.

The essential question at the core of this evolutionary process, in any society, is the following: *How does the society make it possible, for the average person making a transaction in the economy, to trust strangers?* This is a massive barrier in societal evolution and most countries have not yet surmounted it. The reason it is important is a simple matter of mathematics: if the people you can do business with are restricted in number, your transactions are limited in total volume, and so are those of the society as a whole; if there are no limits to the number of transaction partners, there are no limits to the volume of exchange in the society. One of the side effects of this constraining force, when it applies, is a tendency to select certain industrial responses only, for reasons we will come to later. It is, for instance, one of the reasons why there are almost no internationally reputable consumer brand names of Chinese origin beyond Acer, Tiger Balm, and Haier. There is not enough trust in the system to support the necessary degree of organizational complexity at global standards of efficiency.

Those societies that have solved the problem, have done so by inventing systems of order to make unrestricted exchange feasible. This usually means they have made it possible for people to (*a*) have reliable information; (*b*) use standard procedures for exchange that everyone involved understands; (*c*) own securely the fruits of their labor; (*d*) rely upon official support to correct the bad behavior of others; and (*e*) calculate the pros and cons of action alternatives. Recall also that exchange here includes employment—the exchange of work for reward, as well as funding, buying, and selling. All these features rest on a bed of institutions, or rules of the game, and each society has its own set of rules. They may all be designed to serve the same ultimate aim—to expand the range of people who may be trusted in transactions—but the way they work, and the principles within their design, are not at all standard. The institutions of society vary greatly between one country and another. Only the United States has Sarbanes–Oxley. Only China has such a record of executing the corrupt. Only France has the *enarque* elite. Japan is the graveyard of venture capital, while Silicon Valley is its paradise.

The last of the four main causes of societal difference in the organizing of business conduct is the culture. This is the realm of meaning. What it means to be an employee in Japan is very different from what it means in the United States. Firms exist for different purposes society by society: in the United States for shareholder value; in Germany for the community; in Japan to employ people; in Korea to build the nation; often now among the Chinese to make a family secure. There is a whole set of associated implications carried in the minds of individuals, shaping their behavior. Attitudes to working, to discipline, to fitting into a group of others, to loyalty, to cooperation, to reward, and so on are all based in the fundamental ideas of the society about the conduct of life. Such ideas shape the institutions, and become manifest in them. The rules for conduct rest on ideas about what the conduct is for. The means are shaped by the ends, and the ends come from the society's ideals, its culture. This is what allows it to remain a society, for without that integration of accepted meanings, it loses its order and its coherence.

Explaining the Evolution of Business Systems

We turn now to a way of gathering together the components of an explanation and exploring how the evolutionary process works. We need to begin with an idea of certain core features as desirable. If you are designing a car, it has to have certain features: accommodating passengers safely; getting reliably from place to place; easy to maintain; perhaps good looking. Cars are produced in prolific variety, but only succeed in the market on the understanding that they fulfill at least these conditions. Precisely how they do so is a second-order question, and it permits a very wide variety of responses.

It is the same with systems of business—in a sense the vehicles that carry economies. There are certain design principles essential to progress, and they may be seen at two levels: what features do *organizations* need to have; and what features do *surrounding societal institutions* have to have? As with designing cars, there is a variety of ways in which such demands may be met, but the demands themselves do not change or go away. As we shall see, the meeting of the demands often needs other parts of the total societal system to be brought harmoniously into the equation, such as the banking system, the education system, government policy, and ultimately the culture.

There is one overriding pair of conditions to be settled first if the lessons of economic history are to be absorbed, and all that follows is subject to these two conditions being met. Going back to the car analogy, there would be no point in starting to make a car if there were no roads and no fuel. Equally, there is little point in trying to develop an economy toward bettering the human condition unless (*a*) there are vehicles, such as companies, in which work and ownership may be brought together, and wealth held through time; and (*b*) there are markets in which competition can work its effects. Exactly how these conditions are met is immaterial here—although later in this book it becomes highly material—but explaining the workings of business systems is just that. We focus on societal ways of conducting business that bring progress to their people. In particular we take note of the formulae that have worked well in recent decades. We are not explaining the constant series of failed societal experiments that litter the world's history with tales of terror, misreadings of human motivation, abuse of power, or the plethora of good intentions that finished up in societal decline. We are looking at the variety of systems generally known as capitalism.

Requirements of Organization

We speak here of organizations in a loose sense, as they exist in many forms and with many structures holding them together. They may not always be coterminous with some legal vehicle, but they have boundaries and memberships understood adequately by people interacting with them. One might be a clearly defined family business where the owners run it and everybody can see and feel the structure. Another might be a loose conglomerate of interlocked companies acting together in their shared interest, like a Japanese business group or German industrial group.

The features that organizations need to have to survive and prosper are:

1. *Efficiency*. Whatever the organization does, it has to do so by using its resources with the greatest intensity possible, so that its return on those resources is competitive with that gained by other companies. This principle spreads across the use of capital, human skill, technology, and knowledge. It is largely what good managerial administration is about. Competition brings the discipline to achieve it, and reputation is based on efficiency.

2. *Learning*. Any organization needs to know what is going on around it, in order to respond to new challenges and new opportunities. Without constant monitoring of the external world, surprises may result directly in failure, or they may result in the long attrition of competitiveness brought about by missed opportunities. As the

best formula for long-term organizational existence is command of stable, understandable, and predictable relations with markets, then constant learning becomes crucial to the maintaining of such a finely balanced position, under the never-ending threat of disturbance and uncertainty.

3. *Change.* The corollary of learning is that you have to be able to do something about it. If an organization cannot change, the learning is wasted, even if it occurred. Such change can take many forms—new structures, personnel, products, practices, communication systems, attitudes, locations. The list is very long. So too is the manner of changing—fast or slow, benevolent or dictatorial, partial or complete. Again the methods vary hugely—and significantly many of them vary by society—but our concern at this point is simply to mark the need, but with one important caveat: the good organization does not have to be constantly changing, as if it were in a permanent state of neurosis. It has instead to contain the *capacity to change*, in case modification becomes necessary.

Requirements of the Societal Institutions

As we have proposed, there are certain things that work to keep organizations healthy as functioning systems capable of producing value. For the institutions of the society, the requirements are related, but different. They are different in that they play an essentially supportive role, helping (or otherwise) the players in the business arena who are taking action. If a 'good' institutional fabric helps to foster organizations that are efficient, capable of learning, and capable of change, how does that support operate?

Without assigning any order of priority, a number of features of successful societies can be identified, seeing them here in terms of elements that foster certain good outcomes, or certain forces of benevolent transformation. While probably no country meets all these criteria fully, economically successful ones tend to meet a larger proportion of them than those whose economic performance has been lagging.

The core list is as follows:

1. Reliable, available, relevant information about business.
2. Clarity and relevance of laws, and enough discipline to make them work.

3. Allocative efficiency to ensure that capital flows to where it can be best used.

4. Productive efficiency to ensure that when capital has been allocated, it is used in the most intensive way.

5. Encouragement for the growth and application of human talent, including geographical and social mobility.

6. The encouraging of innovation and creativity, and the valuing of change.

7. Clear rules for the ownership and trading of assets.

8. The use of rational calculation of means–end relations, and forecast benefits, to supplement or replace personal judgments about risk.

9. A state administration autonomous from social class, and devoted to the public good, hence modest, honest, responsive government, not feared.

10. A perceived link between individual and collective well-being, and a positive attitude toward wealth.

We now have a basic set of ideas about the struggles of societies across centuries. By trial and error, by learning from others, by the effects of historical accidents, by the conscious pursuit of policies, they stumble forward toward prosperity. Building the qualities of their institutions, stimulating the responses of their organizations, and guided by their cultural ideals, they foster the emergence from within them of certain ways of doing business, certain systems of putting together into stable patterns of interaction the elements at their disposal—money, human talent, technology, and ways of trusting.

We are now faced with three broad questions:

(a) How do the cultural ideals shape the institutions, a question we will restate as: How does the system of meaning help to create the system of order?

(b) How does the system of order, carried in the institutions, shape the conducting of business? What, in any case, is the system of business?

(c) How is it that the systems of business vary so much between societies, especially in terms of what kind of industry a society is 'good at'?

As a framework within which to consider such questions, a picture is presented in Figure 2.1 of the main components of the analysis.

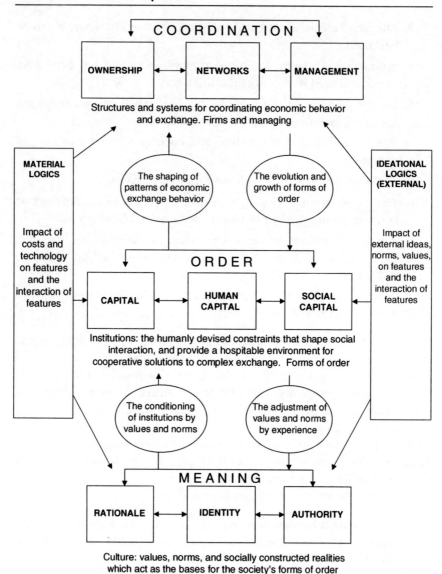

Figure 2.1. The elements of a business system

We will outline its broad meaning and then return to the three questions.

Societies are complex adaptive systems in which change is constant. Such change is generated both internally and from outside. When setting up a picture to analyze the workings of such a system, certain ground rules apply: the categories used are simply convenient boxes for thinking about certain common features; they are all interconnected, with flows of influence in every direction; relations between things change over time and finding stable patterns does not mean that they are stable forever; and yet stable patterns may be traced, with enough staying power to explain a society's business system at present and to help judge its direction of emergence. It is also possible to make sense of the contrasts between systems of capitalism, and so to use comparison (and also, options) as a guide to judging possible evolution. In this study our main agenda is China, but it will be deliberately placed alongside others to bring out both its special nature, and its potential alternative future trajectories.

Culture and Meaning

The theory behind this analysis may be stated in simple terms, in the following way. A society—if it is a functioning society—will be psychologically held together by a culture, and the role of the culture is to interpret 'meaning' for members of the society, in other words to define reality to a point where it can be understood enough to cope with, and to assign significance to certain features and responses. This is the base layer of the model—the realm of *meaning*, or the social construction of reality.

The culture is seen here as working in three main ways in interpreting reality. One is termed *Rationale*, and this captures the agreement (to the extent that it may be discerned) over the core purposes behind economic behavior. Why do firms exist? What ends do people have in mind when they do business, and what means do they think appropriate in its conduct? In simple terms: 'What's it all about?' Surprising variations exist between societies, as we have noted already.

The second and third elements of culture, and therefore of meaning, are those underlying the society's basic social architecture—its systems of order. Horizontal order provides individuals with a sense of belonging in the wider social matrix, but do they belong as individuals, as family members, clan or tribe members, parts of a class, or parts of an occupation group? Where do their primary loyalties and dependencies lie? Because of its force in fixing a person's sense of where he or she fits in society, this is termed *Identity*. Its vertical equivalent also fixes a person's position but this time in relation to *Authority*. Here we see the workings of the power structure. What kinds of people have authority? On what basis? How is power distributed in the society?

Institutions and Order

Over time, as the members of the society conduct their lives, they construct a pattern of stable, predictable rules for conduct, and the purpose of this set of rules is to provide a predictable framework within which people can judge how to behave. This is the realm of *order*, and it can become highly elaborated and specialized, ascending from basic rules for interpersonal conduct such as dress codes or table manners, to the regulations governing financial disclosure in a capital market, or the codified statutes of a legal system. These rules for conduct are discussed as a set of *Institutions*. They help people to know what to do, and—significantly—they help people to judge what others are likely to do. In this book we will be concerned with those institutions designed to affect the conduct of economic life.

The principle issues in economic life are *Capital, Human Capital, and Social Capital*, and these are identified as the arenas in which institutions accrete. The realm of *Capital* is the realm of assets such as money, land, technology, and it contains institutions such as banks, accounting systems, financial regulations, commercial laws. It works to channel capital in various forms into productive use. *Human Capital* institutions do the same things for a society's stock of knowledge, skills, and the attitudes and inclinations that may go with them. It works primarily through the education system and the structuring of labor markets. *Social Capital* is in essence trust, a feature of great significance for economic progress, but whose form does not follow one pattern. Interpersonal trust (as with *guanxi*) works in tandem with institutional trust (as with laws of contract), and the balancing of the two forces—partly affected by the costs of maintaining them—provides societies with many options and eventual recipes.

The Business System and Coordination

The third layer of the model is the business system, seen here as a set of ways in which the necessary components are brought together into stable and understandable arrangements. How, in other words, are capital, labor, technology, and knowledge combined to facilitate their fruitful interaction. There is a wide variety of types of firms, with many interpretations of how ownership and membership operate, and where the boundaries are. Thus the first element is *Ownership*. There are many ways in which firms fit into the surrounding economy, and whether and how they link together, and so the second element is *Networks*. There are many ways in which, inside a firm, the key resources are made to flow together, as managers seek the necessary efficiency, learning, and adaptiveness for the firm to prosper. This is the realm of *Management*. The sum of all these features is a total formula for the *coordination* of economic exchange. That is what a business system is.

In observing the interactions between these three layers of *meaning*, *order*, and *coordination*, the view needed is necessarily historical. The shifts of history are significant here, and they usually dominate in shaping the distinctiveness of each society. They will be seen later in terms of two blocs of influences, placed between the layers of *meaning* (i.e. culture) and *order* (i.e. institutions). These are 'key historical influences', and 'the role of the state'. It goes without saying that China is deeply influenced by its history, and that no account of its current business system can ignore such facts as the invasions of the nineteenth century, the Revolutions of 1911 and 1949, the Cultural Revolution, the Deng reforms. All states have had potent formative experiences, some very clear, such as the Code Napoleon in France, or the reforms of Bismarck in Germany. Others might be less specific but equally momentous, such as the US access to the vast untapped resources of North America in the nineteenth century, or the role of Hong Kong in economic intermediation between China and the West.

The role of the state may well run through the entire set of features in the model, as a universal conditioner of actions and relations, but it needs to be considered a specific topic, to allow for comparison between societies, and to permit understanding of why the depth and extent of its permeation may vary. Some states are highly interventionist, others not. This needs to be acknowledged, but so too do the realms of intervention, and the basic mechanics of the process, need to be seen. If there are influential state policies affecting economic action, sufficient to explain phenomena such as labor markets, taxation processes, access to markets, they would be noted in this part of the analysis. Thus, the decentralization of economic decision-making authority in China in recent years, and the rise of 'tax farming' at the local level, are significant influences on business conduct. French employment laws, with their origin in political ideals, directly affect a great deal of management practice. The contrast between China's 'strong' state, and India's 'weak' state, is significant in explaining much economic action.

We have explained earlier that a societal system is always open to influence from outside, often crucial in its effects, as was for instance the impact of Marxist ideology on Russia, or the effect of access to Western markets and technology on Taiwan after 1950. These influences are seen here as of two main kinds—the material, and the ideational. Material influences are tangible and direct. A new technology comes in from abroad, such as mobile telephones, personal computers, nuclear engineering. Or a new process changes the trading price of goods or services, as has occurred with mass marketing in many fields. Commodity prices rise and fall and are usually out of the control of a single society. All such direct effects are absorbed into the functioning of a country's business system, and cannot be ignored.

The second source of external influence is the arrival of ideas, and although there are often attempts to control their arrival, as for instance with Internet filtering, or bans on media, the patrolling of borders in this way is increasingly challenged by advances in communications technology. The arrival of ideas is persistent and widespread. Teenage culture, aspirations to own certain brands of consumer goods, ideas about freedom, and codes of dress slip across national frontiers in a never-ending stream, affecting behavior in markets, organizations, and homes. These need to be acknowledged for their influence, and they are often harbingers of change.

Tracing Effects

Using an analysis of the kind just outlined introduces complexity at a level not commonly encountered in managerial explanations. It forces the reader to come to terms with a wide range of inputs to the understanding of a present-day phenomenon. It is a long way from the usual two-by-two diagram, or the three boxes with arrows. It therefore needs some justification. That lies in three propositions: first, the world is complex, and oversimplifying is dangerous if it leads to judgments made out of context, and especially when comparisons between societies are being made; second, because societies tend to remain cohesive as they evolve, it is more revealing to sense the total as they change; and third, any judgments about action need to be made against the background of what that action is embedded in, and the fact that many effects are not easily visible.

We posed three questions earlier in this chapter: How does *meaning* shape *order?* How does *order* shape business *coordination?* How does the system of *coordination* influence the emergence of certain forms of industry of relevance to an economy's competitiveness? Why, in crude terms, do the best companies in most main industries, originate in just one or two societies?

Meaning and Order

Meaning shapes order in the following way. The members of a society have an incentive to make their society 'work' as it provides defense against attack by outsiders, and it gives a valued sense of identity beyond the primal group. Language grows to express this and, in the creating of language, meanings take on agreed form. This applies at the level of defining what things are, but it also applies at the level of how life should be lived—against the context that people need to learn how to best adapt to their circumstances, and that such learning needs to be passed on. So, for instance, under subsistence agriculture with crops like rice, it becomes a cultural response to be able to cooperate, and perhaps to calculate the value of such cooperation for reciprocal exchange. These ground rules or 'social axioms' become the guidelines to be absorbed and acted on if people are to fit in, and if the society is to function coherently.

Over time, the world of collective meaning can divide up into mini-worlds of specialized meaning—a process accelerated by modernization, as that brings a strong tendency for specialization of work and skill. These mini-worlds are kept integrated into the total by the penetration into them of the universal social axioms, and the latter hold the culture together, not so much by discipline, but—like a neural network—integrating and maintaining core meaning across domains. Change and adaptation is also never ending, as are also processes of reaffirmation of cultural ideals.

Within the specialist meaning spaces—let us say the world of accounting in China as opposed to the Chinese world of production technology—the members who go in and out of those spaces to earn a living tend to invent stable processes and structures with which to do their work. These become institutions, and as such they guarantee a degree of orderliness within the space. The culture may well have a strong impact on the formation of these institutions and this can be illustrated with two examples from China and its history. In production systems, for centuries, it was normal to employ subcontractors to attend to a specialized part of a production process, and they would bring in their own labor force. This is still visible in many parts of southern China today. It is not 'textbook' production management, but is nonetheless efficient, and it owes its origin to much earlier responses to managing complexity, the shaping of which was at least in part cultural.

A second example of culture shaping institutions comes from accounting. In traditional China, accounts were kept as a means of allocating to partners in the business their annual share of benefits, and it also included the tracking of contributions. So revenues and expenses were the focus, and profit seen as a balance between the two. Accounting for sharecropping and lineage estates was similar, and the legal bodies owning such assets as land, or ferry rights, could exist for centuries as sacred trusts whose asset value was seen as either unchanging or irrelevant. There was no concern for 'institutionalization' of the value of capital in this system. It was simply left out of the calculations. Capital accounting never developed, and the inefficient use of capital, even under conditions of imported ideas about accounting, has remained China's most serious handicap. The massive inflation of assets that led to industrial production capacity rising to double what was needed, and the gigantic figures for nonperforming loans in the state banking sector, are perhaps evidence of some persistence in this combination of system and mindset.

Order and the Business System

The business system (or systems) rests upon a bed of institutions. When private businesses became legal again during the 1980s in China, the return of this institution changed the face of China radically. When Zhu Rongji changed the rules for the allocation and management of capital in the state sector in the 1990s, the new structures changed fundamentally the behavior of many organizations. In the reverse direction, institutions can come into being as a result of issues in the business system, as when a group of companies lobby government to provide new legislation, or, for instance, when they influence syllabus design in universities.

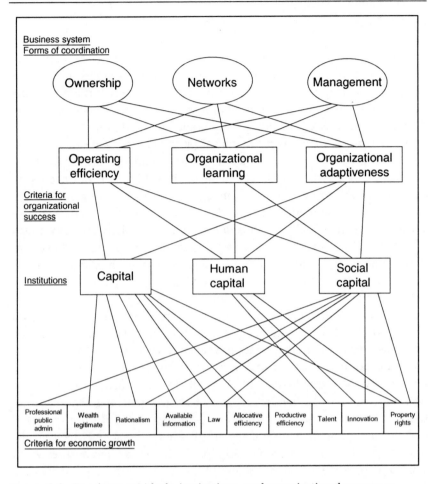

Business system
Forms of coordination

Ownership   Networks   Management

Operating efficiency   Organizational learning   Organizational adaptiveness

Criteria for organizational success

Institutions   Capital   Human capital   Social capital

| Professional public admin | Wealth legitimate | Rationalism | Available information | Law | Allocative efficiency | Productive efficiency | Talent | Innovation | Property rights |

Criteria for economic growth

Figure 2.2. Development ideals, institutions, and organizational responses

This interplay between the world of business and the world of surrounding rules of the game is usually highly interactive, and it is against this context of changing forces that the dramas of competition are played out. In these dramas, we now focus on the interplay between the three requirements of competitive organization and the ten ideal characteristics of the institutional fabric, summarized in Figure 2.2. The way these forces interact may be seen by considering the contents of the three boxes which make up the business system, namely Ownership, Networks, and Management.

Ownership

The creation of legal bodies capable of holding assets through periods of time beyond the lives of their founders and current owners, has always been a crucial step in societal evolution, and no society has a monopoly on the idea. There were temple corporations in ancient Mesopotamia. When Europe was establishing legal bodies to hold the wealth of the Catholic Church in the early Medieval period, so too were the Chinese establishing trusts around temples. There are Japanese craft corporations going back over a thousand years. For much of history it has been seen as an advantage to be able to disengage from personal control of assets, and so from dependence on individuals, at least for certain kinds of assets—those that might be considered communal. This does not mean that personally held assets could not coexist, and they usually have. But there comes to be a difference in the style of behavior in using the assets when comparing the two types of ownership.

The difference, in essence, is that where assets are privately owned their use comes to be privately dominated, not surprisingly, and commonly a single individual will stamp his or her authority on decisions about their use. This results in strategy making that may well be more adventurous and faster to implement. It may also reflect the special knowledge accumulated by the individual about the shifts in an industry. The organization may well also be held together by bonds of personal loyalty, rather than by formal bureaucracy. In the opposite form of organization, held and managed impersonally on behalf of others, the style is likely to be more rational, neutral, objective, and 'professional' as far as business decisions are concerned. Power is likely to be much more widely dispersed. These are of course stereotypes, and rely on simplification. There is also a large range of options mixing the two types along a continuum.

A highly significant societal feature affecting the longevity of organizations, and shaping much of their internal social psychology, is whether inheritance of assets must be shared, typically between children when an owning parent dies. This partible inheritance is mandatory in the world of Islam. It is also traditional in Chinese culture. It is part of the French Napoleonic heritage. It is not so in many other Western cultures, nor in Japan. In the latter cases, primogeniture dominates, and it is common to find organizations lasting centuries, and common also to find a strong concern with managerial professionalism to look after the growth of assets, or at least to assist the formal owners to do so. In Japan, it is not unusual for a family running out of talent to adopt a new member for his (and very rarely her) usefulness in looking after the assets. By contrast, in the worlds of both Islam and China, the common folklore is of 'rags to rags in three generations' as family fortunes rise on entrepreneurship, stabilize, and then fall apart as family tensions erupt or talent runs out. The tensions between personalistic control and professional managerial concerns are often very high, and a great deal of the world's business is conducted as a resolution between these two forces.

The significance of the limited liability formula for incorporating a company, dating as it does from the early nineteenth century in Britain, is that it vastly increased the ease with which investment could be made, accounted for, and safely kept on behalf of a large body of people. This form of enterprise has accounted for much of the economic value generated in many countries since then. Its reintroduction in China in recent decades has been highly influential on growth.

But the success of the limited liability formula does not mean that ownership has moved on a wide front from being personal to being public. It has in certain countries such as the United States, but in most countries laws do not protect shareholders well, and ownership remains concentrated in a few hands in each company. The global average is that the three largest shareholders hold about 50 percent of a company's equity. For the top ten French companies it is 54 percent, in Scandinavia 37 percent, for the group of common law countries 43 percent. It only drops below 30 percent in the United States, Australia, the United Kingdom, Sweden, Taiwan, Japan, and Korea (the latter three being under the strong influence of the United States). This does not mean that the three largest shareholders will necessarily be individuals or family trusts; they might equally be insurance companies, or banks, or other firms. The important point for our consideration here is that the pattern varies across societies and is clearly influenced by both inheritance norms and by legal tradition.

In rough terms, legal systems divide into Common Law and Civil Law alternatives, and within the civil law group are three versions different by virtue of their origins: French, German, or Scandinavian. Centuries of colonialism and globalization have spread the main types out of their European base. Very often there are hybrids: Thailand uses common law but with French overlays; Japan uses a form based in German civil law but with US overlays; Italy uses a form based in French civil law but with German additions. It would be risky to so classify the system now emerging in China, except to say that it is based on a civil code, that it rests on a long tradition of state control over the legal process, and the absence of an independent judiciary, and that it is now incorporating at high speed a great number of new ideas from outside, while interpreting them into a Chinese frame.

Patterns of ownership of economic assets will be reflected in methods to solve the first challenge of economic coordination; that of establishing the primary vehicles for economic action—what is brought together 'under one roof' to be controlled and held in efficient interaction. The obvious solutions are forms we are familiar with, from sole proprietorships up to complex multidivisional, multinational enterprises. But China is now a fertile ground for the growth of new forms of loosely connected firms, whose boundaries and internal connections are opaque. This allows the hedging of bets, the taking of risks, the seizing of opportunities in conditions of weak information, the use of political and other connections, and the avoidance of close scrutiny. Normally an observer wants to know what a firm does—what product fields is it in, what technology does it depend on, what competences can it bring into play. Especially in some systems of capitalism disclosure is crucial to the workings of the system, as the allocators of capital want to know where best to invest the money. But where the system is not dominated by such allocators, the scrutiny cannot automatically take priority there. Firms may then behave in ways that defy the 'normal' rules.

Networks

In some societies, and especially in the US, the full pressure of competition has been orchestrated by the government as a means of driving the business system to higher levels of performance, and in this design, collaboration between firms is seen as a threat to the public interest. It is fairly obvious when prices are rigged, but it may also be so when other deals are cut to affect the market, for example in sourcing material, or skill, or access to knowledge. This does not mean that firms cannot collaborate. It means that when they do they need to be clear about how, and they may need to establish a new firm so that the venture can be tracked and its performance known openly. Where competition is the essence of a system, opaqueness is threatening.

But competition is not always the essence. Some business systems do not exist to drive firms to compete to death. Germany and Japan compete in world markets using a quite different philosophy from that and do well in the process. In these cases, firms collaborate in many ways, and are interlocked across many dimensions—technical, educational, labor relations, funding, knowledge acquisition, etc. These interlocks would be illegal in some other jurisdictions, because their outcome is that it is harder to put a boundary around the firm. When large European firms list on the New York stock exchange as a means of gaining access to capital, the hidden costs of dismantling these connections are often high and seemingly often unanticipated.

In certain economies, based on SMEs, the network becomes the organization, as goods could not be produced by single firms efficiently. Instead the firms specialize and then link, often with the flexibility to adjust to changes in demand, technology, or price. The 'network capitalism' of China is just such a system, and it accounts for much recent prosperity.

We have just reviewed two ways of pulling things together: ties under ownership; and ties under voluntary cooperation. We turn now to the final form of holding things together, namely ties under management or leadership inside the firm. Here the things being tied together are people and their work, technology, knowledge, and financial resources. Issues here are somewhat more micro than in the other two forms. They do however often account for many of the organizational qualities so necessary to an economy—the efficiency, the learning, and the adaptiveness.

Management

As with the other two coordination mediums, it is possible to identify a core feature distinguishing the main alternatives from each other. Here it is the degree to which managers rely on the inputs, creativity, and responsible contributions of the workforce. In some societies the reliance reaches high levels, and one thinks of Scandinavia, Germany, Japan, where the interdependence of white-collar and blue-collar ranks is unusually high. Associated with this also are relatively high wages, high levels of job retention, and heavy investment by firms in skill training.

In other societies workers are treated more as extensions of the mechanical production or service system and are not expected to think for the company to the same degree. They are given tasks, and their work is controlled, but ideas for improvement are expected to emerge from higher ranks, and payment systems reflect this.

These two main alternatives work in different ways to meet the universal organizational needs for efficiency, learning, and adaptiveness. If you analyzed a 'typical' German company to discover where in the organization those three requirements were handled, the answer would be everywhere in the company. The workforce is engaged, in the same way as is the management, with those three issues, and strong worker presence in the boardroom, as well as very high worker skills and knowledge, make it possible. If on the other hand you looked at a 'typical' US company in a traditional industry, you would see that the responsibility for those three challenges lies with management. Their job is to deal with them and to program the response of workers to meet the needs. This is visible in tight specifications of job description, tight performance measurement and control, and highly trained professionalism in management ranks. If you were to go to one of the millions of small or medium enterprises in China that account for the achievement of its being the workshop of the world, and asked who in the organization is responsible for efficiency, learning, and adaptiveness, the average employee would point upwards and say 'lao ban'—the big boss.

These varying formulae result in a selecting out of which industrial type to concentrate on. The German (and Japanese) response places emphasis on job security, training, participation, and reward sharing, and is best suited to industries in which the best competitive strategy is to manufacture complex products that can be kept competitive via continual inventive technical enhancement. This uses the special competences of the organization most fully. In the US case, the efficiency is released best in industries that supply mass markets with products or services at a lower level of technical sophistication, and where a bureaucratic organization can program worker behavior enough to be responsive, but mainly to be efficient in handling throughput. Goods for mass consumer markets are a case in point, as are also hotel chains or insurance companies. A variant in the US case is the organization that relies principally on its managerial ranks to do the organization's value-adding work, as in consultancy, financial services, project management, and entertainment. One final significant US response is that of the Silicon Valley formula, with its highly flexible mass of small enterprises, fed by venture capital and new science, and aiming at initial public offerings (IPOs) to make the risk-takers rich.

In cases where the big boss carries the responsibility for efficiency, learning, and adaptiveness the organizations are likely to display the features that accompany that dependence. They will be focused on industries understood by the boss, and any diversification will be into fields easily understood and managed, such as property investment, or where risks may be hedged and knowledge acquired via friends. Such structures, with their tight direct control and supervision, are ideal for noncomplex manufacturing. The various bosses work out among themselves, on their networks of cooperation, the questions of learning and adjustment. That means making either simple products such as garments, or making components of more complex goods, as part of a network of collaborating units. The efficiency of such structures is visible in their capacity to compete against, and put out of business, whole swathes of industry in the advanced economies.

Each of these business systems is good at certain industrial responses, and not at others. To succeed, they have found the right niches in world markets, and might be thought of as constantly refining their responses to enhance their competitiveness, taking in signals from the market as they do so. But in this process, their repertoire of responses is not entirely open. They are embedded in their societies, and this chapter closes with a brief account of the way they are constrained and reinforced by these roots.

Connections

The idea of 'complementarities' in the analysis of an economy comes from the fact that things are so connected across an economy that they change together. Sometimes the connections between them are not immediately obvious, as when labor market structures echo capital market structures. In other cases, the connections are more obvious, such as that between the education system and the work skills in use. Here we simply point out that in complex adaptive systems, such as societal systems of capitalism, the connections across the system, and 'down into' its heritage are inevitable and significant. People do not have entirely free choices in practice. The effect is that societies evolve following paths that are already largely established, at least in terms of direction. They may make sudden turns, and in some cases may back away from where they were heading, as arguably did China in the 1980s, but in the longer historical view they tend to remain true to certain core senses of where they want to be, and how they want to get there. This is why we began with the rationale.

To illustrate this general point, we take an example of this connectedness in the United States. Here, labor markets are volatile. People move jobs regularly and job retention is low by international standards. Companies fire people, often in large numbers, and explain it as an inevitable outcome of the search for shareholder value. But they can relatively easily find new jobs, given the fluidity of the total system and the institutions in place to help them do so. Pushing them to do so is also the weakness of the welfare system, as it is—certainly by European standards—intolerant of the unemployed. As more than half of the households directly or indirectly own shares and society maintains an ideological belief in equality of opportunity, this logic is accepted as legitimate. Inside the firms, training is—by international standards—light. Giving people new skills is not seen as a good investment in such a volatile labor market, as the investment may well be lost. So jobs are designed not to depend on high worker skills and creativity; there is more programming and specializing of work, and more control. People are expected to bring the right skills with them to be hired, and it is easy for skills to be acquired in the open system of education, on the individual's initiative. In the capital market, money flows to where it can yield the best return to investors; that is, shareholders, and the people who decide its allocation have much power in the total system. They are rewarded accordingly, in terms of both status and pay, and take on the style of a new aristocracy. Their rationally calculated pursuit of return provides immense dynamism in the system, and the pursuit of financially defined performance dominates the definition of strategy at all levels. If the company does not perform in the way defined, it begins to be starved of capital. This locks together the flexibility in the labor market with that of the capital market. In the particular way they function, neither could work without the other. They have evolved together

In evolving together, the systems of capital and labor have engaged other components in connected sympathy. So we see a wide set of linkages between the institutions of capital markets, fund and pensions management, general management in boardrooms, employment, education, and the social mores that legitimize the system, so that the idea of socialism in this environment is seen as quite sinister. An obvious corollary of this is that any substantial change to a component might throw the system out of balance, and be resisted. It might also simply not work.

Systems of capitalism are thus complex, internally integrated, constantly evolving, suited to certain competitive responses, and slow to change radically. They bear the traces of their own histories, and cultures, and their particular modes and ideals of government. This has a bearing on what industries they will be best able to compete in, as we shall demonstrate in later chapters.

Key References

Berger, Peter L., and T. Luckmann. 1966. *The Social Construction of Reality*. London: Penguin.

Beinhocker, Eric D. 2005. *The Origin of Wealth: Evolution, Complexity, and the Radical Remaking of Economics*. London: Random House.

Bond, Michael H., Kwok Leung, et al. 2004. 'Culture-level Dimensions of Social Axioms and their Correlates Across 41 Countries', *Journal of Cross-Cultural Psychology*, 35(5): 548–70.

Coates, David, ed. 2002. *Models of Capitalism: Debating Strengths and Weaknesses*, 3 vols. Cheltenham, UK: Edward Elgar.

Faure, David. 2006. *China and Capitalism*. Hong Kong: Hong Kong University Press.

Hall, Peter A., and D. Soskice, eds. 2001. *Varieties of Capitalism*. Oxford: Oxford University Press.

Landes, David. 1998. *The Wealth and Poverty of Nations*. New York: W. W. Norton.

Meyer, Marshall W., and Xiaohui Lu. 2005. 'Managing Indefinite Boundaries: The Strategy and Structure of a Chinese Business Firm', *Management and Organization Review*, 1(1): 57–86.

North, Douglass C. 2005. *Understanding the Process of Economic Change*. Princeton, NJ: Princeton University Press.

Ragin, Charles C. 1987. *The Comparative Method*. Berkeley, CA: University of California Press.

Redding, Gordon. 2005. 'The Thick Description and Comparison of Societal Systems of Capitalism', *Journal of International Business Studies*, 36: 123–55.

Whitley, Richard. 1999. *Divergent Capitalisms*. Oxford: Oxford University Press.

3

Escape from History?

To understand any society today requires a coming to terms with its history, and this is especially true of China. Few societies have been so shaped by a consistent way of running a country over two millennia, in essence an imperial bureaucracy capable of controlling a stable, meaningful, and humanist way of life. Few societies have achieved the heights of respect accorded to China for these early achievements as a civilization, achievements which remain as foundations for the national sense of pride at being Chinese, and as one respected observer defined it, 'a civilization pretending to be a nation-state'.[1] Few have so arranged matters that a conservative intellectual elite remained in power for so long. Most societies have periods of decline between the high points of their civilization, but China's nineteenth- and twentieth-century experiences of civil war, famine, invasion, decadence, and poverty seem unusually severe. They have left many Chinese people with an understandable urge to recover their national pride.

The idea of needing to catch up on two centuries of lost progress is now deeply implanted, and reinforced by reminders. For at least half of those living today, the last of these all-embracing catastrophes—the Cultural Revolution—remains a memory of personal experience; for a few ex red guards the event is recalled as days of heady teenage liberty, but for the majority, as a decade of psychological torture for families with their internal loyalties destroyed. China lives with, and is shaped by, its ancient and modern history in a very compelling way.

In this chapter we will review in brief terms those aspects of Chinese history with a bearing on the evolution of its present-day business systems. This means paying attention to the socioeconomic dimension of that history rather than to other dimensions such as the arts, or the details

[1] Pye 1992.

of politics. We will then consider in broad terms the implications of this legacy for the culture and institutions of China's present-day business world. This will put us in a position in subsequent chapters, when we describe China's three main business systems, to incorporate these ideas into the explanatory framework.

Early History

Before China became a unified state, its earlier history was one of feudalism, and the first clear records of that period date from the ninth century BC. That structure continued for a further six centuries, and during this time, China was subdivided into separate states run by princes. Following the initial Western Zhou period, there followed the Spring and Autumn Periods (770–476 BCE). At this time, and concentrated mainly in the valleys of the Yangtze and the Yellow rivers, there were fifteen large feudal states and a number of smaller ones. In this period there grew the idea that the core states, with societies following Chinese culture, made up the 'Middle Kingdom', in that it was closer to heaven than the semi-barbarous fringe. The head of this federation was a king but not yet an emperor, and his authority was relatively precarious. Eventually, after three centuries, the fragile stability broke down and gave way to the period known as the 'Warring States' (475–221 BCE).

During these centuries of feudal ministates, two 'wandering scholars', Confucius (551–479 BCE) and Mencius (c.372–289 BCE), developed highly influential ideas about societal governance that have had effects on Chinese life ever since. In the Warring States period there also flourished a further 'hundred schools of thought'. This new thinking occurred at the same time as a similar flowering of philosophical thought was taking place in the city-states of Ancient Greece, half a world away in distance, but an entire world away in thought processes and conclusions. Whereas the Greeks stressed political liberty, citizenship, and democracy, and saw their statecraft and artistic achievements flow together into a single liberated and creative golden era, the Chinese continued to accept the monarchy without question and concentrated on the refining of moral principles to be used as its base. Under this authoritarian dominance, their artistic evolution would take centuries to unfold.

From the earliest definitions, the ultimate source of power was seen in China as the mandate of heaven, conceived not as an inherited divine right, but as a duty to be borne by a virtuous philosopher-king, whose descendants would also have to deserve it. In contrast with the Greek idea of a class of free citizens, Chinese political power was concentrated in an elite. For such power to be retained, and for loyalty to be demanded from subordinate groups, the elite had to govern with justice, benevolence, and sincerity. Law was used to control the behavior of the population, and it became a system of regulations and punishments, with little regard to rights. The elite was above it, but was required to maintain proper behavior among its members, bound as they were by their own codes of conduct and morality (known as *li*). A serious offense against *li* could only be expiated by suicide.

The flowering of various philosophies in this early period prior to the establishment of a single unified state gave rise to all the main ideas that guided Chinese thinking about society for the next 2,000 years. Among these, the leading systems were Confucianism, Taoism, that of the Mohists, and that of the Legalists, although many other specific ideas lie outside these four main responses. At a later date, Buddhism spread from India to become an important component of the set of ideas. It is useful to see that such conceptions were not necessarily in competition with each other: that for many people, a mixture, for instance of Confucian and Taoist beliefs, was quite natural; that Buddhism threatened no other system; and that people need both practical guidelines and spiritual compasses.

The Confucian ideal was based on a return to the perceived virtues of an ancient era. In this, the core unit of society was seen as the family, and the state was seen as a form of superfamily. Power was concentrated in family (or state) headship. Loyalty upwards was exchanged for the downward responsible care of members, and discipline was seen as critical to the maintaining of order. The basis of the system's capacity to perpetuate itself was the indoctrination of individuals into clearly defined roles, the consistent acting out of which defined civilized conduct. To be Chinese is to know how to behave in all circumstances. The key roles specified were: father, son, wife, friend, and subordinate/leader, and the definitions of how they should relate to each other became the ground rules of social order. The core of the system was the concept of 'filial piety', the obligation of unquestioning obedience and respect from a son to a father. In a later amendment to the Confucian doctrine, Mencius—without challenging the core reasoning—added the notion of the natural goodness of man, an idea that later was to be challenged fiercely by the Legalists.

The contrast is sharp in comparison with what evolved in the European alternatives. China's order was based on roles. Discipline supported the written rules of conduct, and the individual was sublimated to that order, in the interests of social harmony. In the Western case, there was greater attention to the cultivation of personally held ideals and principles of conduct, plus the addition of a guiding conscience, leaving the individual in a freer space in terms of conduct, and with a stronger sense of individual rights.

A rarely commented-on feature of Chinese social ordering was that the childhood training of individuals into deference toward parents served to guarantee care in old age—an incentive which fostered the perpetuation of the codes of conduct inside each family for generation after generation, over millennia. Confucius knew that if families took responsibility for the welfare and the social conduct of their members, the society could be both stable, self-sustaining, and to a large measure self-governing. The socialization could take place inside the families and did not need the infrastructure of a large priesthood. The state's role could then be that of making sure the rules were followed, and larger matters dealt with, while the system in the micro detail ran itself. One of the outcomes has been peoples' adoption of family as the primary unit of identity, and as the first source of help, in times of need. A family's respectability within a community then becomes a crucial issue, a point of high concern and of much striving. People are conscious of their family histories, and will work hard to build and maintain the 'family name', often keeping records going back centuries.

Confucianism is not a religion. It has no deity and no explanation of an afterlife, no answers to the many mysteries about life and death that occupy the minds of people. It is instead an elaborate code of conduct governing social life, and a set of moral principles designed to support harmony. Put together, these are designed rationally to produce a good society. In consequence it is not threatened by systems of thinking which address the mysteries, and in fact it lives in harmony with them. Chinese people do not have to choose a single belief system. They adopt any of the ones that they find useful or consoling, and their mental world is one of mixtures of interconnecting influences. The systems of thought also interpenetrate: thus filial piety heads the Ten Virtues of Taoism, and so serves to complement Confucianism. The spiritual world—excluded from the pragmatic and 'this-worldly' realm of Confucian thought—is well represented in the magic gardens of Taoism, fortune-telling, *feng shui*, and calendar readings. The practical application of such beliefs, as for instance in Chinese medicine and acupuncture, and the widespread resort to astrology, continues to foster their serious acceptance. The spread of Buddhism from India added a further complementary spiritual world, and that too became absorbed into the total. A Chinese person entering a temple is likely to go in as a member of a Confucian family, to buy incense sticks and offer prayers to gods chosen from a wide pantheon, to pay tribute there to deceased family members, to seek the counsel of fortune-tellers nearby, with the whole process dominated by a golden and revered Buddha. This is how the pains and the questions of life are dealt with, and how people come to terms with their place in the natural world.

Taoism provides a counterbalance to the tight rules and roles of Confucianism. It does so by emphasizing individual freedom and spontaneity, mystical experience, and the possibility of self-transformation. Associated with the philosopher Laozi, the pursuit of 'The Way' encourages a harmonious coming to terms with nature, with its changing rhythms, and an accommodation with the cycle of life and death. It stresses simplicity, purity, and naturalness. Like Buddhism it emphasizes accommodation, self-denial, and the elimination of desire. It stands against assertive action and organized knowledge.

The Mohists taught doctrines which were those of a sublime universal love, extending beyond family and state to all mankind. They believed early on that all you need is love. This system, preached by Mozi five centuries before the birth of Christ, foreshadowed much of the Christian message, but without including ideas of immortal life for the blessed and eternal damnation for the wicked. As a distinct school of thought it faded from view in the time of emperors, but its traces remain in the ideals of 'human-heartedness', affability, and tolerance which characterize much Chinese social life, and which are needed to balance the potential aggression of competing families and clans and the domineering state.

The Legalist school, which was the last of the major indigenous philosophies to emerge, ran counter to Confucius and Mencius, and argued that man's nature was essentially evil. Nothing effective could be achieved by preaching ideals as a basis for societal reform, and the behaviors of past leaders were seen as no longer relevant. Strong law was the best protection for societal order. Using such ideas, in 221 BCE, the first of China's great revolutions ended the feudal period, and ushered in the Qin (rapidly to become the Han) imperial dynasty. The first emperor, Qin Shi Huang, a man of formidable and aggressive energy, set about the founding of the first recognizable state of China. He did so with notorious cruelty and violence; for instance, sacrificing a million lives in building the Great

Wall. He also imposed universal standards for language, commerce, currency, transport, and administration. He had the traditional aristocracy, 120,000 families, seized en masse and deported to what was then the edge of the nation in Shaanxi, with a single blow destroying the ancient landed power of the noble clans of the feudal era. He gathered together all the nation's books of ancient wisdom, and—in a gesture for which his reputation was forever damaged beyond repair—he had them all burned. Moreover, 460 scholars were put to death for concealing their books. Even so, his legacy was the unified state that his successors in the Han dynasty controlled centrally from Xian or Luoyang for the next four centuries, and that would survive intact as a political unit to the present day.

Over the succeeding four hundred years, the Han state gradually returned to the earlier Confucian ideals, and away from the oppressive Legalism with which it had begun. To find administrators it encouraged the selection of educated 'gentlemen', and enough of the lost philosophies were recovered from their hiding places in peoples' memories and secret vaults, to foster the slow reemergence of an intellectual elite—the early mandarins, many of whom could trace their ancestry to the old noble families of earlier centuries. Slowly Confucianism returned as the state doctrine. The elite would not be chosen by examination until much later, in the Tang dynasty, but at least there came into power a body of scholars able to influence policy and maintain a steady adherence to the core ideals of Confucius. The difference was that now, the condition of the national economy was a core concern, and the influence of merchants would challenge the Confucian monopoly on state policy. The feudal economic system of autonomous fiefdoms had given way to a national economy.

It is unnecessary here to detail the transitions of power over the succeeding dynasties. Suffice it to say that great flowerings of civilization, and also periods of decline, came and went as the dynasties succeeded one another. One clear trend later in the second millennium was for a gradual change in the nature of the autocracy, whereby the central power came to be exercised with less awesome strength, eventually leading to an essentially weak state resting only on tradition for its authority. The last dynasty was that of the Qing (1644–1912), and it came to represent the dangers of a state closing itself off from the world, and remaining proud and unchanging. With a very clear image of itself, shattered by a long series of unexpected defeats and humiliations brought by the West in the nineteenth century, but unable to adjust, it declined slowly but inexorably toward its eventual collapse in 1911 under an onslaught of

41

new ideas. The essential dilemma was how to modernize a society under totalist bureaucracy. It still is.

Let us now take note of certain key elements in the traditional formula used by China to run its economy and society, and then consider the resulting legacies of that history for the present day.

The Idea of the State

As noted earlier, China is a civilization rather than a state. The state is defined by the culture.[2] A culture is also more likely to survive threats than a nation-state, and this may explain the Chinese state's capacity to survive intact longer than any other, and to withstand immense pressures from the invasions of both armies and ideas. Nor has dramatic internal change affected a view of the state as a functioning unit. Pressures for federalism, unlike elsewhere, have never succeeded in diffusing power. The culture was always especially strong, with a built-in capacity to survive, and its strength derived from the long-established certainty that China held a special place among nations, not so much from its size or military power, but from the conviction that its own form of order was closer to the natural order of the cosmos. It was surrounded by lesser countries, with weaker stability, that would acknowledge its greater centrality, its greater similarity to heaven. Proper conduct and social order, as indicators of superior statecraft, were therefore of high significance, and, by extension, the rules of conduct became sacred. The genius of Confucianism lay in making those rules clear and transmittable, and in providing a moral base for their use. The power of right conduct in influencing others was seen as superior to the power of reward and punishment. China understood both hard and soft power a long time ago.

Power was always centralized, and this is traceable to the same worldview. The emperor was the transmitter of the cosmic order. His example of virtuous conduct was the standard to which others should aspire. Without the emperor figure, the keystone would be missing and the whole structure threatened. It is hard for outsiders to appreciate the peculiarly high degree of control over society which the Chinese state was designed to achieve, but a number of its design principles will be taken for comparison to illustrate the point.[3]

---

[2] Fairbank, Reischauer, and Craig 1965; see also Pye 1985.
[3] Ideas on this are drawn especially from Jenner 1992.

First, however, is the matter of the surrounding conditions for thinking. Unlike in Europe, there were no alternative political structures for comparison, no neighbors with comparable civilizations. It was not possible to observe how other states could accommodate the demands of oligarchies with vested interests, or of a powerful church, or of chartered groups of burghers. China, for most of its history, was seen by its people as having the only respectable government in the civilized world.

The Effects of Totalism

The assumption that only a single central government power was appropriate was implanted from the beginning and has survived to the present day. It carried significant implications: there was no sense of personal private space which the state could not invade; there was no sense of citizenship with individual rights; the safeguards against abuse of power were aimed not at the structure of power itself, but at its abuse as judged by the rigorous standards of the high culture; diversity in the political arena was seen as inherently wrong; the politics of bureaucratic control became highly refined, and one of its outcomes was skill in maintaining the advantage by fragmenting the activities it supervised into an infinitely large number of tiny units. Sun Yat-sen's metaphor of the 'tray of loose sand' was apposite for the state he attempted to modernize in 1912. The extreme diffraction of China's industry today suggests the absorbing of the same instinct. Bodies that might grow to significant scale and might challenge the state continue to be either co-opted or brought under strict control. The current experimenting with much greater business independence associated with WTO is a particularly adventurous route to take in this regard. So too is the recent allocation of economic power to provincial governments and municipalities. Despite changes over the various dynasties in the amount of government control over daily life and work, the usual lesson taken by Chinese from their history seems to be that giving away too much discretion will weaken the state's ability to master its fate, order will be threatened, and the mandate of heaven will be seized by somebody else. The imperial bureaucracy becomes agonizingly difficult to move from, even today when a flood of new ideas is pouring in, and as W. J. F. Jenner observes, 'It almost makes one feel sorry for China's rulers, caught as they are between a played-out past and impossible futures.'[4]

[4] Jenner 1992, p. 36.

The Supporting Apparatus

The will of the emperor was transmitted through a supportive elite chosen for the faithful adherence of its members to the state ideology. That ideology contained the moral justifications that made the power structure acceptable. The dogma which flowed from the interpretation of the ideology was a monopoly preserve of China's gentry—an elite chosen continually for its intellect, and acting in the name of the emperor. Confucian scholarship could only be practiced after years of training and the acquisition of high literary skills at a level simply not available to the mass of the public. Social peace was maintained by the local and provincial work of magistrates. At a high point of imperial rule, around 1800, with a population of about 300 million, those qualified for appointment to imperial office numbered around 40,000, but resting on a substratum of aspirants numbering a further million. Without such a supportive elite, China was (and is) ungovernable. With it, and assuming tight control of it from the center, China is governable, but designed to maintain its status quo.

The function of the Party in modern times is similar to that of the mandarinate in earlier periods. So too are the essentials of its makeup. To be a member of the elite requires absorption of the state ideology and the ability to interpret it in ways which fit with the imperial will. Elite status brings privileges, as earlier. But also, as earlier, any challenge to orthodoxy becomes a highly dangerous and political matter, and this is not a control structure conducive to adaptability. Change will wait for a sign from the top, such as Deng Xiaoping's famous tour of the south. Nor is it a structure that can comfortably accommodate any *radical* change of core purposes for the society as a whole. With the best will in the world, and with the highest intellects brought to bear, the challenge of fundamental societal change, for such a structure, remains far more complex than copying success elsewhere. The stealthy revolution of the last two decades must be seen as a formidable achievement, but its continuation still remains a design challenge for the state's control structure.

The Family in Chinese Society

It is perhaps understandable that, in the face of such an authoritarian context, the family came to play such a crucial role. It was, in any case, an extension of the state structure. In the family milieu, for all the subordination and discipline that went with membership, the individual could find a secure base for identity, security, emotion, economic support, recreation, social contact, education, and the 'religion' of ancestor veneration. In addition, a family was normally part of a larger descent group or clan, capable of promoting the welfare of families inside it. In seeing this specific social network, defined in clear relationship terms, as a refuge from or alternative to the controlling state, it is important to see also that there were virtually no other sources available to the average person in need of help. Other than the larger clan bodies and trade guilds, the society produced little in the way of 'community' in the sense thought of in many other societies. It should be noted here that the traditional guilds in China worked in a somewhat different way from those of Japan and Europe. The Chinese form was one of local monopoly licensed by, and responsible to, officials, and judged on its merits as a responsible local body. This allowed little room for free private enterprise.[5]

Conservatism

The conservatism that provided so much of the state's stability was based on a bond between the emperor and the scholar elite. This united the state and the culture. With the emperor at the pinnacle of the structure of education and the examinations, the great tradition of cultural superiority could be kept alive. But a devastating side effect gradually began to undermine the perfection of the design. The reverence for tradition blocked out new learning. It also smothered the idea of progress, and left China isolated in its complacency. There is no more telling sign of such introversion than the treatment of the huge volume of new knowledge acquired from the sea voyages of the great Ming fleets under Admiral Zheng He in the early 1400s (including by some controversial accounts the mapping of continents not known to Westerners for a further seventy years in the case of the Americas, and a further two hundred in the case of Australia). All this new knowledge was destroyed, in another devastating burning of the books, as for at least a century China turned back in on itself, later opening cautiously to restore its traditional trading patterns but not to expand them. Lord Macartney's attempt in 1793 to open up trade with England and the East India Company was a notorious

[5] Fairbank, Reichauer, and Craig 1965, p. 73.

failure. He was told that the celestial empire had everything it needed, in abundance, and that future trade must remain under the control of the regulated system of Canton.

The Use of Science

One of the great puzzles in Chinese history is the society's inability to make full use of the scientific knowledge that it had accumulated. Why did technology not progress? Why did business not exploit science for commercial ends and generate new societal wealth? Why did Chinese scientific knowledge, starting as it did five hundred years ago far ahead of the West's, not continue to outpace it? Making full allowance for China's skill in adapting knowledge from outside, why is there still dependence on the skills of other societies in fundamental research and the funding and commercialization of basic science?

The answers to these questions remain under constant debate, but there is enough agreement on some of the causes to hazard a summary. It is of course impossible to point to a single cause, as the explanation contains many features, but among them are the following:

1. The overwhelmingly dominant feature of the economy, until quite recently, was agriculture. In this the tendency was for land to be limited, and capital scarce, but for labor to be plentiful and well skilled in traditional methods. In circumstances like these there was little incentive for labor-saving innovation in farm technology.

2. The continued breakdown of family wealth, under the system of dividing it among the sons, inhibited the accumulation of capital which might otherwise have gone into experimental ventures.

3. The world of farmers and artisans, most of whom were illiterate, was at a different social level from that of the literati, and the latter were therefore in a weak position to combine theory and practice.

4. The world of commerce, which might be thought of as a source of demand for new technology, was as handicapped as the farming world when it came to the accumulation of units big enough to justify new technical ventures. Nor was there a national market to aim at, except in very few industries under state control.

5. Property rights were not secure in the absence of laws to foster them, so risk-taking was inhibited. This may well have been exacerbated by

fears of unpredictable taxation, and an inhibition about appearing rich enough to draw the attention of the government.

6. No bodies existed in the society equivalent to the 'philosophical societies' of Victorian England, that brought together the scientists, businessmen, and capitalists, and so stimulated the first Industrial Revolution.

7. There was no lead from government to stimulate science.

8. There were no great regular trade fairs, such as those of Europe, at which new ideas and techniques could be exchanged and connected with the world of commerce.

An Economy of Merchants

The traditional organizing of the economy was, as earlier suggested, highly diffracted. Instead of creating organizations to integrate, rationalize, and streamline the production processes done in myriad households, the only coordination was done by merchants doing the buying and selling. Factories did not emerge, except under state control. As Mark Elvin has suggested, commerce substituted for management.

The merchants, in turn, were dominated by officials, on whom they depended for protection. Rather than becoming risk-taking investors, they were better off becoming semiofficials. Economic growth was not on the government's agenda, and its concerns remained stability, tax gathering, and infrastructure such as waterworks and granaries. Under the traditional dynasties this economy did not so much fall behind that of the West as time went on, but it proceeded on entirely different terms. Inward looking, without scientific institutions, uncoordinated, labor-intensive, capital-starved, and efficient only at a stationary level of technology, the economy kept reproducing itself in a preindustrial condition.

The Mao Legacy

Mao Zedong remains for many a revered figure because of a single achievement—the restoration of China's pride as a nation free of invaders and able to 'stand up' alongside other nations. This required immense reserves of toughness and single-mindedness, and he seems to have possessed those in large quantities. The people of China believe in strong leadership, as do most Asian societies, and they are generally prepared to live with its consequences. When those consequences include extremes of domination, and subordinate dependence, that instinct to follow the strong leader is turned into subservience on a large scale. Mao was the arch manipulator of the forces of subjugation and was prepared to use fear as his main instrument. It reached a point where he was eventually able to reach into every household and control its revenues and food intake.

It is not our intention here to describe the Mao years, for which other detailed accounts are available.[6] But it is necessary for us to note the aftereffects in the economic domain. Of these there are three that stand as continuing legacies of modern history. They are the retention of state dominance, the splintering of the economy into fragments, and the self-preserving and mistrusting conservatism of an entire generation. This is not to say that the effects remain permanent, as they are slowly being washed out of the society with the new generations. It is instead to say that they have affected much that happened in recent decades and much that was unspoken but thought about among people with influence at all levels, from the small shopkeeper to the regional governor. The society's institutions and many of its systems of managing and organizing bear the imprint still of that age of noble ideals, but also of propaganda, dogma, fear, and subservience.

The dominance of the state remains the centerpiece of societal design, as it always has, but the special feature in the twentieth-century interpretation of it has been the use of the Party as the instrument of control. Unlike the earlier mandarin elite, chosen competitively for its austere scholarship, Party membership was open to anyone willing to espouse the ideology and represent it locally. It has to be said that if many members were inspired by the social ideals, many were also inspired by a wish to survive the hostile circumstances they were immersed in. In more recent years the extra dimension has been added of access to opportunities presented under economic growth. But nobody can know the salience of these tendencies at either the individual or societal level. One of the authors was at a lunch party in Guangzhou years ago, as China was beginning to open up, and when the Party man left the table, an old professor leaned over to him and whispered 'Please take this message away

---

[6] We would especially recommend reading each end of the spectrum, from the massive assault launched in Chang and Halliday 2005, to the detailed political account revealed in MacFarquar and Schoenhals 2006.

from here and explain it to people trying to understand China: for the past twenty years we have all been "acting".'

The second effect stemmed from the nature of the communes as self-sufficient entities, and the consequent dispersal and multiplication of production systems. This paid no regard to economic efficiency and was not intended to. Its result was a huge number of small factories all over the country, most of which could not survive the arrival of widespread market forces. The aftereffects of this are still visible. Similarly, but at a higher level, the development of autonomous regions, each able to sustain itself industrially, began as a response to fears of invasion. Its effects remain in the continuing 'regionalism' of the China market, and the weakly developed national market in almost any goods.

The third effect, the conservatism of a generation, is less visible with every passing year. But its effects are similar to those stemming from the dominance of the state via the Party. It has contributed to the low level of upwards communication in the managerial process, and perhaps also to the urge to control one's own fate manifest in the explosion of entrepreneurship.

The Challenge of Modernization

As we have pointed out earlier, the difference between a modern and a premodern society is that a modern society is able to maximize the use of the resources at its disposal by raising both (a) the intensity and (b) the extensiveness of economic exchange; anybody can do business with anybody else. There is a quantum difference between that and a society where the full potential of exchange options cannot be realized; too many people cannot be trusted. To meet this fundamental modern design principle requires a system for the rational allocation of both financial and human capital to places where their use can be most fruitful. This will rest largely on a fabric of institutions, such as law, to foster trust between strangers, and to give people the information they need to make informed judgments. Another core need is for science and business to find ways of turning inventions into extra value for the society. Finally there needs to be a way for people to keep the fruits of their labor. As one lay philosopher observed—'Communism doesn't work because people like to own stuff.'

Key References

Chang, Jung, and Jon Halliday. 2005. *Mao: The Unknown Story*. London: Jonathan Cape.

Elvin, Mark. 1973. *The Pattern of the Chinese Past*. Stanford, CA: Stanford University Press.

Fairbank, John K., Edwin O. Reischauer, and Albert M. Craig. 1965. *East Asia: The Modern Transformation*. Boston, MA: Houghton Mifflin.

Hamilton, Gary G. 1990. 'Patriarchy, Patrimonialism and Filial Piety: A Comparison of China and Western Europe', *British Journal of Sociology*, 41(1): 77–104.

Jenner, W. J. F. 1992. *The Tyranny of History*. London: Allen Lane.

MacFarquhar, Roderick, and Michael Schoenhals. 2006. *Mao's Last Revolution*. Cambridge, MA: Belknap Press.

Pye, Lucian. 1985. *Asian Power and Politics: The Cultural Dimensions of Authority*. Cambridge, MA: Belknap Press.

_____ 1992. 'Social Science Theories in Search of Chinese Realities', *China Quarterly*, 132: 1161–70.

Spence, Jonathan D. 1990. *The Search for Modern China*. London: Hutchinson.

4

The Legacies of History

We have in Chapter 3 implied that China cannot escape from its history, and we have outlined briefly the main elements of that history. It is necessary now to identify what is carried into the present day and is as a result deeply embedded in the society and unlikely to change quickly. As we are concerned particularly with China's business life, we will concentrate on aspects related to organization and economic behavior. As a result, we focus on six crucial features affecting the society's emergence toward a new condition. These are as follows:

1. Retention of control by the state
2. Endemic mistrust and its connection with social structures, information access, social norms, and institutions
3. Hierarchy and its effects on organization
4. Individual entrepreneurship and opportunism
5. Technological dependence
6. The desire to make up for lost time

All these flow forward from its history, and in a sense all of them make China what it is. Attempts to make it what it is not—such as a replica of a Western-style liberal market economy—run into two massive concealed obstacles. First, the features of the legacy are all interconnected, so that change requires movement on a very broad front and is unlikely to work partially. Second, radical societal change requires a new definition of ideals, and one that does not require the abandonment of heritage. Walking away from a proud culture is simply not feasible. A nation's construction of reality is not negotiable. It was tried before in various phases of the

Mao era, resulted in killing of up to 45 million people,[1] and reduced the country to deep poverty.

Retention of Control by the State

The state has a *duty* to control. That has always been the first principle of Chinese statecraft. Loss of control over order is deeply threatening. In recent years this duty has been discharged in the economy by four principal means. First, the state owns all land. It also owns a large sector of the economy, and especially the industries seen as strategic. Second, it devolved economic decision power to the provinces by use of the Party as its agent in controlling developments. Third, it sanctioned the emergence of the new and vibrant private sector but retains rights to intervene through licensing and taxation, as and when any threat to central authority might emerge. Fourth, it has so far maintained a monopoly control over bank lending, and over access to the stock markets.

Two things are missing from this picture when making comparisons with other countries' paths to modernization. The nascent bourgeoisie is not coalescing to put pressure on government in any coordinated way, and the 'tray of loose sand' again comes to mind. Nor is there evidence of the emergence of a truly independent society. In business this would be visible in strong independent coalitions such as confederations of business leaders, or a national chamber of commerce with voting or lobbying power, a freestanding stock-exchange council, and a free press. The government does not yet welcome intermediaries with serious influence. While numerous business associations have sprung up over recent years, this has often occurred at the behest of the state, which tends to penetrate and control these associations.

And yet, potentially monumental changes are afoot, and cannot be denied. The opening up to WTO rules of conduct is very highly significant. The success of the market-driven private sector is undeniable, and so too is the success of the hybrid sector in which local governments ally with entrepreneurs to bring together state assets and astute management. The new stress on building professions, such as accounting, indicates a readiness to move toward rationality and objectivity in the use of resources. A further consciously induced catalyst for change has been the

---

[1] Estimates of the death toll of the individual policy disasters vary. For instance, estimates for the Great Leap Forward range from 20 to 43 million dead from starvation. Chang and Halliday 2005 accuse Mao of fostering the deaths of 70 million people.

use of foreign technology, both practical and managerial. All these show that a massive experiment is underway. But its nature, as Deng Xiaoping observed, is that of 'crossing the river by groping for the stones.'

At this stage in our argument, we would observe only that the eventual pattern of the economy will still be one in which the state can control what it needs to control. We will later open up the question of options for doing that, when we consider the various business systems and their trajectories.

Endemic Mistrust

Totalitarian states induce mistrust. People in them usually have few resources with which to build a sense of security, are competing with others for these scarce common resources, and usually lack the support of institutions which might help them to trust others they do not personally know. To survive, they get whatever they can from the system, but they know that others are doing the same, that obligations extend to friends and to partners in exchanges, but no further. The assumption in viewing strangers is that they have the same mentality, and will also get whatever they can. So, you have to be careful.

This mindscape is normal in many communities living at the subsistence level, and human beings cope with its stresses by behaviors that ameliorate them. Within a restricted community like a village, elaborate rules come into play to govern reciprocity in exchange: people with sudden wealth are expected to have a good reason to explain it, and also to share it—if only symbolically; status is claimed by simple displays of consumption; obligation exchanges are accounted for over decades. Above all, key social groupings such as family are expected to look after individual welfare. In larger social bodies the finesse of this social balancing is more difficult and the competition for the scarce resources is more crude.

In many states, the government will construct institutions to take responsibility for welfare across a large group of people, under ideals such as Communism, or in paternalist welfare states, and China's record in this, although turbulent, nevertheless affected much of the population, and still does for the tens of millions in the state sector. This system of welfare is now being dismantled, and the responsibility passed back either to new employers, or to the people themselves. So where do they now turn?

The traditional refuge in China is the extended family. Inside it, one is safe. Such membership then entails certain rules for trust and they work in concentric circles. The inner circle is family and the members are deeply trusted. You also trust, in a different way, a second circle of proto-family members; these are close friends of long standing, perhaps key employees or business partners, and people you knew at school; then there is a third circle of people with whom you have a relationship of reciprocity, your *guanxi* connections. These are people you transact with, in business or in other fields, and their connections with you are built over time as deals are done and trust accumulated via buying and selling, exchanging information, borrowing and lending, coinvesting, committee and charity work, etc. Critically, many of them are in a field of influence, like a government position, or a bank, and their help to you at some point may be crucial. An effective navigator of this social context will have cultivated several hundred of such connections. But three conditions also apply to this scene: first, it takes much time and effort to build and maintain such a web; second, its reliability is stronger when the network is of people who know each other across the structure, as in a trade, or a district, because a reputation for trustworthiness is an important source of capacity to do things in business, and the loss of it in a business community is highly damaging; third, and crucially, that is all with which you have to work. Outside your three concentric circles is quite a dangerous jungle.

Economists talk of low transaction costs as contributions to efficiency in an economic system, and the Chinese *guanxi* networks are the basis for this in many parts of the economy. They explain much of the success of the original equipment manufacturer (OEM) supply chains which link small enterprises into clusters and then chains, and which have helped China to become 'the workshop of the world.' There is also evidence that much entrepreneurship is now based in family enterprise, as the traditional structures of society reassert their ancient roles.

One of the most significant sources of influence on the architecture of trust in a society is the way information is handled. If it is highly codified, as in a well-defined legal system or a detailed book of instructions governing an accounting system, and if the codes are made to apply throughout the society, then the behavior of other people, and the standards of their conduct, become reliably predictable, and in some sense 'trustworthy'. Such means of guaranteeing information and its meaning, and ensuring its application, apply in many fields: educational qualifications, assessments of corporate performance, and legal systems are just three where the conduct of business is affected by the reducing of risk.

In China, although much has been achieved recently in the direction of freeing the flow, and the reliability, of information, it must be said that the limitations are still dominant and trust still severely inhibited. The absence of a strong and independent profession of accounting, taking responsibility for the quality of reported corporate data, remains a handicap. The absence of a free press denies the kind of commentary that assists in the judgment of information, although that vacuum is now being filled to some degree by active use of the Internet. The quality of many statistics remains suspect. The concern with control and with protection against interference (exacerbated by much experience of interference from authorities) brings out a natural tendency to keep things secret. In a society where information is problematic, useful information becomes a strategic advantage, and must not be given away to just anybody. Secrecy is standard in many business dealings.

One of the common features in high-trust societies is the sharing of norms across the population. It is clearly no defense against the unscrupulous, but the sense that people share ideals gives a starting sense of trust that their behavior will be within certain bounds. This is especially visible at a societal level in Japan. By contrast, it is far less visible in China, and that may well be due to the absence of a clear national ideology in this age of experiment and radical change, and in the face of a collapse of prior ideologies, a collapse not yet fully acknowledged.

The last cause of trust being so weak is the poverty of the institutional fabric required to sustain it beyond the arena of personal connections. This fabric may not be poor in the sense that there is not much of it visible. It may in fact be quite visible, as is the legal system. Its poverty lies in its incapacity to protect, to provide predictability, or to reduce uncertainty. Much of this weakness stems from the absence of the large bodies of people needed who are capable of ruthless objectivity, professional pride in standards, and the rational pursuit of evidence-based judgment. Again, much is now happening to meet this need, but the size of the task remains monumental.

Hierarchy and Its Effects

In any managed activity with a need to be competitive, there are three requirements that we have earlier pointed to: the efficient organizing and coordinating of activities; learning by the organization about external worlds having an impact on it; and the ability of the organization to change if it has to. These challenges are met in different ways in different societies, as suggested in earlier chapters. Management itself is a culturally influenced process.

There are two basic formulae in use in the wealthy economies, and it could be argued that they are wealthy partly because those responses have been refined to a high level of application. The first response is for managers as a group to take responsibility for all three fields of action: coordinating, organizational learning, and organizational change. The workforce in such circumstances tend to follow the responses designed by managers, and leave the responsibility in the managerial ranks, where it is arguably well rewarded. Preparation of people for such roles is also usually well developed, as for instance with MBA degrees. This response is found most commonly in liberal market capitalism of the kind found in the United States and United Kingdom. It has the ability to produce large complex organizations that are capable of flexibility and learning, as well as efficiency in coordination. The Fortune 500 contains many.

Another formula, favored especially in Germany and Japan, is one where the workforce becomes heavily engaged in all three fields of action. Those thinking on behalf of the organization—in the sense of learning what it needs to know and being interested in its adaptability—are spread throughout all ranks. There is commonly here a high level of involvement of workers in technical innovation, or market response, and much of the brainpower of the employees is engaged in solving company problems. This results in organizations with high levels of adaptiveness, especially in the incremental improvement of technical products, where worker ingenuity is brought to bear on the creation of machines, or systems.

In each of these two alternatives (acknowledging of course the immense variety of options and combinations which flourish in reality) there is an implicit recognition that the sharing of power works better than the concentration of it at the top of the hierarchy. In the first case, with a dominance of managers taking care of the three roles, there is nonetheless usually an acknowledgment that workers need to be motivated, to participate where feasible, and to be empowered enough to feel responsible. These themes are easily seen in any textbook on management, designed for application in the liberal market economies of the Western world.

In the second case, where influence is spread among both management and worker ranks, as in Germany and Japan, that power sharing derives largely from the surrounding institutional fabric of the society. German labor unions, for instance, are heavily represented at board level. Long periods of employment in the same firm make it worthwhile to build high levels of worker skill. So too in Japan, the custom of 'lifetime employment' for a considerable proportion of the workforce makes it possible to reach higher levels of worker commitment and skill relevant to innovation.

The position in China is different from that in either of the two broad types just described. There is a strong tendency in Chinese organizations, at all scales from the family business to the large conglomerate group, for decision-making to gravitate to the top of the organization and not to be dispersed downwards. The tradition of the 'big boss'—*lao ban*—is deeply entrenched. With it goes a culture of dependence on the receipt of directions from above, and a reluctance to risk the taking of initiatives. This would be normal anywhere for nonskilled or semiskilled workforces, but in China it extends also through the ranks of management. There are many reasons for this phenomenon, but perhaps three are worthy of special note. First, the tradition of centralized authority is deeply embedded in the society's norms for the constructing of order. Second, many of the older generation have suffered from the deeply threatening pressures of the Communist era, and especially the Cultural Revolution. They have learned not to stick their necks out for fear of getting their heads chopped off. The unpredictability of reactions from the powerful in that earlier era, and the possible severity of punishment, led many to shelter behind conformity in order to stay out of trouble. Third, there is little developed managerial professionalism, and very few advanced skills in the workforce, on the basis of which an independent perspective might be constructed. Hard work in itself is neither enough to take care of coordination across an organization nor organizational learning or organizational change, and when these are left to the big boss the organization at large scale is weakened more and more as it grows. At small scale it may well be nonproblematic and that is the theme to which we now turn.

Entrepreneurship and Opportunism

Most of the world's societies are built around families, and there are numerous structures for fitting together the instincts of people toward family membership, and the creation of a stable wider society. Few societies, however, have laid quite the same degree of emphasis, as has China, on family membership as the key source of identity for a person. The strength of this structure comes from a continuous history of millennia in its use, an elaborate set of moral and behavioral codes to maintain it, and the stimulus to its self-replication (as the guarantor of security and welfare) built into the design. The family is the state in microcosm, and the state as superfamily (or more accurately the Chinese notion of civilization) is sacrosanct.

Equally part of the societal design is the competition between families for the scarce resources available in a relatively poor country. This is exacerbated by the fact that connections between the families are based on specific ties of reciprocity rather than an overall sense of community. The competitive relations between these social units become more intense than in some other societies in the absence of sources of status in the society more generally. There are not yet the developed professions in which status might be acquired. The traditional route to status via education, although now opening up, still only caters to few people, with 6 percent of the relevant age group in tertiary education compared to the US equivalent of 77 percent. The strong sense of hierarchy built into Chinese sensibilities, as in most Asian cultures, raises the significance of status and respect, but instead of its being focused on the person, as might occur in the 'individualist' cultures of the Western world, it focuses on the family. Concern for the dignity of family pride, of 'the family name,' is high in the system of ideals.

The Chinese entrepreneur, whether acting alone, or in partnership with family or friends, tends to think in terms of family security via wealth as a primary rationale for the work of building an enterprise. This application of filial piety is instinctive after years of socialization into the values surrounding it. Even though the same pattern occurs in other societies, it is unusual for it to reach the levels of implementation achieved in China. The explosive growth of the private sector since 1980 is a reflection of this drive. Within that sector lies the secret of China's success in becoming the world's favored source of consumer goods and components. It is here, with the efficiency of flexible networking between independent small firms, that OEM reaches its highest levels of scale and world market penetration. The searching for opportunity, which is part of this approach, rests on a willingness to take risk, a perspective often founded in fatalistic beliefs derived from the surrounding belief systems. But at the most fundamental level, much of the success, as we shall examine later, is founded in the entrepreneurial drive of individuals acting honorably to build and protect their family reputations.

Technological Dependence

For science to become commercialized successfully in any society, a number of features have to be in place. Basic research needs to be accessible, even if not directly conducted in that society, although having 'one's own' scientists is likely to offer an advantage in the world of networking which fosters and monitors scientific progress. Inventions need to be protected from being stolen for exploitation, and there need to be incentives for those doing the inventing. There needs to be an interface connecting the scientific and commercial worlds so that ideas can flow both ways. There needs to be a system of funding that allows ideas to be pursued. And there should be a source of funding, such as venture capital, that encourages the linking of new products to markets. There is often also, in successful cases, support from government for research with longer term or more basic outcomes.

The combination of these components in one society is rare, and China is lacking in most of them. Much work needs to be done to reach reasonable levels of technological independence and competitive competence in invention. In the meantime China will borrow much technology. It will also be handicapped by its reputation for intellectual property rights infringement, but that phenomenon needs to be seen in context, though it rarely is. The context is that the major multinationals, because of their accumulated scale, have a virtual stranglehold on science as it might be applied in the commercial world. The world's high-income economies, currently with 16 percent of the world's population, contain 99 percent of the world's top 300 companies by R&D spending.[2] To protect this monopoly by extending 'their' rules of the game to all countries, is, to say the least, self-serving, and has the effect of giving them bigger arenas in which to exercise their dominance. Such a case is rarely made, but it does at least serve to explain certain responses in developing countries, and the guerilla warfare over intellectual property that is constantly being fought.

In practice, the development of scientific invention proceeds by hybridization in China. Many scientists are trained outside and bring back what they have learned, keeping in touch with their foreign colleagues and collaborating in the making progress. Also many foreign firms enter alliances with specific technology-transfer clauses. New science parks have sprung up to foster transfers, and a flow of information between them and

---

[2] Nolan 2004, p. 214.

places such as Silicon Valley need not always be one-way. The reproduction of venture capital systems in the US style will await the development of China's financial infrastructure, but small-scale entrepreneurs will in the meantime find capital on their own networks.

Key References

Chang, Jung, and Jon Halliday. 2005. *Mao: The Unknown Story*. London: Jonathan Cape.

Foster, George M. 1967. 'Peasant Society and the Image of Limited Good', in J. M. Potter, M. N. Diaz, and G. M. Foster (eds.), *Peasant Society*. Boston, MA: Little, Brown.

Guthrie, Douglas. 2006. *China and Globalization*. New York: Routledge.

Naughton, Barry. 2007. *The Chinese Economy*. Cambridge, MA: MIT Press.

Nolan, Peter. 2004. *Transforming China: Globalization, Transition and Development*. London: Anthem Press.

OECD. 2005. *OECD Economic Surveys: China*. Paris: OECD.

5

The Regional Ethnic Chinese in Business

All societies receive influence from outside their borders, from the direct pressures of world markets to the more subtle pressures of the world of ideas and alternative techniques and practices. China is no exception, and has responded to such influences by slowly opening its doors, since 1980, to a point where they might be considered now almost—but not quite yet—fully open. Significant influences brought in have been (*a*) the logic of prices in world markets for goods made in China, and for materials needed by China; (*b*) the acquiring of new technology over a wide range, and by a variety of methods; (*c*) the importing of institutional structures— often for local amendment—in fields such as financial regulation, commercial law, and education; (*d*) foreign direct investment (FDI) and all the influences that go with it; and (*e*) ideas and ideals about the individual in society, many of which confront Chinese tradition, not least among which is the open communications possible on the Internet.

But, in relation to outside influence, China is distinct from many other developing nations in having a special feature in its recent history, and one with a substantial impact on the manner of its recent evolution. The 'Overseas Chinese'[1] have assisted in two major ways: firstly by being intermediaries between China and the markets of the developed world; and secondly by investing massively in their home country and tying the Pacific-Asian regional economies together with it.

In this chapter we examine this phenomenon, and in doing so bring into the account the varying formulae of Hong Kong, Singapore, and

---

[1] The title 'Overseas Chinese' is deliberately placed in quotes to indicate that it is no longer entirely acceptable, especially to those who might be placed in the category. They might well retain strong affiliation with Chinese cultural traditions, but over decades and generations they have become citizens of other countries, and the implicit denial of this acquired citizenship is unwarranted. In normal description of their category we use the term 'regional ethnic Chinese'.

Taiwan as possible influences on the homeland's business systems. We note also the role of ethnic-Chinese entrepreneurship in the other Association of Southeast Asian Nations (ASEAN) states. In the laboratory of China, here is a box of sometimes-powerful catalysts for the experiments being conducted there.

At the heart of the set of issues is the question of whether the large private business groups, which emerged from among the ethnic Chinese of the countries around the South China Sea are capable of sustained growth as significant global corporations, with long-term viability; and what are the implications of that organizational skill for China? Related questions flow from that. Are such organizations essentially products of an earlier postcolonial era? Can they adopt forms and practices suitable for future, more 'modern' conditions, especially those brought by technology, information advances, and global markets? Are they essentially mercantile rather than industrial capitalists? Are they capable of acting as models for China to emulate as it engages with globalization? Assuming that they are products of the circumstances of their emergence, how has that experience marked them? If they have to change, can they? If they do not, what are their competitive advantages in today's world? Are they tigers or dinosaurs, or perhaps chameleons?

It must be acknowledged that there are already on the world scene large organizations with global impact, created by ethnic Chinese from the region. Companies such as Acer, Cheung Kong, Evergreen, and the CP Group have grown to prominence under powerful leaders, not only in ways that embrace modern principles of managing and organizing, but also in ways that do not mean straight copying. In cases such as these, the inspirational leader remains crucial, ownership is usually concentrated, and succession to a new generation is still under test. The questions remain: is this a form of enterprise that displays historically short-term brilliance, and then breaks up and gives way to newly created alternatives, allowing the surrounding economy to benefit from creative destruction? Or is this a form that will make a transition to professional management, widespread ownership, and greater longevity? Or will a hybrid emerge that takes the advantages of both approaches, thereby not abandoning its cultural heritage? In any case does it have a choice, given that it is embedded in a set of cultural assumptions from which it cannot easily escape?

In viewing the regional context against which such questions are posed, two formative periods are distinguished: first, the 'nationalist' era, from 1945 to around 1980; second, the 'modern era' after 1980. The watershed between these two is Deng Xiaoping's initiation of ideological change in China. The division also coincides loosely with what might be termed the colonial and the postcolonial periods of different kinds of learning for business people. The passage of time suggests that Deng's revolution changed the region more than any other factor, as it presaged the reentry of China to the global arena. Nothing conveys better the massive shift around this period than the rebalancing of ownership in the exploding economy of Hong Kong. In 1976 the market capitalization of the top ten companies was $41 billion and Chinese-owned companies accounted for 10 percent of that total. By 1986, the top ten companies had a market capitalization of $256 billion, and Chinese-owned companies accounted for 54 percent of the total.[2] During those ten years the Chinese took command. The watershed coincides also with the gradual decline of nationalist economic policies in the region, and the rise of globalization. But we begin with the longer historical context.

The Traders of the Southern Ocean

Chinese traders from the southern coast of China have traveled into the region of the Nanyang, or Southern Ocean, for well over a thousand years. They typically brought with them Chinese medicines, silk, porcelain, furniture, and other products of the Celestial Empire, and returned with spices, rare wood, foodstuffs, and other commodities. The trading firms known as the *nam pak hong* (north-south companies) clustered in Hong Kong's Western district today, with their displays of such wares, show how that old tradition has not died out. Indications of the strength and stability of those mercantile ties are visible in the historic 'Chinatowns' of the ports of that long era: Jakarta, Semarang, Manila, Iloilo, Malacca, Penang, Bangkok, Saigon; parts of cities in which Chinese people could settle and find their familiar temples, relatives, teahouses, cemeteries, moneylenders, and people who spoke their own dialect.

The colonial era, especially in the second half of the nineteenth century, provided an opportunity for two further developments affecting this ancient pattern. First, it coincided with a mass exodus of people from China, predominantly young males, seeking a livelihood so as to support their families back in China, a nation which at that period was descending into severe disorder. That decline in what had long been

---

[2] Much of this was achieved on property revaluation, but the entrepreneurial *élan* is nevertheless stunning.

an orderly civilization, busy with commerce, came about because of overpopulation, decadence, extreme conservatism in the administration, invasion, civil war, and technical backwardness affecting both agricultural and industrial productivity. These pressures produced a series of famines, mass unemployment, and severe hardship. People left, bringing little with them except a will to work and to save, strong family dedication, a talent for entrepreneurship, and respect for knowledge. All these features are variations on the theme of how to deal with insecurity. The arrival of tens of thousands of migrants from China between 1850 and 1900 changed the demographics and labor markets of the region, but more significantly it increased the propensity to handle commerce and industry.

The second change in the colonial era was the incorporation of Chinese 'middle men' into the economies. They took on the roles of go-betweens (*compradors*), supervisors (*kapitans*), bookkeepers, or office managers, etc. They also set themselves up as independent business owners, beginning usually at microscale. In most such roles they would act as the key connectors of the colonial owners to the local employees, customers, or suppliers. Until World War II they built up their experience of the international business world and its techniques, honed and developed their own in parallel, and began to coalesce as an early stage *bourgeoisie*, their rich leaders forming a small new elite. Many families continued to send money back to China, keeping their links with the psychological homeland. Much philanthropy also flowed along that channel, visible still in university campuses such as Xiamen and Hong Kong.

Related to this intermediary role in the colonial context is an older tradition which developed in China in the nineteenth century and spread into parts of the region. It is known as 'bureaucratic capitalism' and it was a way for the government and the world of business to cooperate for the good of the society. Essentially, bureaucrats, often tempted by knowledge gained in their roles as controllers of licensing, or of trading, would convert into businessmen, or in reverse, businessmen would become commercial agents of the state. In the latter case the rewards of status could be high. Many examples of this were visible in late nineteenth century China, but the pattern also repeated itself in the region. An example is available in the Khaw family, whose empire based on tin mining, straddled the border between Thailand and the Malay peninsula. The family's relations with King Chulalongkorn were such as to lead to the royal gift of a special burial ground—a matter of high significance in Chinese culture—as well as the royal 'bestowal' of several wives into the family's clan structure. This industrial dynasty lasted from 1797 to 1932.[3] It is clear from such accounts that many Chinese had gained knowledge of large-scale business under their own impetus, and were not dependent on the support of the colonial powers, even though ready to take the opportunities which colonial order brought.

A radical change to their environment followed from the end of World War II. The colonial era was over. The United Kingdom began to dismantle its empire. The Netherlands was forcibly evicted from Indonesia, France from Indochina. The United States stood back from the Philippines. At the same time, a strong sense of nationalism drove the emergence of new governments. This was not a stable period, given the surrounding Cold War, wars in Korea and Vietnam, *konfrontasi* between Indonesia and Malaysia, Communist insurgencies in the region, and a constantly threatening and unpredictable China.

But, as the Chinese know well, there are opportunities within danger, and they were in a position to take them. Four factors in the environment helped to stimulate this process: a new injection of immigrants from China, fleeing the reprisals of the Communist revolution; the product demands brought by war, and by access to Western markets; the exit of colonial companies; and the nationalist encouragement of indigenous industry in the countries of the region. These years, from 1945 to 1980, have been termed the 'nationalist period', and it was a time of formative influences on the type of Chinese capitalism that would emerge to dominate the region later.[4]

New Immigrants

The new immigrants from China in the late 1940s and early 1950s included a high proportion of Chinese *bourgeois*. These were the industrialists whose factories were being expropriated under Communism, the landowners whose farms were being collectivized, the government and military officers of the Kuomintang. There was also a large group of ordinary people who feared the uncertainties of the new regime and its radical plans for the redesign of society. (It should be noted that the traffic was not entirely one way, and a small number of people, motivated by

---

[3] For an account of this see Cushman 1991.

[4] The account given here is drawn mainly from four sources: Redding 1990; Carney and Gedajlovic 2002; Elvis 1999; Whitley 1992.

idealism and nationalism, went into China from the region. Accounts of their drift into disillusionment make tragic reading.)

There were four main destinations in the exodus from China. The largest movement was to Taiwan, led by the deposed leader Chiang Kai-shek, and in this group were military and government officials, many industrial leaders, and much of China's heritage of cultural artifacts. They were to make a fiercely independent state with claims on China, and would create a political tension still unresolved. They would also supervise an economic miracle and grow one of the leading 'little dragons.'

The second destination was Hong Kong, with its promise of stable British administration, its tempting proximity, and its commercial and industrial opportunities. In 1945 its population was just over half a million. It grew to 1,800,000 in 1947, 2,424,700 in 1953, and 3,209,500 in 1961. Even under this pressure the political stability remained. The huge flood of refugees was absorbed, rapidly employed, and eventually housed. The inflow never entirely stopped. By the end of the century their average income would exceed that of most European countries. Hong Kong made itself into an industrial base of world significance, and has since expanded that base into China's Pearl River Delta, and along the southern coast.

The third destination was to the countries of Southeast Asia, joining those already there from earlier times, and focusing especially on Singapore, the latter being (and still remaining) an essential refuge from the unpredictable political oppressions suffered by ethnic Chinese in surrounding countries in the postwar decades. Lastly, and in smaller numbers, there were movements to the Western world.

The result of these migrations is a region in which the ethnic Chinese proportion of populations varies greatly. Taiwan, Hong Kong, and Singapore together accounting for 33 million people, are essentially Chinese, even though Singapore has slightly more than a fifth of its population ethnically Malay or Indian. In population terms elsewhere the ethnic Chinese are not significant: Indonesia about 4 percent, Philippines about 1 percent, Thailand about 9 percent, Malaysia somewhat larger at 35 percent, for a combined total of about 55 million across the entire region. But their economic significance is universally high in the region, and clearly dominant in the ASEAN economies. In the Philippines, for instance, the 1 percent of the population considered ethnic Chinese in 2002 accounted for about 40 percent of gross national income. Much of this stems from the postwar migration of China's entrepreneurial class in the 1940s and 1950s.

Demand for Products

The Korean War of the early 1950s, and US war in Vietnam, which escalated through the 1960s to its conclusion in 1975, both created heavy demand for supplies, and provided important stimuli to infant industry across a wide spectrum, from uniforms to armaments. At the same time, the slow return of prosperity to the postwar West was creating demand for low-cost products, as consumerism reappeared. Plastic purses, wigs, all forms of clothing, toys, electrical gadgets, plastic flowers, could be sold at prices which startled—and sometimes put out of business—their Western competitors. Key to this was access by Asian firms to markets in developed countries, and for all the years of growth in the second half of the twentieth century, and still on, this access has remained crucial.

The Colonial Retreat

The colonial economies had been constructed primarily to serve their home countries, and secondly to grow local prosperity, the balance between these varying greatly between the British, Dutch, French, and US versions. As a result colonial companies tended to fall into three main categories. First, the extractive industry and agribusiness companies, for instance, established palm oil or rubber plantations, or mines, and connected these products into their home industries as key supplies. Typical here would be Sime Darby and London Tin in Malaysia. Second were the early multinational manufacturers, such as Lever Brothers (later Unilever) or Imperial Chemical Industries, based in Europe, but taking their products into the world, and locating themselves abroad mainly in familiar colonial environments. Third were the regional companies established to facilitate trade, such as the Hongkong and Shanghai Banking Corporation (HSBC) in banking, Swire in shipping and airlines, Jardine Matheson in trading, and American International in insurance.

When the emerging nations of the region began to form postindependence economic policy, they would almost always give priority to indigenous industry, and in effect attack the colonial firms. In some cases, they also adopted policies, popular at the time, of import substitution. In simple terms, the reactions of the colonial companies followed different tracks depending on their larger strategic roles. Companies extracting products to send home, in the main withdrew, sold their assets to locals, and sometimes left their corporate names. In 1971, 30 percent of company directors in the top 100 companies in Malaysia were British, and 32 percent Chinese.[5] Companies selling into the region adapted to the threats by forming joint ventures and alliances, and many survived, coming back more strongly as market forces later returned to overturn the nationalist political agenda. Many retreated into the hospitable enclaves of Hong Kong and Singapore. The service companies facilitating trade were in the best position to adapt, as their portfolios were so varied, but the survivors of the colonial era now are associated mainly with Hong Kong, where they were safe from government policies of expropriation, and where they could take part in the local economic explosion, building heavy investments in industrial or property ownership, from which to move globally. The strongest examples here are HSBC—now one of the world's largest banks; the Swire group—the creator of Cathay Pacific and the second largest bottler of Coca Cola in the United States; and Jardine Matheson—key to the founding of Hong Kong, and now holding foreign assets of $6 billion.

This restructuring of the regional roles of the colonial companies provided an opportunity for ethnic Chinese entrepreneurs to fill the vacuum. This was done either by acquisition, by alliances, or by received training into large business administration and then new start-up. Either way the opportunities were taken, as the Chinese instinct for business asserted itself.

Nationalism in Economic Policy

Two economies in the region were not nationalistic in the postwar period. Both Hong Kong and Singapore remained open to the world, and although the Singapore government became strongly interventionist, it nevertheless encouraged competition and especially capital investment from abroad. The other countries of the region, however, turned inwards and protected their industries against any further invasion from outsiders. For periods of time they also turned against their own ethnic Chinese, treating them as outsiders, and bringing in discriminatory legislation in the Philippines, Indonesia, and Malaysia, although Thailand remained tolerant. Such legislation eventually faded away, as the Chinese learned to circumvent it, to act as good citizens, and to present no political threat. Many also learned to co-opt political support among the new elite, and in

[5] Lim 1983.

consequence found the freedom to take the opportunities in the protected economy, in exchange for the risks of opprobrium associated with crony capitalism.

The abuses of the Marcos and Suharto regimes were often explained locally in terms of the wealth accumulated by the elite with the help of the ethnic Chinese, and although Thailand has not suffered quite so severely from crony capitalism, it is nevertheless seen to operate as an alliance of ethnic Chinese business and local political power. The essential point here is that the period of nationalist economic policies between roughly 1945 and 1980 was one in which regional Chinese business people could find and take opportunity without the direct threat of competition from world players.

Historical Influences

It was noted earlier that the 'middleman' role in business dealings, which had been fostered by the colonial powers, was a valuable step in preparing the ethnic Chinese for subsequent business dominance. An extra element in the history of this evolution was the stimulus provided during the Japanese occupation of the region in World War II. The new military rulers were unable to handle the economy directly and they looked to the Chinese as convenient agents to serve their purposes. The traditional colonial structures had collapsed. The continued running of the economy needed Chinese help. This four-year period of opportunity to learn would be the one in which many organizational skills would be acquired for later use, although that does not imply that the Japanese had been welcome masters.

A further historical influence, from much longer incubation, was the collective wisdom of the Chinese emigrants about the handling of business in conditions of political turbulence and absence of status. The events of Chinese history, and the traditional structure of its society had taught people how to cope with the two overriding conditions which permeated their family histories: uncertainty; and the need to co-opt political support if you wanted to grow a large business. They coped with uncertainty by the careful management of trust, using relationships, and by the hedging of risk through diversification. The leaders of larger firms also knew that a close relationship with the political elite was essential to the finding of opportunity spaces, and the retention of the right to use them. In the circumstances of the nationalist era, those political elites were often military in origin, and bureaucratic in the ranks dealt with directly. They were, in other words, not business oriented. At the same time, however, the government in most countries in the region had taken ownership of the strategic industries. The old lessons for dealing with such circumstances, learned in China, and passed on as the family wisdom, were perfectly adapted to helping them cope with the Southeast Asia of the nationalist period. More recently, the same skills are being carried back into China.

The Modern Era

Since the early 1980s, as China began to open, a new phase of progress has been visible, as the ethnic Chinese have come to add the enormous opportunities available in China to those in the other countries around the rim of the South China Sea. Trade and investment now flows region-ally at a high rate, and the 'bamboo network' is vibrant with activity. This has enlarged the scale and scope of many enterprises, and has led many to become serious contenders in the new global patterns of business. What factors affected this, and what implications does it have for China?

The period in question was punctuated by the 'Asian crisis' of 1997/98, and many of the emerging changes were accelerated by that experience. They had however already been gathering momentum from the previous decade, as globalization brought new forces for change along with its waves of new investors and buyers. A simple example of that is the sudden firing in 1988 of the entire 5,000 officer staff of the Indonesian Customs and Excise Service, and its replacement by a Swiss agency. This came about because the foreign multinationals there had issued an ultimatum to the government: clean this up or we leave. Such reform accumulates and spreads. The 1997 crisis gave such processes legitimacy and injected urgency, but it was already a clear trajectory, as the old crony capitalist autocracies began to crumble under the scrutiny of modern communica-tions, global interest, and more democratic politics.

Three significant shifts affecting business are traceable across the region, from the 1980s onwards: (*a*) a weakening of the structure of alliances between economic and political players—the basis of the old cronyism; (*b*) the much stronger penetration of global business interests, techniques, 'emerging markets' investments, and corporate FDI; and (*c*) the rise of China. The result, in broad terms, is that the traditional large family business groups from the earlier period, have adjusted into a new 'hybrid' form, with some features of their original character and others imported from an array of external models, usually Western, but at times Japanese. It should be noted that slightly ahead of them, in the race for global business, were the Korean *chaebol.*

The context of this emergent new form of Chinese capitalism is not that of China, but there are enough parallels for the process to be of strong interest for comparison. The new 'dragon multinationals' of the region might well become examples of what can be done to handle the challenges of efficiency at large scale, organizational learning, and adaptiveness, using the given social psychology and institutions of the Chinese economy. We now examine the phenomenon in that light.

It should also be noted that we have so far mainly considered the large organizations. But much of any culturally Chinese economic system is bound to be made up of SMEs—the quintessentially 'family businesses' of network capitalism. This form of enterprise, designed as it is to be below the government radar, and designed also to adapt to high levels of surrounding uncertainty and risk, is likely to retain its essential characteristics wherever it operates. The natural affinity between 'cousins' when the owner-managers of such companies interact between China and the region is likely to account for much of the business that takes place. They understand each other and they run similar organizations. This partly explains why of FDI into China over the years since 1980, about 65 percent has come from these overseas cousins.

But China's problem is that of organizational coordination at large scale, and we consider now the regional 'dragon multinationals', for the lessons they offer in that regard.

A list of some of the firms of interest is given in Table 5.1. In this list, a noteworthy feature is the significance of Hutchison Whampoa. Its foreign assets, at $48 billion, compare with a total of $29.6 billion for all the others combined. This company is the globally successful hybrid *par excellence,* a fact that accounts for much of the respect accorded to its guiding spirit, Mr Li Ka Shing. For this reason, it will justify some scrutiny in its own right.

The original Hutchison company grew to prominence in the 1970s when Hong Kong's economy was booming and busting, and when speculation in share dealings was rife on its four stock markets. Run then by Westerners in a 'colonial' mode, Hutchison was brought to near bankruptcy in the mid-1970s, by a stock-market collapse, but rescued by HSBC, on the security of its head-office building. At that point it had become a 'casino' where salaried entrepreneurs running divisions could start up

Table 5.1. Ethnically Chinese-owned 'Dragon Multinationals' from the UNCTAD list of top 50 MNEs from developing economies

Rank	Corporation	Home base	Industry	Foreign assets (US$ b)	Trans-Nationality Index
1	Hutchinson Whampoa	Hong Kong	Ports, diversified	48.0	71.1
8	Neptune Orient Lines	Singapore	Trade Shipping	4.6	94.8
9	CITIC Pacific	Hong Kong	Construction	4.2	58.4
11	Shangri-La Asia	Hong Kong	Hotels	3.7	78.9
14	Flextronics Int	Singapore	Electronics contract	3.5	81.5
15	Capitaland	Singapore	Property	3.2	48.1
16	City Developments Ltd	Singapore	Property, hotels	3.0	62.5
20	First Pacific Co. Ltd	Hong Kong	Electricals & electronics	2.3	66.1
32	UMC	Taiwan	Electronics semiconductors	1.5	28.9
35	Nan Ya Plastics	Taiwan	Rubber & plastics	1.4	15.3
37	Orient Overseas Int	Hong Kong	Transport & storage	1.1	59.6
38	CP Pokphand	Thailand	Food	1.1	98.7

Sources: Mathews 2006; World Investment Report 2004, Table 1.3.1.

companies, play the market with their shares, and try almost any form of industry in which to speculate. There were approximately 160 uncoordinated companies in the group when it ran into the ground. HSBC brought in an Australian CEO with a record in effective turnrounds and he set about rationalizing the group into a set of divisions, and introducing professional standards and classic bureaucratic practices in finance, control, marketing, planning, and human resources, in the process appointing a set of divisional heads, eight of whom were Westerners and two Chinese. He fired most of the earlier heads. The newly rationalized and professionalized company recovered, and stabilized around a set of industries—retailing, wholesaling, engineering, building supplies, ports and terminals, telecommunications, and China business. Dealings in property were kept separate.

With no interest in long-term control, HSBC a few years later sold its stake to a Chinese entrepreneur who had established a reputation in Hong Kong for great probity and flair, Mr Li Ka Shing. Of Chiu Chow origin (a southern Chinese coastal region, east of Hong Kong), he had by then built the Cheung Kong organization into a fledgling business empire, initially in manufacturing but then mainly in the field of Hong Kong property. His acquisition of Hutchison marked a key turning point in the switch from colonial to Chinese domination of the Hong Kong economy. In parallel, and in his role as a director of HSBC (where he served for a time as deputy chairman), he became closely familiar with the world of global finance.

Mr Li, by his consistent behavior and decisions, made it clear that he understood the need for the organizing skills of the team he inherited with the acquisition of Hutchison. He kept the key people and the systems they had constructed in the turnround period, and he has continued to rely heavily on such expertise in the decades since. The heads of the retail and ports divisions, for instance are the same Westerners who were there at the time of the acquisition decades earlier, and his chief operating officers and directors of finance have been for decades Western. He has not avoided Chinese executives, but has not filled the boardroom with them. He is apparently unaffected by the issue of ethnicity. His behavior suggests a combination of (a) delegation under conditions of clear performance control and participative planning; (b) a willingness to trust; and (c) structuring the organization in such a way that it fosters effective interfaces with the global world of finance, and of strategic cooperation.

The expansion of Hutchison Whampoa into global markets was driven by specialists who understood industry in global terms, and who could handle dealings in other continents. The global expansion of port operations has been driven by a British divisional CEO. Expansion of telecom into Europe was pursued by two other British executives, and founded on the technical competence of a US executive. Retailing expansion in the Asian region has been driven by an executive brought up in the world of UK chain-store retailing. Matters of finance, or legal affairs, have for decades been handled at board level by executives from the United States, United Kingdom, Australia, and South Africa. The day-to-day running of the group was for decades in the hands of a highly trusted British, and earlier another Australian, 'right-hand man,' whose remit was to maintain the rationality acquired with the company. And yet, strong Chinese figures have always been also present, especially in dealings with the mainland, and the vast majority of employees are ethnically Chinese.

Now one of the richest people in the world, Li Ka Shing has a business empire across the globe, and the issue of succession looms. His solution is to divide the empire between two sons, one taking industry and the other property. As in all Chinese family successions in the world of business, personality will play a large part in determining the corporate future.

The creation of such hybrid organizations—many at large scale—in the region, has been described by Henry Yeung as a means of escaping from the limitations of what was once termed 'ersatz capitalism.' The term refers to the kind of business system in which, between the 1950s and the 1980s, entrepreneurs, specializing mainly in the tertiary sector, would manipulate their alliances with a political elite, so as to maximize returns from rent-seeking. The favorite arena for such activity was property development, where licenses could lead to lucrative oligopoly positions, but it also extended to natural products in certain countries, or to protected national markets. Given their access to capital, and their seeming mastery of 'emerging markets', they were able to pursue strategies based on high barriers to entry (due to need for both capital and political backing) in industries turnable into cash cows in conditions of prosperity, for example, power, telecom, property, infrastructure, commodities, retailing, and distribution. In each case the technical skills needed could be hired in, and the boardrooms could remain the domain of the deal-makers.

The breaking down of these oligopolies took place in a number of ways. Societal resentment of the elites grew in many countries, especially Indonesia, Malaysia, and the Philippines. The markets became saturated as both local and foreign competition grew. Movements toward democracy and transparency came in with the ideals of marketization, deregulation, and liberalization. The growth of organizational complexity made necessary by the rising tide of business with China, and the rest of the world, required more professional management and more outside capital.

In the Chinese ethnic regional heartlands of Hong Kong, Singapore, and Taiwan, the same pressures were being felt, but with less emphasis on the need to escape from the political effects of cronyism. For these ethnic Chinese states, the issue was more one of keeping up with the demands increasingly made by the foreign multinationals as they poured into the region. Such demands now included attention to technical education, management training, efficient infrastructure, and light government. The responses of Taiwan and Singapore were roughly similar, although Singapore has relied much more on the hosting of foreign MNEs. Their governments created 'developmental states', in which aspects such as the construction of modern infrastructure, the growth of scientific and research capacity, and the allocation of capital in accordance with development objectives all fell under the national planning bodies and received government funding. The state shaped many of the market forces. So too did those governments take direct risk through ownership of key large firms and groups. In the case of Hong Kong, the government stayed out of business investment per se, but retained very close links with the major companies. It also poured investment (largely recycled from its monopoly-based revenues from land sales) into education, infrastructure, and the modernizing of the finance sector. This policy of 'positive nonintervention' was consciously designed to leave the forces of the market to do most of the work needed to create growth.

The result of these regional forces for change, from 1980 onwards, has been fourfold. First, the reliance on ties with local political elites has declined, as the firm-specific advantages brought by that have been found increasingly irrelevant in doing business more globally. Also, as noted earlier, the secrecy involved in maintaining such local understandings has been undermined. Second, the rise in bureaucratization and professionalism in the Chinese business groups has been greatly speeded up by the 1997 crisis, and by growing organizational complexity. Helping with this has been the availability of a growing class of managerial professionals, trading on their MBAs, ambitious for performance opportunities, and often less sycophantic toward the owners/employers than might be the inside executives brought up in the older traditions.

The third shift has been in corporate governance. As companies turn more toward international sources of capital, and away from their traditional networks of personal backers, that brings with it widespread reforms, both to corporate practices—especially disclosure, but also to the surrounding fabric of supporting and controlling institutions. Regulations get tighter, controlling bodies get more teeth, more people need to know more things, and more people have a say.

The fourth shift is in the constitution of the networks over which many deals are put together and made to work. Originally local and often subethnic (all Chiu Chow, all Hokkienese, all Cantonese), these grew into regional ties connected by mutual trading or rent-seeking interests, and are now undergoing global stretching into not just other countries but other languages and cultures. For this, the networks now need to include non-Chinese participants.

Although these hybridized regional multinationals are latecomers to the world of global business, they are nonetheless capable of finding a way to penetrate the world outside and compete. Around 13 percent of the world's FDI comes from developing countries, amounting to about $83 billion in 2004. Of that, about 80 percent comes from Pacific Asia other than Japan. John Matthews has described how this is achieved, and argues that it is based on organizational strategies to counteract the typical handicap of latecomers, namely the absence of a strong organizational resource base. Such strategies entail tapping the resources of others, imitation, and transfer. A clear example is the grafting on of essentially Swiss or German skills in hotel management to a chain of Chinese-owned hotels.

Another is the acquiring of high-tech skills in information technology (IT) by hiring personnel from Silicon Valley. Another is the local distribution of an outside brand.

There are many ways in which the strategies of the big established MNCs can be complemented: contracted services, licensing of technology, joint ventures, and formal alliances of many kinds. In making such arrangements work for both parties, the ethnic-Chinese partner brings two things to the table. Local knowledge of how things work and with whom to connect is a first obvious offering, but bundled with it is also commonly the offering of local distribution facilities that are otherwise inaccessible because of special local agreements. The second offering is not so much a bargaining point but an organizational capacity: the ability to make things happen fast, because the boss has decided. This distinct advantage in fast-moving environments is one of the key features retained in the hybridization. It remains one of the most powerful weapons in the business armoury, as it allows for the gearing up of entrepreneurship to levels not attainable in either Western or Japanese bureaucracies.

The Nature of the Hybrid

The hybridization process in the large conglomerate enterprises built by the ethnic Chinese has been described by Henry Yeung and other scholars in the following terms. They began under the influence of certain institutional contexts, and cultural conditioning, varying somewhat between specific country environments but usually including (a) family- and kinship-based entrepreneurship; (b) the use of personalistic networks; and (c) tightly controlled, centralized coordination of their organizations. Taking the opportunities available in the earlier conditions of ersatz capitalism, they learned to connect well with political elites, and to take the opportunities for rent-seeking that were available. They also hedged risk by diversifying investments, while retaining a core focus in one industry, usually—but not always—in the tertiary sector.

As time went on, and their local environments came under increasing influence from global forces—political, economic, and social—their organizational responses began to change. What was retained was their essential Chineseness. The central controlling role of the owning group—in most cases members of a family—was not given up. Neither was the sense of specific cultural identity in relating to the outside world. In many dealings, and especially with China, this became a strategic resource, in contrast with its having been a handicap earlier in many of their host communities.

What was new were the four things noted earlier: the reducing of reliance on local elite connections; the introduction of more professionals and managerial bureaucrats; venturing out into the world of global financing; and the adding of non-Chinese to the networks. What then did these new elements bring to the mixture? How do these organizations now deal with the fundamental organizational challenges of efficiency, learning, and adaptiveness? The subtext to these questions is: What might China learn from this process of hybridizing?

In terms of the first challenge—the efficiency of the organization in its use of resources, no studies exist that compare such features as productivity across business systems so as to answer this question unequivocally.

The China Circle

To understand the fruitfulness of the interflow between these regional large firms and the mainland, it is appropriate to bring into the account the notion of a 'China Circle' proposed by Barry Naughton in his major work on the Chinese economy. This describes the flows of business dealings over time, linking Hong Kong, Taiwan, and the mainland; but let us begin with the end result, and work back from there. Of the top ten firms in China now exporting high-tech products, nine are foreign—four from Taiwan and five from the United States. The Taiwanese dominate in the value of their exports and account for 52 percent of the group's total volume.

When Hong Kong was at its peak as a manufacturing base—before China opened—it had an industrial workforce of just under a million. The movement of this industry to the mainland has sponsored the creation of around eleven million jobs in the nearby coastal provinces of Guangdong and Fujian. Much of the reason for Hong Kong's continuing prosperity is the de facto extension of its industry into China.

What happened, beginning in the early 1980s and accelerating ever since, was a process of increasing integration. In the early stages of their industrialization, in the 1960s and 1970s, both Taiwan and Hong Kong came to master the skills of labor-intensive manufacturing for export to developed country markets. They prospered in consequence and—albeit with different specific societal formulae—created institutional frameworks to support the growth. What they had in common in these societal designs were: an emphasis on technical education; investment in infrastructure and communications; good legal structures; and an efficient system for the allocation and use of capital. They also shared an economic structure made up of a small number of large firms, and a very large number of small and medium firms, the latter able to network among themselves to achieve high transaction cost efficiency combined with the benefits of specialization.

This success acted as a demonstration to China of what was possible, and led to the stimulus within the mainland of the famous speech by Deng Xiaoping after his Southern Tour, where he saw firsthand what was going on in places like Shenzhen. This slow opening then coincided with a new trend in the organizing of international business driven by the new possibilities for the coordination of industrial processes in the age of IT. The information revolution made it possible for the geographical dispersal of world industry via 'commodity chains'. The making of an article could be broken down into stages and components, and in such a chain the intermediate goods, such as small electric motors, disc-reader heads, or logic boards, could be sourced where costs were lowest. The chain could be managed by logistics specialists, and the links to market by other extensions of the chain, using either the big brand houses or intermediaries such as buying agencies.

This redesign of the industrial structure resulted in the shifting of labor-intensive manufacturing from offshore into China, often leaving the managerial coordination in either Taiwan or Hong Kong. These latter locations also accumulated new surrounding structures for design, accounting, information processing, and technology development. Over time these skills are slowly leaching into China. In Taiwan the government was active in orchestrating the response, in taking investment risk, and in sponsoring such supports as science parks and links with Silicon Valley. In Hong Kong the government took less direct measures but was very active in the fostering of appropriate education, infrastructure, and in providing a tax regime to encourage entrepreneurship.

Some indication of the power of this China Circle is visible in the figures for FDI. Investment by the category of 'overseas Chinese' sources (Hong Kong, Taiwan, Macau, and tax havens) is running at about $35 billion per year. The annual total for the industrialized triad of the United States, EU, and Japan is running at about 15 billion. A further 8 billion comes from Korea and ASEAN. The favored vehicle now is overwhelmingly the wholly foreign-owned enterprise, accounting for over 70 percent of the deals. Equity joint ventures—a standard response at an earlier stage—are now down to about 25 percent, and falling.

As to sources of this flow, the dominant player is clearly Hong Kong. Between 1985 and 2005, the combined investments of Hong Kong, Taiwan, Macau, and the tax havens accounted for about 60 percent of all FDI into China. Further analysis suggests that within this 60 percent, 47 percent is attributable to Hong Kong, and 12 percent to Taiwan. (It is necessary to note here that there are about a thousand multinationals with their regional headquarters in Hong Kong, and that some of this investment is being made by them, and counted as coming from Hong Kong.)

We see here that the economies of China, Hong Kong, Taiwan, and—not so strongly but still significantly—the ASEAN countries, have become fused together. The 'sojourners of the southern ocean' have come home, bearing capital and know-how.

Key References

Carney, Michael, and Eric Gedajlovic. 2002. 'The Co-Evolution of Institutional Environments and Organizational Strategies: The Rise of Family Business Groups in the Asean Region', *Organization Studies*, 23(1): 1–29.

Chen, Xiao-Ping, and Chao C. Chen. 2004. 'On the Intricacies of the Chinese Guanxi: A Process Model of Guanxi Development', *Asia Pacific Journal of Management*, 21(3): 305–24.

Cushman, Jennifer W. 1991. *Family and State: The Formation of a Sino-Thai Tin-Mining Dynasty*. Singapore: Oxford University Press.

Elvis, P. J. 1999. The Strategy and Structure of the Large, Diversified, Ethnic Chinese Organizations of Southeast Asia, Ph.D. thesis, University of Hong Kong, Hong Kong.

Lim, M. H. 1983. 'The Ownership and Control of Large Corporations in Malaysia: The Role of Chinese Businessman', in L. Y. C. Lim and P. Gosling (eds.), *The Chinese in Southeast Asia*. Singapore: Maruzen.

Mathews, John A. 2006. 'Dragon Multinationals: New Players in 21st-Century Globalization', *Asia Pacific Journal of Management*, 23(1): 5–27.

Ralston, David A., James Pounder, Carlos W. H. Lo, Yim-Yu Wong, Carolyn P. Egri, and Joseph Stauffer. 2006. 'Stability and Change in Managerial Work Values: A Longitudinal Study of China, Hong Kong, and the US', *Management and Organization Review*, 2(1): 67–94.

Redding, Gordon. 1990. *The Spirit of Chinese Capitalism*. New York: de Gruyter.

Sung, Yung-Wing. 2005. *The Emergence of Greater China*. New York: Palgrave Macmillan.

Wang, Gungwu. 2003. *Ideas Won't Keep: The Struggle for China's Future*. Singapore: Eastern Universities Press.

Whitley, Richard. 1992. *Business Systems in East Asia*. London: Sage.

Yeung, Henry W. C. 2006. 'Change and Continuity in Southeast Asian Ethnic Chinese Business', *Asia Pacific Journal of Management*, 23(3): 229–54.

6

The State-owned Enterprises

It is not possible to argue that there is only one business system in China. There are many. The problem is to find categories in which to describe what is going on there, in ways that are at least a reasonable starting point of understanding, always on condition that there are plenty of exceptions and special cases. We are especially concerned in this book with how different forms of business system are evolving in China, and for that reason our focus is on kinds of organizations, ways of their connecting, and ways in which they organize internally. These are dimensions of organizational style, and patterns have formed that allow rough but useful distinctions to be made between three dominant organizational responses to what the environment and history of Chinese business has both permitted and encouraged.

The three main forms are as follows:

1. The *state-owned* sector, now shrunken from its earlier dominance of the economy, and under pressure—since the mid-1990s reforms of Zhu Rongji—to perform at competitive standards of efficiency or go out of business. The sector is also responsible for certain strategic industries protected by the state from outside ownership, as occurs in many societies. Most state-owned enterprises (SOEs) are large, bureaucratic, and capital-intensive.

2. The *local corporates* is a category embracing substantial internal variation and complexity, and it is the result of a long transformation of what use to be termed 'the collectives'. These owe their origin to the 1949 revolution and the subsequent setting up of the communes, each of which had its own set of industries. The key features here are the blending of private-sector initiative and investment with the local government use of essentially state resources. These resources, including industrial plants, land, labor skills, and state

banking capital, have come to be used in radically new ways by local entrepreneurship. The rights of local workers over the assets, which they see as collectively owned, have often been overridden in this development. Encouragement of such local initiative has been consistent government policy for nearly two decades.

3. The *private sector* in China, now accounting for about two-thirds of the economy, has come from being illegal in 1980 to being the main engine of growth. Typically—but not entirely—made up of SMEs, it displays features such as personalistic authority, selective networking, and unusually strong entrepreneurial drive.

In Chapters 6–8 we consider these three quite different systems, in an attempt to locate them in their context. They are not just products of the laws of economics, although those laws are clearly very much at work. They are also products of their history, culture, and external influences, and these need to be factored in, before attempting any estimate of their trajectories from now on. We begin in this chapter with the state sector.

Industries controlled by the state have a long history in China, as have also attempts to find a blend between state interests and market forces as a means to improve commercial performance. The great early silk and ceramics industries were traditionally state-controlled. Under the late nineteenth-century wave of globalization and industrialization, several hundred companies, in armaments, railways, telegraph, banking, shipping etc., came to be registered as *kuan-tu shang-pan,* denoting official supervision and merchant management. But in those days, as Albert Feuerwerker observes in a classic study, they did not induce a revolution radically altering the basis of China's economy and fostering its modernization. History is likely to reach a similar conclusion about the late twentieth-century experiment in state control of industry, as the state's sector of the economy comes down from its 75 percent dominance in 1980, to its position today with about 15 percent of the economy, now largely restricted to industries judged strategic to the national interest (see Figure 7.2). This takes no account of the state interest in many other companies in the 'collective' sector associated with local government, some of this latter also spilling over into partial interest in the private sector (see Chapter 7). The 'central' state portion is also likely to decline as the banking sector, among others, comes under the competitive and acquisitive forces unleashed by the WTO agreement. It is likely that the state sector of China's economy will level off at below 10 percent of value-added, by around 2015, if present trends continue, and assuming other sectors continue their incursions into the growing market. By then the state will be left in direct control of the industries it deems strategic, and will use other methods, such as taxation, to influence the patterning of the rest.

The essential dilemma for China has been that the fundamental purposes for which the state sector was established under Communism were disconnected from market discipline. Nowhere are the consequences of this more forcefully stated than in Peter Nolan's description of Citigroup's annual global profit per employee at $55,800, (with Bank of America at $50,600, and Credit Suisse at $54,300), while that in the Bank of China was $2,600. Using purchasing power parity comparison the Bank of China figure still only reaches $11,500. Low allocative efficiency in such companies in China is evident also in the data for nonperforming loans, reported to have swollen to somewhere between 23 and 43 percent of loan value, for the banking sector, before becoming the focus of recent very severe scrutiny.

The dilemma comes to a head in state companies such as those described in the fine-grained study of Shanghai industry by Doug Guthrie. Here he explains the slow rationalization of the Chinese economy, and how the 'shock therapy' of sudden confrontation by the market hinders the internal adjustments needed for productivity improvement. His advice about understanding the transition is that 'we need to examine the extent to which rational institutional structures are replacing particularistic authority relations in ways that are meaningful for individuals.'[1] This theme will serve as a guide to our analysis of changes in the state sector of China, and will serve to illuminate the old saying that contrasts China's 'tray of loose sand' with Japan's 'piece of granite.'

A significant shift of pace in reform took place in 2003, with the establishment of the State-owned Assets Supervision and Administration Commission (SASAC), a body with ministerial-level authority reporting directly to the State Council. Dealing with industry other than the finance sector (handled separately and in parallel), this body manages the assets of the state, by performing the responsibilities of investor. Its mission reads as follows:

SASAC guides and pushes forward the reform and re-structuring of state-owned enterprises; supervises the preservation of and increase in the value of state-owned assets for enterprises under its supervision and enhances the management work

[1] Guthrie 1999, p. 209.

of state-owned assets; advances the establishment of modern enterprise system in SOEs, and perfects corporate governance; and propels the strategic adjustment of the structure and layout of the state economy.

When it was set up, SASAC was made responsible for 189 enterprises, a set considered the chosen 'national team' as far as industry was concerned. The number of firms under such control is constantly shifting as they get reorganized, and the original number before SASAC was higher. Some estimates consider that round fifty will survive the process, but this depends on their speed of learning and of change. SASAC has pursued its aims with vigor, and by the application of strong discipline. The rest of the state sector—swollen as it was by excess assets, debts, and labor—has been subjected increasingly to the laws of the market. At one stage, around the year 2000, the assets in production facilities were calculated to be about double those needed in the economy. Many firms have been sold, merged, broken up, and dispersed. Well-managed state enterprises have often found themselves forced into absorbing badly managed ones, filled with excess labor and underused factories. Much of the pain of these adjustments has been borne by the ninety million workers whose jobs have been at stake, and without the surrounding growth running at 10 percent it would not have been possible to absorb the pressures of such an adjustment without widespread disorder.

Figure 6.1 shows a picture of the elements in the business system called 'China state-owned enterprises'. It should be noted that the category SOE contains two main segments within it. This simple division allows us to consider a first set noted earlier as the 'national champions', and containing around 100 enterprise groups, chosen in 1991 and 1997 by the State Council and being readied for world competitiveness. In the early 1990s this group accounted for about 25 percent of all sales in the total state sector, but for 50 percent of the profits. They employed about a quarter of the workers in China's large-scale enterprises. There is also a second set of more problematic SOEs whose fate now rests largely on their performance, but with a high probability of extensive failures, as the government dismantles the old policies and prepares for global competition. The Organization for Economic Cooperation and Development (OECD) reports that in terms of value added to the economy, the SOE sector, strictly defined, declined from 29.1 percent in 1998 to 10.2 percent in 2003, and that during the same period the 'private-controlled sector' went from 27.9 to 52.3 percent. The object of our study is clearly in the process of massive transition.

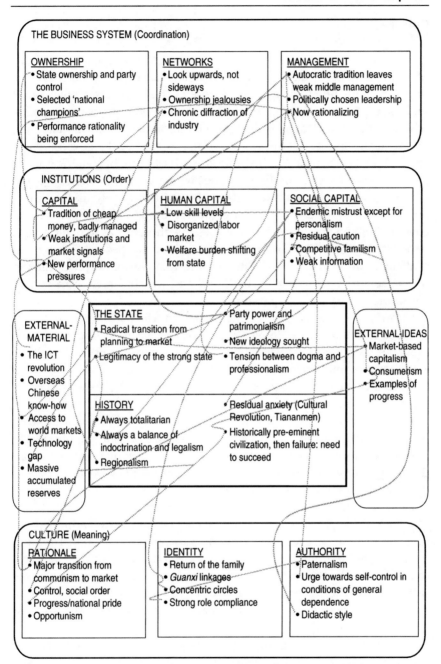

Figure 6.1. The Chinese state-owned enterprise sector as a complex adaptive system

Culture

We considered in Chapter 4 how Chinese history and culture—in our terms the layer of meaning—shapes a societal reality. We consider now the way in which Chinese people make sense of those aspects of their world that have a bearing on the structuring of the instruments of economic action by the state. Dominant here is the notion of the patrimonial state, a view of the society that makes it normal to look to the government— rather than to other societal institutions such as those of civil society—to provide the order the society needs, but which as well as allocating that duty to government, allocates with it the right to largely unquestioned power. Limits to the use of that power are traditionally thought of as being governed by the 'mandate of heaven'. A government has to demonstrate responsibility and human concern. This gives the people the right to challenge and overthrow an elite abusing that power—a phenomenon which punctuates the history of China and which serves to make any government wary for its reputation.

A Confucian-style system of ethics underpins the patrimonial state and serves to legitimate the holding of power by one group, seeing the vertical exchange as one of downward benevolent concern for people's welfare, and upward compliance and orderly behavior. The core idea is extended when economic assets are seen as being owned by the state, the use of them serving the people.

As part of this traditionally strong role of government, Chinese political power has always been buttressed by the seizing of a monopoly on the interpretation of the state ideology. For centuries the mandarinate's control over society on behalf of the emperor was based on society's dependence on the mandarin interpretation of the Confucian-inspired laws. A remarkably small elite could control a remarkably large country that way. The state was kept in balance by a managed tension between indoctrination and regulation, the latter including punishment. The indoctrination rested on the interpretation, and these twin roles were, in the twentieth century, seized by the Party, as interpreters of the Marxist ideology, and are still retained. The current challenge is to replace the Marxist ideal with a legitimate alternative, the present best attempt at that being the 'socialist market economy'.

This power structure is one of the bases for the 'didactic' style of leadership often described as widespread. One of its outcomes, especially in the state sector of industry, is that key leadership roles in organizations are filled by the faithful (or by the politically astute) and business performance is not the only criterion for appointment. Acceptance among subordinates is made easier by the high levels of role compliance, into which people are so strongly socialized. It should be added also that the majority of state industry leaders appear to have taken inspiration from the Communist ideal and conducted themselves as protectors of the people, thus being accepted as legitimate. Corruption came in later and—although problematic—is still by developing country standards not out of control. Adding to the compliance of so many with this state-run structure, was the relative insecurity stemming from poverty, but the recent years of prosperity for many are now encouraging independence, assertiveness, and individualism, especially among the young.

The mental universe of many Chinese people, as well as containing the core idea of the legitimacy of the strong state, and the state's right and duty to provide order, also contains a pent-up sense of its being time to restore China to its proper place among world civilizations. Status is significant at all levels in the Chinese world, and is part of the instinct for hierarchical ordering which so permeates Chinese life. The Chinese people want to catch up, and are fiercely consistent in this view. Here the ideal attaches to the state itself, and the interpretation is that if the reputation of China in the world is increasing—which it clearly is—then the government has the right policies and is 'good'. In contrast with Russia, which denounced its earlier regime and broke with it, China has not publicly renounced its immediate past. Instead it has implied a new ideal symbolically, slowly, and incrementally, by its new actions.

Key Historical Influences

Significant historical legacies affecting the state sector today (in addition to those noted earlier related to the patrimonial state) must include the aftereffects of the Cultural Revolution. The risk aversion that this has induced in many decision-makers of the older generations is unmeasurable in its effects, but arguably significant. Many people will still not 'stick their necks out' in case history repeats itself. The fact that that revolution still cannot be discussed openly, after thirty years, is an insidious sign of the damage done to the psyche of so many. Many state firms have been described as full of middle managers able only to pass down orders and to keep discipline, with little sign of questioning of the status quo or of the taking of initiative.

In more recent history, one of the most crucial acts by the state has been the decentralization of much economic decision-making into the provinces. The ideal of regional autonomy had been established early in the Communist era, as a reaction to fears over national defense, but the more recent extension of this was a response to the need for a better decision mechanism to stimulate business and risk-taking. It let the genie out of the bottle, and produced much stimulus to growth, as it pitted municipalities, counties, and provinces against each other in a competitive battle for investment. They had to behave in such a way as to attract business. But one of the features of the state sector now is the strength and potential divisiveness of these regional powers. In intriguing testimony to the real effects of this, the 2005 OECD report on China, revealed that the local share of government expenditure, at 68 percent, was higher than that of any of the twenty OECD countries studied.

We now turn to the institutional layer of the model and examine how China orders the sourcing and allocation of (*a*) capital and (*b*) human capital, and how (*c*) social capital plays a part. The latter, more than any other, is the arena in which to seek understanding of China's 'loose sand' and its effects.

Capital

In very crude terms the allocation of available capital within China works as follows. The people put their savings into the banking system, having few alternatives for its safekeeping, and the sum is around $800 billion and growing. The foreign reserves swollen by export success now exceed $1 trillion. The nonperforming loans in the banking sector amount to around $500 billion. The cumulative amount of FDI so far arrived, most of it from the regional ethnic Chinese, comes to around $600 billion; United Nations Conference on Trade and Development (UNCTAD) statistics suggest that in 2004, the current stock of inward FDI in China is about $250 billion.[2] And the accumulated welfare obligation is also around $500 billion, although estimates vary greatly. These figures will naturally change. The financing of the SOE sector has been about 90 percent dependent on the state banks.

Taxation is now largely decentralized, and reflects the ancient tradition of tax farming. About half of national revenues are raised locally—far

---

[2] The causes of the discrepancy of cumulate inflows and existing stock are not clear. It may be explained by a combination of factors, such as investments announced but not fully made, investments devalued after maturity, or withdrawals.

more than in other OECD countries; the United Kingdom figure is 5 percent, Germany and the United States are at 30 percent. Local authorities are charged with meeting centrally established budgets for tax gathered, but informally given leeway to negotiate with the taxpayers over rates. The tax laws are for guideline purposes. There is consequently a market in destinations for investment and a high level of competition, as local governments outdo each other in bidding for what investors can offer.

The two internal stock markets, originally intended to alleviate the very heavy reliance of state industry on bank loans, have failed to do so for a complex of reasons. Among these might be noted: the tight government restrictions on listing and the prevention of the market from funding other than state organizations; the withholding by government of most shares from being traded; the weakness of surrounding institutions such as accounting, financial analysis, press commentary, and related professions; and the low level of development in the flow of high-quality information. These weaknesses are now being addressed and changes in the direction of greater market discipline are predictable.

The financial balancing act in recent years has been one in which the massive nonperforming loans have not bankrupted the system of capital sourcing and allocation because the government has transferred money into the banking sector to alleviate them, handing over 60 billion dollars of foreign reserves with which to (indirectly) do so. It has also sanctioned the use of the peoples' bank savings for investment in low-return activities. The banks have also been major sources of government tax revenue, in conditions where tax collection elsewhere has not proved easy.

The banks have remained under the control of supervisory committees, via which the Party has influenced loan decisions, as a result of which much capital allocation has been based on administrative considerations. The consequent bad management of cheap money (in terms of external criteria of financial management) contributed to the national buildup of excessive industrial capacity. The absence of market signals in the capital allocation system, and the inability to coordinate investment planning when faced with the diffracted and compartmentalized nature of much Chinese industry, mean that waste has been endemic and financial discipline lax. The role of banks in controlling and stimulating the performance of industry has so far been largely missing, and because banks are the principal sources of capital to the state sector, there have been no other sources of pressure for efficiency and effectiveness except exhortations or threats from the supervising boards.

To put this inefficiency in perspective, let us consider comparatively what it takes to produce the national GDP. In terms of allocation of capital to industry, China uses around 50 percent of its GDP, whereas Germany uses 26 percent, Japan 32 percent, and the United States 28 percent. In terms of productive efficiency, to generate $1 of GDP, it has been costing the United States $1.5, India $2.8, and China $6. Two powerful forces are now converging to squeeze out this slack. The first is the work of SASAC described earlier. The second is the arrival of foreign banks with permission to lend to industry. This latter force is of less direct relevance to the state sector than to other sectors, but it is predictable that it will bring with it an indirect force of changed expectations about performance in the use of capital, and that this will be especially public in the context of the stock markets where the state firms are listed. This second force is a part of the wider WTO impact, and as the state firms begin to compete for investment with other sectors, in an open capital market, they will be entering a new world.

Human Capital

Within the field of human capital two issues are worthy of note for their effects on SOEs. The first is the welfare dependence that still hangs over much industry, with millions of employees still relying on firms for their basic needs, and with firms run in such a way that those needs are accepted. Despite the recent reforms, which have reduced the state workforce by more than half since 1998, there still remain state-employed populations the size of the total national workforce of many other countries. Although policy is to reduce this weighty obligation, it is clearly not a matter of short, or even medium-term solution.

The second aspect of human capital is the shortage of professional skills in administration and technology. Dramatic expansion in training is now taking place, but the amount of catching up to do makes this also a problem to be solved in the longer term. Its effects are made worse by other managerial challenges to be considered shortly.

Social Capital

Social capital is essentially trust. Each society has its own architecture for the reliable relations of exchange necessary for its economy to work. In

China, trust is mainly based on interpersonal bonds of reciprocity, and the glue holding both the economy and the society together is the universally required *guanxi*, or connections. Outside such connections, and exacerbated by the competition for scarce resources, mistrust is endemic. This particularist response stands in stark contrast to the universal trust found in Japan, and more than any other factor accounts for the radical contrasts in economic structures that result. Given its significance, some explanation of its origins, and its enduring nature, is called for.

The Chinese traditional social structure is one in which power is centralized in, and monopolized by, the state. The exercise of it has always been a matter of strong control, and delegation under conditions of surveillance by the center and its agents. No alternative bases for stable, lasting power have ever emerged. The state has never permitted the growth of independent institutions of civil society, of local administrations making their own laws, or of powerful intermediaries in the economy such as an independently-managed central bank, a strong stock market, independent professions, or a free press. This controlling tradition has always been excused by the concern for maintaining order in a country capable of breakdown, and there is some inevitable logic in that.

One of the features of the traditional structure was its reliance on socialization within families as the basis for order. The ideals of social harmony and consideration for others were as much the message of the Confucian socialization as were the concerns with obedience and respect for authority and status. But, the realities of life at the subsistence level, which has been the condition of most people for most of the time, meant that each extended family competed for scarce resources with others. Each family was its own welfare state. The sense of communal solidarity was undermined by this need for survival, as the essentially utilitarian nature of relationships was forced to dominate in how they worked. A crucial outcome, as we have said earlier, is that Chinese people trust others to the extent that there are personal connections, and this means placing people in concentric circles. A successful business person will have a wide circle of personal connections and will spend much effort building and maintaining it. Outside that is the region of unknown people, and because all people are competing for the same scarce resources, these outsiders cannot be trusted. There are no obligations to or from them, and the rules of mutual exploitation are understood.

The picture just described is not unique to China. In different versions it accounts for much of the social psychology of people living at the subsistence level in many societies, in fact the majority of the world population. As George Foster, in a classic paper, points out, much of this psychology and the elaborate systems of reciprocity that go with it, derive from an 'image of limited good', in other words a belief that there is only a fixed amount to go around among everybody, and it had better be distributed fairly if society is to be stable.

There is much to be said for *guanxi*-type trust-bonding as a basis for transaction cost efficiency in economic exchange, but only within limited circles of exchange processes, as with a locality, or a specific trade, or an OEM commodity chain. Beyond that the inability to do business with strangers becomes a severe handicap. It puts a cap on the total volume of exchange a society is capable of carrying. To get over this obstacle would require movement on three fronts. First, the idea of limited good would have to give way to a belief in expanding good, or 'progress,' an idea which lies at the core of much Western rationale. China's experience since 1980 is causing this change in perception, especially among the younger generation in the cities that have benefited most from the recent prospering. The second requirement is growth of the institutions needed to foster a new form of trust in China, known as institutional trust. Leading this set is the legal system, but also in it are independent professions such as accounting, whose work is to provide reliability of data and standards objectively patrolled and guaranteed. The third requirement is the opening up of flows of information, including commentary, so that independent and informed judgment may be encouraged at the individual level. The dilemma faced by the government over the second and third of these requirements is that they each pose a threat to the power of the hierarchy, and thus to the state as it has always been conceived. The solution that emerges may not replicate what developed elsewhere.

Ownership

Majority ownership of the SOEs by the state has been normal, but when the state owns so much, its interest is then spread very wide, and no one company can benefit from the focusing of an owner's attention and concern. In consequence the kind of ownership structure found in many other contexts, whereby owners take a strong interest in fostering the value of their investment because that is the only investment they have, is muted in China's state sector. Although supervisory boards may well represent state interest, they may not act with the same zeal as if their own money were at stake.

A valuable insight into how the government keeps its access to the strategic decision processes of firms in this sector is provided by Guthrie, from new research on the vertical 'stacking' of state ownership. In a 'nested hierarchy' of bureaux, the power of government ownership descends from central to provincial to municipal to district to township to village. Key components in this new architecture, and crucial to its controlling function, are the state-owned Asset Management Companies that now appear in the structure.

A large part of the state's concern in its supervision of industry has been the retention of political control, and the top ranks of the companies in this sector are deeply penetrated by the Party faithful, especially the position of president in each company or bank. One of the outcomes of this politicization of firm strategy is that decisions were made, and resources committed, in ways that did not always match the normal logics of effective management. Liabilities came to be amassed. Good assets might be transferred into the hands of more market-sensitive outside bodies with tenuous (or sometimes corrupt) connections maintained. Alliances might be forced on good companies in order to solve the problems of bad ones, often seen in swollen workforces. Irrational diversification commonly took assets out of a familiar industry into an unfamiliar one, so that dreams of quick returns might be pursued. Very heavy investments of capital might be made beyond normal criteria for assessment, if state policy is dominant in the decision process. One of the end results of such weaknesses is that the state sector as a whole has been yielding a total of 3 percent return on assets, compared to the private sector with 7 percent, it being noteworthy also that the good state-sector performers tend to be in protected industries, whereas deregulation and competition is now causing severe stress to the others.

One of the main determinants of success in other Asian countries that adopted the principle of the 'developmental state', was the high quality of the planning staff in the state bureaucracy. In Japan, Korea, Taiwan, and Singapore these planners were seen as the intellectual and social elite of their societies, much of their authority stemming from this. Acquiring deep knowledge of industry and strategy as they rose through the ministerial ranks, they worked between the senior levels of government and industry to shape progress. Their policies were not imposed by externally derived economic orthodoxy (and in fact there were hardly any economists per se in their ranks). Their judgments were usually tested in clearly understood markets. They also took much influence from other countries, often cosmopolitan in their personal training and education.

In none of the four cases did they produce a copy of an outside business system seen as a whole. The contrast is stark, and crucial, between this use of special bureaucratic skill in other countries and the situation in China where such skills are limited, generally inbred, and often colored by political influence. This weakness is now a matter for urgent rectification, and may be expected to change, but it nevertheless accounts for much that has shaped the current position, and change will inevitably be slow. The creation of SASAC, and its status so close to the State Council, was significant in symbolizing that many of the old orthodoxies had gone, but its task remains immense.

A further feature of the ownership structure for SOEs is its commonly diffracted nature. Ownership here is not simply a matter of controlling shares. It extends into the perceived right to have a say, and that may well be influentially expressed by bodies outside any legal definition of ownership. In consequence, policy is subject to pressures from (1) ministries in charge of certain industries; (2) regional bodies protecting local interests; and (3) the Party protecting its own position. These often conflicting perspectives penetrate at all levels from the main board down to the factory floor. The result has usually been compromise, but not competitiveness. Again though, the picture is now changing, and these interest groups are shifting among themselves as power comes to be slowly redistributed in the society, and the Party itself slowly changes its role.

Networks

We consider now how alliances bring things together, and will conclude that in general they do not. China's state sector is an arena of divisions, not of cooperation. The tray of loose sand is nowhere more apparent than in the absence of horizontal webs across the economy holding things together. This is not to say that there are no horizontal networks more broadly in the economy, but those that do exist tend to cluster around clear leadership and production synergies, and to be driven by new owners stitching together collaboration across the no-man's land left by the evaporation of so much state industry. We consider these as a separate system in Chapter 7. The more normal SOE tendency is still to look upwards not sideways.

Among the reasons for this divided industrial structure—and the doubling of industrial capacity beyond need which it gives rise to—are the following features: the heritage of ministerial or regional command; policy promoting regional autarky in case of an outside attack; the endemic mistrust in a society without institutional trust; the legacy of totalitarian control and risk aversion; the absence of market signals fostering efficient integration; the absence of finance-market mechanisms fostering alliances; and the deep concern with control which so pervades Chinese social psychology and which comes to the surface in ownership jealousies inhibiting mergers, a result of which is that only the weak get merged.

The results of such forces for state-owned industry have been described by George Gilboy as the creation of an 'industrial strategic culture' in which, with few exceptions, Chinese firms focus on developing privileged relations with Chinese Communist Party (CCP) officials, 'spurn horizontal association and broad networking with each other, and forgo investment in long-term technology development and diffusion'.[3] Again, the contrast with Japan, Korea, and Taiwan is stark. Analyzing this in more detail, Gilboy[4] goes on to say:

Firms that can develop strong links to research institutions, financiers, partners, suppliers, and customers have an advantage in acquiring, modifying, and then commercializing new technology. Such horizontal networks are essential conduits for knowledge, capital, products, and talent. Yet China's unreformed political process suppresses such independent social organization and horizontal networking and instead reinforces vertical relationships. China remains a fragmented federal system, its fractious regions unified by a single political party. The CCP controls all aspects of organized life, including industry associations, leaving few avenues for firms to work together for legitimate common interests...political obstacles prevent firms from associating, sharing risk, and taking collective action.

In a study of the emergence of corporate groups in China, Jean-Philippe Huchet came to a similar conclusion. To indicate the chronic splintering of industry he used the example of China's cement industry, which at the time of his study had 8,000 independent producers, compared to a total for the rest of the world of 1,500. The Chinese government had clearly set out in the 1990s to find an equivalent to the Korean *chaebol*, and the earlier Japanese *zaibatsu*, which had played crucial roles in the economic development of each society. This is how the notion of the team of national champions came into being. The subsequent effort led to 'considerable changes in the way of conceiving economic organization, property relations, the working of markets, and company

---

[3] Gilboy 2004, p. 9.   [4] Gilboy 2004, p. 41.

strategy'.[5] But results have been mixed. In industries close to the customer, such as domestic appliances and consumer electronics, concentration has increased to a point where the ten biggest firms hold 80 percent of the market. This suggests the picking up of market signals. In industries that are geographically concentrated, there has also been the imposition of rationality, and for instance in tobacco—concentrated in Yunnan— reform and restructuring is advanced. In other industries, remote from direct market pressure, and geographically spread, local protectionism has caused resistance, as is visible in automobiles and in construction steel. The cement industry was subject to twelve different ministerial offices, as well as local and provincial governments. In cases where an industry is not nationally strategic, as for instance with most consumer goods, it is possible for a firm to benefit from local government protection, or 'cover' and to use this as a basis for rapid expansion and integration to large scale.

A further aspect of local or regional government support is that an SOE which becomes a mainstay of regional or local government finances, may well become protected against the inflow of goods from other provinces, the means used being both visible and invisible barriers. This dividing of markets adds to the difficulties of making national competitive conditions do their work.

Management

A number of recent studies agree on certain features traceable to the history of the SOEs, and amounting to a widely shared corporate culture. Among the dimensions of this culture, Lieberthal and Lieberthal (2003) identify the following:

1. A premium on good political skills rather than on modern management capabilities.

2. Middle managers as information links and discipline enforcers in a top-down decision system, but not partners in a search for new ideas and improved processes.

3. 'Stovepipe' structures inside which is an emphasis on obedience to higher authorities. This may be coupled with high technical competence in discrete tasks, but at the same time suffers from an inability to optimize the workings of a total value chain across an organization's components.

[5] Huchet 1999, p. 9.

Further studies, such as that of Desvaux, Wang, and Xu (2004) provide complementary evidence in describing the widespread occurrence of unclear authority structures, absence of accountability, resistance to change, absence of incentives, and a shortage of strong CEOs.

China is now moving fast to strengthen its middle and senior management ranks, by formal training. But the addition of new knowledge, and new techniques of behavior, is only a small component of the set of changes which are needed to prepare this sector for post-WTO competition. The condition of management in China today is a product of its context, and that context is not just the last fifty years, but the last thousand. In both the ancient and modern legacies, hierarchy and control were norms and became instincts.

One of the outcomes of this hierarchical tradition in management is that it inhibits the growth of close interdependence between management and workforce. Instead managers tell workers what to do and then supervise the doing of it. This works well in certain kinds of industry where products change little, where work processes can be broken down into specifically defined jobs, where control can use obvious output data, and where market forces penetrate little or slowly. This is true, for example, in industries such as steel making, power generation, oil and gas, mining, and basic food processing. It is not true in industries dependent on consumer taste, or on response to rapid technological change, or on complex production systems requiring initiative and cooperation on the shop floor. Nor is it true in the service industry, as anyone staying in a state-run hotel would (until very recently) become aware. It is largely for this reason that SOE management now finds itself running companies that cannot compete. The old style does not fit the new circumstances. The style is also deeply embedded in a whole set of surrounding features and expectations and is—even with a powerful motivation—hard to change.

The Changing SOE Business System

The picture drawn above is not flattering when seen from the standpoint of the MBA textbook or the investment analyst. China's large-scale industry looks unprepared for WTO. The main industrial sectors of the economy are filled with inefficient companies, and given the propensity to build excess capacity, access to those sectors by other firms with different approaches has so far remained blocked. Most of China's large industrial firms (with some exceptions) have remained dependent on external technology. Exports of high technology and industrial goods are now dominated by foreign companies. There is little effective diffusion of technical learning within the state sector. The market is fragmented to an extreme degree. Integration of firms under ownership is hampered by the absence of institutions to facilitate it. Overcapacity is endemic. Firms can make money when they are protected, but rarely otherwise.

In judging the nature of change to the state system, two new features need now to be added to the account. One is negative, the other positive. The negative feature, most completely argued by Nolan, is that the world's large corporations outside China (in simple terms the Fortune 500) have since 1990, and because of the new power of information technology, gone through 'the most revolutionary change in the history of capitalism'. This has resulted in such an accumulation of scale and efficiency that no new entrant to that arena is likely to be able to compete. To assume that a labor cost advantage might be used by Chinese companies is to ignore that the outsiders will also have direct access themselves to that advantage, as many have already shown. More than half of China's exports of advanced technology industrial goods come out of firms with foreign ownership. They are already inside.

China does have an answer to this dilemma, and it lies in the two alternative forms of capitalism now emerging as dominant—the local corporates and the private sector firms. We consider these in Chapters 7 and 8, but before doing so, it is necessary to review the question of change in the state sector.

Change and Embeddedness

Nolan, in his authoritative but cautionary study of the team of 'national champions,' suggests two features, which are not always taken into account, to affect Chinese industrial evolution. One is that the negotiating power of Asian countries may grow to counterbalance the current dominance of Western capitalist ideals in the design of WTO influences. This may permit acceptance of a greater role for the state in an economy, and would follow from the relatively successful cases of Singapore, Korea, France, Germany, and Japan.

The second influence might be a nationalist backlash within China if its main industries come to be either taken over or eliminated by newcomers from outside, especially from the West or Japan, against both of whom historical resentments can resurface. A number of incidents might be pointed to as signs of this high sensitivity. Attacks on the

Japanese embassy in 2005, or the resentments surfacing over the presence (no matter how discrete) of a Starbucks branch within the Forbidden City—these all speak of the reassertion of cultural confidence and identity, and are of course fueled by the success of a quarter century of growth.

The salient facts give a picture of reforms moving at a fast pace, the speed being consistent with the overall economy's long-maintained 9 or 10 percent expansion. The impending arrival of effects from full WTO membership is also a form of deadline. The key features of the reforms, as described by Takeuchi and by Tang and Ward, are:

1. The identifying of the team of 'national champions' to be supported in their buildup to world market competitiveness.
2. Attempts to rationalize the remaining state companies, many of which are in industries where China has no comparative advantage.
3. The privatizing, stock-exchange listing, selling off, opening to investment, and enforced merging of state enterprises.
4. The large-scale moving of employees, by layoff and market rehiring, out of the state sector.
5. Reductions in the direct use of state capital.
6. The building of links with foreign companies, especially for technology, and including the option of foreign control of certain SOEs, but still protecting against foreign dominance of an industry by that route.
7. A general reduction in government intervention, and a consequent release into the market of otherwise trapped financial and labor resources.
8. The establishment of asset management companies to supervise and rationalize bank lending.
9. Simplifying the maze of bureaux controlling state industry.
10. Building an independent accounting profession, and investing heavily in professional (including managerial) training more broadly.
11. Adopting a form of corporate governance, which—while paying lip service to Anglo-US ideals—in practice (as in Japan) leaves control largely in the hands of insiders.
12. Permitting entrepreneurial dynamism to emerge from state enterprises with new organizations.

These reforms are deep and radical, and as a total they would appear designed to change the nature of the SOE sector into something unrecognizable from its past. But two questions arise: Will the transformation happen? Does China's future progress depend on it? The latter question arises because China has other options within its portfolio of systems, and their availability will inevitably affect government policy, even though the other options take China away from its tradition of tight central control. Let us now consider the SOE sector in isolation and return to the wider question when concluding the book.

Hovering over the entire scene is Nolan's point that the global game of big business has made a quantum leap in competitiveness from which China's large enterprises have been largely 'protected'. In itself this is enough to condition seriously any optimism about the creation of world champions, and it has nothing directly to do with China. An invisible but crucial aspect of the challenge posed lies in the culturally conditioned capacity for the efficient large-scale coordination of complexity, a skill seemingly instinctive to both westerners and Japanese, and an important foundation of their global competitiveness. In China, by contrast, large-scale organizations only operate at high levels of competitive efficiency under limited conditions: the tight focusing of skills in one field (thus reducing complexity) often combined with heavy capital investment and foreign technology (as with Baosteel); or with dependence on charismatic leadership, often using a military-inspired corporate culture, as with Hua Wei, or Broad Airconditioning.

Any complex organization, as we have stated earlier, has to compete by the use of capacities to (*a*) coordinate its resources efficiently; (*b*) learn about relevant change; and (*c*) change itself. These are universal principles. Large-scale organization in China, especially in the state sector, faces these demands with certain handicaps. The authoritarianism that typifies organizational behavior stifles communication by preventing the independence of thought that accompanies empowerment. The stovepipe structures prevent the flow of ideas and information across the organization and so inhibit learning. The conservatism that comes from mistrust and a legacy of unpredictable intervention, inhibits organizational adjustment to change. The personalized nature of many relations in the organization structure inhibits the full development of a performance-based professionalism in management and in operations.

The surrounding institutional fabric, although changing, is still not providing stimuli to change the deeper instincts. It will inevitably stabilize as a Chinese form of institutional fabric, reflecting for instance

Chinese beliefs about law, morality, priorities in relationships, identity, and rationale. Although the individual's relation with the state can be anticipated to evolve into a new accommodation, it is unlikely to take on an altogether new form, given the amount of cultural tradition that lies behind it.

The state-owned sector of China has proven seriously handicapped at technical innovation for reasons connected with its structures and managerial responses. The provision of education by the state, although now increasing rapidly in scale, has only met a small portion of the demand. Rational reward systems are still not the norm in most of state industry, nor is the exercise of initiative normal among many executives. Competition has been met with substantial struggling in organizations not designed for that purpose. Property rights are still in evolution, but the new psychology they bring is unlikely to penetrate business decision-making in the state sector to any serious degree.

The SOE sector of China seems likely to continue its decline. Certain components of it will survive, specifically the members of the well-supported national team that respond managerially to the new challenges they face (and this will predictably be a minority of the starting group). Others may be saved because of the strategic nature of their industry, or the state's acceptance of the welfare burden they carry for it. China's future growth is likely to depend post-WTO on the other business systems within it, the private sector, and the entrepreneurial semigovernment local corporate hybrids. These equally are products of their society's history and culture, but are also proofs that variety in responses is possible in conditions of the massive discontinuities that China's history displays.

Key References

Allen, Franklin, Jun Qian, and Meijun Qian. 2005. 'China's Financial System: Past, Present and Future', Working paper, Wharton School, University of Pennsylvania.

Desvaux, Georges, Michael Wang, and David Xu. 2004. 'Spurring Performance in China's State-Owned Enterprises', *McKinsey Quarterly*, Special edition: 96–106.

Feuerwerker, Albert. 1958. *China's Early Industrialization*. Cambridge, MA: Harvard University Press.

Foster, George M. 1967. 'Peasant Society and the Image of Limited Good', in J. M. Potter, M. N. Diaz, and G. M. Foster (eds.), *Peasant Society*. Boston, MA: Little, Brown.

Gilboy, George J. 2004. 'The Myth Behind China's Miracle', *Foreign Affairs*, 83 (4): 33–48.

Guthrie, Douglas. 2006. 'Governance, Not Ownership is the Issue: Explaining the Success of China's Publicly Traded Firms'. Keynote presentation, Conference of the International Association for Chinese Management Research, Nanjing, June 16, 2006.

Guthrie, Douglas. 1999. *Dragon in a Three-piece Suit*. Princeton NJ: Princeton University Press.

Huchet, Jean-Francois. 1999. 'Concentration and the Emergence of Corporate Groups in Chinese Industry', *China Perspectives*, 23 (May–June): 5–17.

Lieberthal, Kenneth, and Geoffrey Lieberthal. 2003. 'The Great Transition', *Harvard Business Review*, October 2003: 3–14.

Nolan, Peter. 2004. *Transforming China: Globalization, Transition and Development*. London: Anthem Press.

Redding, Gordon, and M. Witt. 2006. 'The Tray of Loose Sand: A Thick Description of the State-Owned Enterprise Sector of China Seen as a Business System', *Asian Business and Management*, 5: 87–112.

Takeuchi, Junko. 2003. 'Trade and Investment Liberalization and Industrial Restructuring in China', *RIM Pacific Business and Industries*, 111(8): 2–22.

Tang, Jie, and Anthony Ward. 2003. *The Changing Face of Chinese Management*. London: Routledge.

Whitley, Richard. 1999. 'Competing Logics and Units of Analysis in the Comparative Study of Economic Organization', *International Studies of Management and Organization*, 29 (2): 113–26.

7

From Collectives to Local Corporates

It has been a long-standing convention, in describing the Chinese economy, to divide it into three segments: state-owned, collective, and private.
The middle one of these was originally clear in what it conveyed. It
included the organizations owned collectively by all the residents of an
urban or rural district or village, but controlled by government agencies at
that level. This category has, since market structure reforms accelerated in
the 1990s, undergone major transition, and is unrecognizable from what
it was. In simple terms, much of it has been hybridized with, or sold to,
the private sector. While still retaining some government involvement,
it has been transformed into something now identified as 'local corpo-
ratism'.[1] Elements of it have expanded massively in new conglomerate
forms. Other elements have declined in the face of new competition from
the private sector in an overcrowded market.

The changes have gone further in some parts of China than others,
so that the sector's significance varies geographically, it being especially
important in the industrial coastlands. This chapter tells the story of this
transition, and treats this complex segment of the economy as a discrete
business system undergoing radical change. To see it as a distinct system is
an analytical convenience, and in reality the boundaries of the category
are porous, and its internal contents now mixed. The organizations in
it, however, share a clear heritage going back to the communes and
brigades of the Mao Revolution, and the hand of government is still in
the background, even though no longer always controlling things in an
obvious way. We do not include here firms under full private ownership—
some of which may well have been separated out from this sector. We treat
these within the private-sector category in Chapter 8.

[1] Cf. Nee 1992; Oi 1999.

There is a complex interface between the state assets held on behalf of the people and the market-driven dynamism of the entrepreneurs, and many observers see this as an opportunity space for corruption and opportunism. Certainly there has been an increase in corruption over the past decades, and much of it has been associated with transfers in this arena. While saying that, it is also valid to observe that many municipal officials in China work hard to improve the lives of the local inhabitants and are inspired by central government incentive structures to compete over progress with other municipalities. The ideals of societal solidarity have not entirely disappeared, and corruption is in any case a highly elastic notion, with a long transition between minor bribery at one end and outright embezzlement at the other.

A further crucial idea in this context is that of 'clan capitalism', first outlined by Max Boisot and John Child in their work on the changing Chinese economy. This suggests that—in the absence of established institutions supporting trust (such as a sound legal system protecting rights, a good information system, and the availability of professional standards throughout)—people will resort to local networks and extended personal connections to establish economic order. Effective local officials can keep government off people's backs, but still get government money. They can also develop a town or an industry by pulling together the components it needs for success. When the domains of local politics and the economy begin to overlap, the effects may cause two plus two to equal five.

History of the Collective Sector

Before 1949, China's agricultural sector was poor and technically backward, relying on heavy inputs of manual labor, using little in the way of machinery, and supporting a subsistence level of survival for most of China's people. Historically, farming had suffered for centuries from the 'high-level equilibrium trap', whereby the cost of labor was so low that investment in labor-saving technology was pointless. In those days, there would be a scattering of small workshops, processing centers, and simple handicraft businesses in most areas, and major industrial centers were concentrated in a few cities, and the industrial Northeast.

One of the earliest initiatives under Communism was, perhaps naturally, the creation of communes, beginning in 1955. This achieved its intention, in that it brought under government control both the growing and disposal of food, and the use of labor. It also brought under the same control the simple industrial facilities and the labor that went with them. They became the collective and brigade enterprises which from 1958 became the initial units for a nationally orchestrated campaign to turn China into an industrial power. This 'Great Leap Forward', ignoring all the basic laws of economics, psychology, management, and processes of exchange led to chaos in the distribution of goods, and it turned the people of China into overworked and undernourished victims, assigned to production teams, inside brigades, inside one of the nation's 26,000 large communes. Cities were included in the treatment. Control was exercised by the commune cadres from the Party. People were required to report on each other, and terror was widespread. Famine reached its worst point in 1960, with a national average daily calorie intake of 1,535 (the norm for active adults is around 2,800 per day, and effects are cumulative— the level at Auschwitz was between 1,300 and 1,700). In the four years of this experiment, an estimated 20 to 43 million people died in excess of the normal rate, from the combination of starvation and overwork. Contributing to this was the policy of exporting grain to earn foreign currency for arms and equipment purchases. China was closed to the outside world in those years, and its people starved of information as well as food, so that even today there is little understanding there of the full scale of the horror. But personal and family histories accumulate, and when Chinese people see collective assets being taken out of collective ownership in later years, they do not forget how those assets were created.

In a subsequent major act of orchestrated destruction—the Cultural Revolution of 1966–76—the commune strategy was reasserted. It failed again, but this time a lesson was learned and that period ended with rural reforms. These were aimed at the comprehensive development of agriculture, industry, and commerce and the promotion of small towns as focuses for growth. Further reforms dating from the 1980s stimulated township enterprises, and also built on the fact that allowing farmers to own some of their output led to increases in productivity. The private sector was reborn in China, although it would be twenty years before one of its members could take a senior public position in the Party.

Throughout the 1980s and 1990s what became known as 'the collective sector' performed well. In 1980 it contributed around a quarter of industrial output, growing to 36 percent by 1996. Over the same period the private sector grew from nothing to 31 percent, at the expense of the state sector, that shrank from 77 to 33 percent, all these movements taking place in a general atmosphere of stunning overall growth.[2] The critical

---

[2] Naughton 2007: 300.

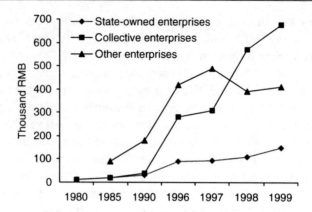

Figure 7.1. Trends in value of production per worker by enterprise type
Source: Takeuchi 2003.

feature of interest, however, is the growth of productivity, illustrated in the above graph (Figure 7.1). Here the collectives are seen to have outperformed the other sectors in the value of production per worker, starting at around 20,000 RMB in 1985 and rising to 675,000 by 1999. The state sector over the same period would reach to no more than a quarter of that productivity and went from 15,000 to 150,000 RMB.

During the 1990s, two features of the business environment began to put the collective sector under pressure. The first was the difficult transition from the earlier protected markets to those driven by demand and competition. Learning the meaning of the words 'market' and 'customer' can be painful for those who have only ever known 'the plan' as a guide to action. The second factor was the tightening of access to credit as the banking system came under pressure to behave rationally. In the earlier phase, innovation and product quality were of little consequence, as patterns of supply and demand were still largely shaped by the state. But, in the later phase, buyer power became a factor, and product quality a big issue. The sector was not at first well prepared for this switch, and it affected both industrial and consumer industries. It was made worse for them by the rapidly growing private sector. In the event, the town and village enterprises (TVEs) did learn to respond competitively, as the graph shows, often bringing in expertise from abroad to help, especially from their ethnic cousins in Hong Kong or Taiwan, but as this happened, the enterprises became more attractive to acquire, and their ownership structure began to change. These were seen by many astute entrepreneurs as golden years of opportunity. State assets could be acquired at low cost,

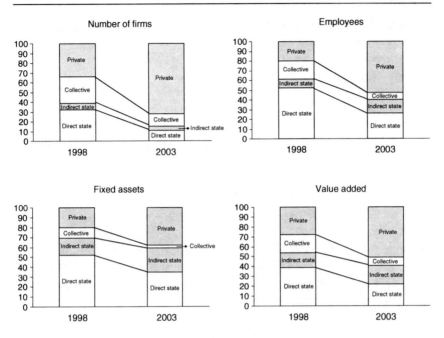

Figure 7.2. Changes in types of organization in the Chinese economy

Source: OECD 2005.

political connections could secure cheap loans from state banks and also give protection from the central authorities, and wealth could be pursued by those with the skills to stitch together all the connections. In this transition, local officials became what Peter Li calls 'privileged agents,' but the ordinary people in the workforce were in the event deprived.

By 2005, the great majority of the TVEs had been privatized. They had been in a transitory form and had served the purpose of maintaining stability and starting growth. A 2005 OECD report on China illustrates the dramatic scale of the changes between 1998 and 2003, and shows clearly (Figure 7.2) that in terms of value-added, the private sector (to be discussed in Chapter 8) now accounts for about two-thirds of national performance, and about 75 percent of all firms. The collective sector, down to 7 percent of national industrial value-added in 2003, is evaporating as the private sector takes it over. In this taking over, it is common for some equity to be held by local government, and for the result to be a hybrid. It is this new hybrid form that we term the 'local corporate', using the word 'corporate' in the sense of an instrument to extend government interest into the economy. That interest may now be down to a minor percentage of equity, but it does give the Party a voice at the boardroom table. In exchange, the entrepreneurs across the same table can ask for the firm's concerns to be looked after in other councils. Both parties have interest, and their coming together creates a hybrid which leaves neither dominant.

The Local Corporate Sector as a Business System in Transition

As previously we will consider first the realm of meaning in culture, then of order in institutions, then of coordination in the business system itself, taking account here of the local corporate sector in its own right (see Figure 7.3). In essence this sector began as a manifestation of state interests, but at the local level. Much of its character has stemmed from that, and all that it implies for access to land, trained labor, industrial plant, and bank loans, and especially for the independence of action away from the state's center. We will conclude that its transformation into a hybrid with the private sector and/or with foreign investors has produced an especially potent force for economic growth, and a highly significant new formula emergent from a distinct history. We should at the same time warn that there remains much variety within the type and that not all organizations inside it will match what is given here as a set of tendencies.

Rationale

China's Maoist experiment in redesigning the ends and means of economic life ended not with a sudden event, such as the collapse of the Berlin Wall, but with a long-drawn-out period of trial and error and adjustment, punctuated by occasional highly symbolic gestures, such as the various sayings of Deng Xiaoping that led to China's turning to a new direction. Of equal significance have been the welcoming of foreign investment ('opening the window and letting the flies in') and the opening up to WTO processes. Experimentation has been encouraged: 'What does it matter whether the cat is black or white, as long as it catches mice?'; 'We shall cross the river by groping for stones.' The mental landscapes of many people contain the sometimes counterbalanced features that result. They grew up with a China devoted to a Communist ideal, and to the suppression of individualism entailed in that, and yet they now live in a 'socialist market economy', itself moving faster

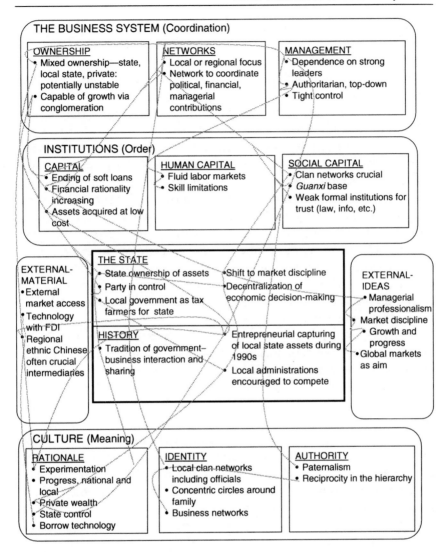

Figure 7.3. The Chinese local corporate sector seen as a complex adaptive system

every day toward a nonsocialist version. In this, their individual skills are crucial to their standard of living. They respond instinctively to the totalitarian condition, with its insistence on conformity, but at the same time they are now surrounded by the most rampant private opportunism and adventurousness, and a newly wealthy *bourgeoisie*. Trained to see the state as the sole protector, they have now had to relearn that family has recovered that traditional role. Across all these conflicting perspectives is the generation contrast, here much sharper than in most societies; the older generation has lived through turbulence and often misery, while the younger generation raised in single-child homes and at times of relative prosperity sees the world very differently indeed.

The rationale in the minds of many of the key players now shaping this sector is divided into three main ways of making sense of what they do. People have different degrees of each, and as with many such rationales there are, for many, unresolved contradictions to be lived with.

The first desirable end envisaged is the continued progress of China toward its perceived rightful place as a great and influential civilization, and as the natural 'middle kingdom'. This remains a great driving force, and it reflects the high sensitivity—very rarely expressed except in gestures—about the state's decline over the past two centuries, and about the costs to the society's reputation of the civil wars of the twentieth century, and of the years under Mao. Chinese executives, especially those engaged with state assets, will talk quite openly and emotionally about improving the society.

A second implicit intention, which is a variant on the first, is the improvement of the *local* society. There is commonly a strong sense of place, and of regional belonging, for many Chinese. They always know their family's place of origin, and they commonly go back and support a home village. In a wider regional sense this feeling is enhanced by differences in language that often go well beyond differences in dialect. For decades it has been difficult to move around in China (although controls are no longer strict), because easy and quick transport was not available, and this adds also to the sense of belonging in one place. Migrant workers are usually planning to return to their home villages, and the US-style geographical mobility of entire families is not replicated here. So local identity is strong, and with it goes a strong interest in locally defined progress. The government policies of recent years, in which local officials achieve promotion by developing their own towns in competition with each other, also enhance the significance of local loyalties, networks, and cooperative ties. It is not always appreciated just how *decentralized* China is in its day-to-day administration.

The third deep-seated aim is—inevitably—personal wealth, or more accurately wealth shared within a family, and capable of enhancing a family's status. Poverty has been the condition of so many for so long that the escape from it is pursued with a rare intensity, and the sense of this subterranean pent-up force is manifest all over China and at all levels. This is clearly a dominant feature of the private sector, to be discussed Chapter 8, but with the flowing together of the collective and private sectors, it has percolated into the collective sector and been absorbed. It is this that perhaps best explains the immense dynamism the sector has unleashed. Officials and entrepreneurs can share this common ground. The urge is strengthened also by the fact that wealth-seeking is now legitimate and encouraged within the societal system. An economy growing for long periods at 9 percent per year is bound to be full of tempting opportunities.

So there are three primary *ends* within the overall rationale in this sector: build the state, build the local economy, seek personal wealth. But what of the *means* seen as appropriate ? Again there are paradoxes of the kind that China is accustomed to living with, and in this sector they stem from the use of state assets for private gain, often resulting in people joining the ranks of either the privileged, or the deprived, depending on their connections within the 'clan'.

The accepted *means* that appear to have crystallized out in this sector under its radical transition might be summarized under four headings. First is the feeling that local initiative is to be encouraged. In fact, the state pits towns against each other in competition, and rewards successful officials with promotion and rising benefits. Some of the initiatives that result are visible in the sparkling new shopping centers, highways, factories attracted to the area, and clean, flower-filled cityscapes. Occasionally the competitive bravado is astonishing. Visitors to the small town of Yiwu in Zhejiang province are usually stunned by the scale and modernity of the wholesale market buildings there, now covering space the size of the Pentagon. Nearby is another town with a full-scale replica of the Forbidden City, designed to attract tourists and filmmakers.

The second legitimate means is the acceptance of the state's right to control things. In practice this is exercised by the Party maintaining discipline over its members, who are in key positions spread throughout the society. This is an ancient principle in China. The state is required to maintain order, and the widespread fear of chaos explains much of the capacity people have for accepting what other societies might define as autocracy. The weakness of property rights is related to this, as one of its effects is to rob people of a base for protest. The rise of a bourgeoisie with significant impact on the structures of power, depends in turn on the securing of such rights, and on the opening of debate across the society. Any emergence of 'civil society' (i.e. institutions outside state control) could become one of the highest points of tension as China's modernization proceeds, but for the moment it shows little sign of challenging the old tradition. Civil society is, of course, a crucial ingredient in Western societal designs, but that does not mean it becomes a universal requirement. Singapore, for instance, runs with controlled politics and has no free press; but then, Singapore does not have 1.3 billion people.

A third legitimate means within the rationale of the transitional collective sector is the borrowing of technology. This includes not just techniques of production and design, but also techniques of organization, marketing, and logistics, especially those associated with connecting into world markets. More than half of China's FDI in 2003 came from Hong Kong, Taiwan, and Singapore suggesting (but not proving conclusively) the links with the globally connected overseas Chinese industrialists. It is one of the arguments of this book that the skills accumulated by the regional ethnic Chinese, and especially their mastering of technology and of the understanding of market access to the developed world, are key to an understanding of much of China's recent growth. Capital itself was also significant, with a cumulative inward flow of approximately $70 billion from Hong Kong alone between 2000 and 2003. Many of the initiatives taken by local governments using the assets of the collective sector were instigated by foreign investors (most of whom were ethnically Chinese) for whom a substantial tax advantage—of less than half the normal rate—was available. Such connections also allowed local officials to gain access to bank accounts outside China—a crucial feature of what went on below the table.

A final legitimate *means* adopted within the sector has been the resort to the 'clan' as the alternative unit of identity to that of the family. More can be done with clan relationships than with family alone, especially when officials control access to key assets, and the details will be considered in the next section on Identity as a feature of culture.

Identity

Chinese people have traditionally seen those surrounding them as belonging within a set of concentric circles. The inner core is family, seen in extended terms and with close attention paid to rank. Inside this network of blood relations the ties of loyalty, obligation, and dependence are very strong. The workings of the wider society have to a great extent depended on the stability, and self-sustaining nature, of family units.

Beyond family lie other forms of bonding and identity, and in the case of people involved in the local corporate sector of the economy two features have affected the architecture of the evolving social ties. The first is that property in China was collectively owned within the local jurisdiction, and, as noted earlier, the disposition of its use was in the hands of local officials acting on behalf of the state. The collective ownership gave people practice in thinking of cooperative systems with local boundaries. The state's role as ultimate owner gave local officials a great deal of power. The second feature was that an entire set of surrounding institutions made it necessary to co-opt the support of local officials if the assets were to be used. Such assets included not just land, buildings, and labor skills, but also access to state bank credit, and even more crucially, political protection in the face of possible interference from state government.

A clan network would typically emerge in a locality such as a county, bringing together the assets, the political cover, the necessary licenses, the technical know-how, and the market access. In many regions the networks might become highly complex, as industries built of flexibly linked firms become part of the local scene. The clan membership would then include the officials, the entrepreneurs, the bankers, those enabling access to markets and technology, and all the suppliers of components and related services needed. The essential dilemma would be the stabilizing of reliable transactions. Without good-quality information about other people or their goods, without predictable and stable legal supports, without property rights, without the intermediation of neutral professions, and always subject to unpredictable government intervention, the average business person would seek stability of commitments using bonds of interpersonal obligation. Without the kind of stable codified bureaucratic order typical of modernized societies, and all the institutions attached to such order, China found another solution. The clan is an alternative to the Western formula for a modern economy. It may prove to be, as Boisot and Child suggest, a postmodern alternative with serious staying power, as it fits well with the accompanying destructuring of much of the world's advanced industry.

Authority

In this local corporate sector, authority flows from (*a*) government connections, and from (*b*) market and technical know-how, with the two streams coming together in the alliances made so often between local municipalities and local or foreign entrepreneurs and investors. It is likely that the balance between these two sources of power has been shifting, and that the logics of technology and market will now be claiming equal consideration with those of the political structure. This will especially be the case where finance is concerned, as the days of soft loans come to an end, and hard budget constraints come in. Increasingly performance will count, and those able to deliver it will share authority with those with friends in high places. The heads of the emerging 'local corporates' usually—of necessity—have plenty of both.

In the day-to-day use of authority, the return of paternalism is virtually complete, and so too its moral underpinning within the Confucian-style system of reciprocal obligations between boss and subordinates. It is however predictable that over time (and probably long time) as demands for performance drive managers toward more measurement and more objectivity, a cadre of professional managers may emerge, carrying their MBAs and moving between firms to enhance their careers. This phenomenon may well first appear as a significant feature in the larger hybrid firms, because many of them have the scale to need it. Also many of them are exposed to the outside influences, such as joint-venture partnerships, which usually demand it.

Historical Influences and the Role of the State

The history of this sector was described briefly earlier and it is perhaps useful here simply to identify the more significant prior events without which this sector would not exist in its present form. The idea of a balance between local initiative and central control has a long history in China. These simultaneous loose–tight properties result from the sheer size of the state, and the relative lightness, in number terms, of the traditional administrative bureaucracy. Governance was by the (often severe) punishing of deviations and the making of examples, and it remains so. It was not by detailed on-the-spot supervision, except in the extreme case of the Mao experiments with collectives. The normal position taken locally has been that 'The heavens are high, and the emperor is far.' At the same time, the existence of the Party is crucial here. Because the Party machine is in place, the government can be reassured of enough control over events to continue with its encouragement of local initiatives, as long as those initiatives present no political challenges.

The simple fact of state ownership of virtually all land and buildings is a significant feature derived from Chinese history, but equally so are the more recent experiments in the introduction of modes of ownership.

Rights to the use of such property are now extending for much longer periods, not yet reaching the freehold ideal common elsewhere but certainly moving in that direction. Most significant, however, as recent historical events, have been the shifts of policy away from Marxism, and especially the moves toward market discipline instigated by Deng Xiaoping, Jiang Zemin, and Zhu Rongji.

Capital

We come now to the societal institutions surrounding the business system of the local corporate sector and begin with those concerned with the sourcing and allocation of capital.

In the first instance, prior to 1980, the assets of this sector, such as land, factory buildings, trained labor, and bank lending arrangements were owned by the state, but operated on behalf of the state through the collectives. All members of the collective shared in this ownership, and—at least nominally—had rights to take part in decisions over the use of the assets. They would, for instance, elect managers to run the operations. In practice, however, the power to control was inevitably concentrated in a few hands at the top of each enterprise, as mass control would have been unworkable in conditions of competition. Inevitably also there would be an overlap between that executive group and the Party.

It is impossible now to find authoritative data to explain the sourcing of capital in the local corporate sector, as the boundaries of the sector are impossible to fix clearly. As the collective sector transmutes into different forms, the reporting of it also splits up. Even so, a number of surveys have thrown light on two features of the supply of capital. First, there appears to be heavy reliance on retained earnings. These account for about 60 percent of capital needs in the 'hybrid' sector (which includes the TVEs) for the years 1994–2002, as reported by Franklin Allen, J. Qian, and M. Qian. The same authors, in a separate detailed study of seventeen new firms in Zhejiang and Jiangsu, report a pattern of entrepreneurs gaining prior experience in state enterprises or TVEs (80 percent of the sample) and drawing their start-up capital primarily from banks (45 percent of firms). The financing of growth later was not through bank finance, but instead through private credit agencies (28 percent), friends (24 percent), and regional ethnic Chinese (15 percent). Relationships with local government were reported in 70 percent of cases. This suggests (without proving) that start-up loans from banks were being used to set up new ventures by people with strong connections in the collective sector. Between 1998 and 2003, according to OECD data (see Figure 7.2), the share of national value-added in the collective sector fell from 17.3 to 7 percent. In those same five years in the private sector it rose from 27.9 to 52.3 percent. In fact, 80 percent of this explosive growth took place at the jurisdiction level of townships or below. The state's local assets were moving into private hands.

We need now to distinguish between categories. Those parts of the private sector which have resulted from the breaking away of pieces of the old collective sector, and are now in entirely private hands, are treated in Chapter 8 on private companies. Those parts of the old collective sector that have become hybrids, or that have been revived as effective firms, and which still have a clear government interest in their ownership structures (even though perhaps small), are the firms we now consider as the local corporates.

Human Capital

For the kinds of industry found in the local corporate sector, human capital needs are mainly for labor able to learn manual skills. This is available in great volume as people move from agriculture to industry. Unions provide no countervailing power against management, and there is much fluidity in the labor market.

The demands for managerial and supervisory skills are now increasing, although the tendency for many of the newer organizations to be start-ups at small scale, means that entrepreneurs themselves handle most managerial issues. In large organizations, middle management is a serious challenge. The attention of government to the provision of education at higher levels is visible in the investments being made there. In 1985, two million people were enrolled in higher education. In 2003, the figure had risen to eleven million, with average annual growth of 23 percent between 1997 and 2003. Clearly China is serious about catching up, and has noted the lessons from elsewhere—that investment in education is fruitful. Not that China ever believed anything different; it simply lacked the allocating of the money to make access widespread. Traditionally also it educated people in subjects a long way removed from the economic world. Getting your hands dirty was low status. Long fingernails meant scholarship, status, and separation from manual work.

Social Capital

There are two major forms of social capital: one, based in relations of obligation and reciprocity between individuals, is called the *personal* form; the other based in societal systems of stable order such as law, good information, professional standards, and bureaucracy, is called the *institutional* form. The two forms normally complement each other, although in some societies, (e.g. the United States) the institutional form has tended to predominate. In China this latter form is hardly yet available, and the entire country tends to find the trustworthiness needed for transactions to proceed in the realm of personal trust. The term for the bonds built with it is *guanxi*, and it is the foundation stone for much of the efficiency in certain of the business fields. The networking of small enterprises depends on it for efficiency. It is also the source of much inefficiency in other fields. The managing of large complex organization is bedeviled by it for its interference with rationality.

In the context of the local corporate sector we see the blossoming of what Boisot termed *network capitalism*, arguing (from the standpoint of information theory) that until a society is able to build the institutions to enable a full codification and diffusion of the information needed for a national market to function spontaneously, and at full intensity, then there is a vacuum. Without reliable information, clear predictable rules, and stable institutions, a person doing business is faced with too many uncertainties to be able to grow the business. A clan-like network is able to fill that vacuum. Such a social grouping takes on extra depth and strength when it has local boundaries as not only do members know each other, but they also share connections with many third parties.

Although local officials cannot give guarantees of future government action, they can give early warnings and some protection. Although local banks cannot grant loans with government money without a rational case being made (or seeming to), they can still underwrite risks taken by people whose record is known to them. A clan structure of personal connections can often help with the question of whether to trust a stranger. Personal trust is a workable alternative to institutional trust, but it operates best in limited domains such as a trade, or a subregion. By this means, uncertainty—instead of being overcome—is absorbed, and its effects subdued.

The workings of the system have been well described by Peter Ping Li. His account is summarized in the statement that the earlier partnership between business and government was a positive one, aimed at achieving a public alliance for wealth creation. As the economy began to open up in the 1990s, this turned into a negative one, and it became a matter of private collusion for the transfer of wealth. An early warning of this was given in a remarkable expose by He Qinglian in 1998—a book at first banned and then later adopted for publication by the state—and translated as *China's Pitfall*. In this she described the raids on local state assets by the new entrepreneurs, and their co-opting of local political support.

The surrounding context in which the clan connections worked was one where the typical local government acted as an industrial corporation, competing with equivalents around it. It became de facto the board of a conglomerate whose subunits were the local TVEs. It was encouraged in this by new fiscal incentives flowing down from Beijing, all of which were aimed at the growing of local industry. As well as providing strategic guidance and performance evaluation to the units, the county government would work to foster appropriate local infrastructure, such as power and highways. It would also support initiatives to connect with global markets, such as delegations to and from China, exhibitions, and publicity. Perhaps most critically, it played a pivotal role as guarantor of bank loans. A further crucial contribution was that of acting as a political shield against a predatory central government. Local government could, for instance, interpret central policies in different ways, and it could implement them selectively. The resultant potential for tax evasion is suggested in 1995 figures that show the TVEs as accounting for 30 percent of GDP, but only 17 percent of tax revenue. The value of the strategic advice given by officialdom in this transformation is attested to in Guthrie's fine-grained study of eighty-one Shanghainese state enterprises.

There is no clear division between the early phase of wealth creation that occurred in the early 1990s and the later phase of wealth transfer that followed, but those who acquired assets did so with a sense of urgency— here was an opportunity that would not recur. The massive privatization that resulted was much affected by competition between the elites for the best deals, by regional rivalries, and by jealousies over the accumulation of wealth in the new entrepreneur class. The motivation of the business people entering the game was the buying of future political support— a sign that personalism would still triumph over rationality for a long time to come in China. So officials became directors, with fees, expense allowances, and foreign trips, and they transferred their Communist privileges into capitalist equivalents. They had brought their political power to market and sold it, and with it, they sold the assets of the people.

The reasons why this happened are multiple. First, it permitted the retention of public ownership (albeit with reduced equity percentages), while at the same time fostering local initiative. Second, it fitted with the culturally compatible ideals associated with clan membership. Third, and negatively, it provided organizations, including some of those known as 'red hats', capable of covering the internal transfer of public assets into private hands. Last, it allowed a response to the societal dilemma of limited institutional trust, by providing a complex set of social bonds which did the job of providing order and predictability. Elsewhere these might be looked for in the workings of strong institutions, such as law and a free press, but not in China.

Ownership and Networks

We come now to the three forms of coordination (ownership, networking, and management) that together shape the business system, in this case the radically changing local corporate sector as it emerged from the old collectives. The first of these, ownership, lies at the center of a huge drama, in which economic rationality is served by the efficiencies which flow from privatization, especially as the marketization of the economy proceeds, but where closer scrutiny would see illegitimate transfers, in a context where the society's control structures allowed for no appeals for fairness to be made. This period is referred to by those taking the advantages as 'the seven golden years'.

The private sector has, in effect, acquired the collective sector, but it has not been a matter of total elimination of the earlier collective interests. The representatives of such interests have instead been co-opted, and still have a role to play, usually as company directors, or 'friends in high places' who are looked after. The end result is that both political and economic forces are aligned to exploit the opportunities available. Perhaps the most important impact of these new forms of ownership is the capacity they inspire for adventurous growth, in conditions where full disclosure is avoidable. A study of such an outcome is provided by Meyer and Lu, who describe the dramatic growth of an organization, that growth having been aided by the obscure nature of its shape, its ownership structure, and its boundaries.

That organization is China International Marine Containers (CIMC), based in the SEZ of Shenzhen, near Hong Kong. It makes marine shipping containers, and from near bankruptcy in 1987 it has grown to dominate the global market. It has done so using organizing skills adapted both to its context and to the world of global competition. The first of these is the ability to resist interference from state owners, one of whom tried to turn it into a captive supplier. Second, it has developed a means of exerting full operational and financial control over subsidiaries, despite their independent legal status, partial local government ownership, and local government representation on their boards. Last, it has successfully funded and executed an aggressive acquisition strategy. CIMC does not fit neatly into any of the general categories—state, collective, or private— being used to bring some order to our analysis, but it provides vivid illustration of the interweaving that occurs between such sectors, in the massive laboratory of experiments which China's economy has become. It is an SOE, with a large number of local corporate components, operating with a market-driven and dominant CEO. The latter—acting as an agent of joint-venture owners, and working to maintain political cover from the Organization Department of the Shenzhen Party Committee—is a professional manager with a high level of autonomy. His professionalism, though, is defined in Chinese terms.

The example of CIMC illustrates what can be done when a company sets out to grow by acquisition in the present-day environment of China, but its very success points to its unusual nature, and to the constraints that many other organizations have failed to get around. The majority of firms wanting to grow by integration across China face the following hurdles:

(a) most markets remain local or provincial, often reflecting local languages and limited transport options between geographical regions;

(b) local governments, competing with their surrounding equivalents, are usually reluctant to give up control of key assets used for such competition;

(c) local governments are responsible for corporate taxes gathered (or tax-farmed) locally, a portion of which goes to Beijing. They, therefore, tend to protect their revenue sources;

(d) stocks of state capital are politically controlled at local levels, and cannot easily be used across regions;

(e) economic reform, in decentralizing decisions, has tended to exacerbate the localism of Chinese institutions, and in turn the hypercompetitive and fragmented markets that result.

The 'clan capitalism' of China is a reflection of these forces. Organizations are built of largely local connections, and holding them together requires political, managerial, and social skills of a high order. In consequence, they are somewhat delicate structures, in that they may be subject to interference from government, to defection by other ownership interests, and to high dependence on individual strong leaders. The latter weakness comes about not just because of the normal risks of mortality, but because the web of connections holding the organization in place are often personally created and maintained. Transition in such circumstances is always hazardous.

Management

There is prima facie evidence that the old 'collective' sector, as it made the transition toward market efficiency and saw its assets privatized, became very efficient in the use of its resources, when compared with other sectors in China. As the OECD report states:

The number of collectively owned enterprises has fallen rapidly over the past five years. The productivity of the remaining firms controlled by collective owners is impressive, and raises further questions. While they have not been counted as part of the private sector, their productivity is nearly as high as domestic and non-mainland private firms, and is consistent with the contention of a number of case studies that argue many operate as *de facto* private firms. Such firms may operate under leases or other informal arrangements, despite their residual property rights belonging to local governments.[3]

To give some ideas of the parameters in this judgment, the state-owned industrial firms in 2002 averaged 8 percent for return on assets (ROA) and 7.5 percent for return on equity (ROE), whereas the equivalent figures for private firms were 13.5 and 13.0.

The management of enterprises in China has always tended to follow a pattern consisting of (*a*) authoritarian control by a strong head; (*b*) downward vertical communication; (*c*) the gathering of control data to ensure predictability; and (*d*) the employment of specialists to handle technology. The style of management is often militaristic in feel, with emphasis on discipline. In the larger organizations managers in the middle and upper-middle ranks tend not to communicate among themselves horizontally across the organization. Instead they inhabit 'vertical silos'

[3] OECD 2005, p. 98.

in which their role is to pass downwards the instructions coming from above, and ensure compliance with what is required. This habit, and the corporate culture typically surrounding it, prevents the emergence of iniatives, and 'intrapreneurship,' and of thinking on behalf of the organization.

One of the outcomes of such structures is that workers and managers tend not to establish the closeness of cooperation seen in Japan or Germany, as their organizations deal with complex technology. Instead, in China the success stories lie in mass production of mid- or low-technology products, where there can be high dependence on the machines themselves to handle the processes, and where jobs can be highly standardized and specialized. This is where their world competitiveness lies, and it rests on production discipline, standardization, and low-cost labor, as well as effective access to market demand.

There is another somewhat different form of network capitalism linking the smaller private firms, and we turn to that in Chapter 8.

Key References

Boisot, Max, and John Child. 1996. 'From Fiefs to Clans: Explaining China's Emerging Economic Order', *Administrative Science Quarterly*, 41(4): 600–28.

Chang, Jung, and Jon Halliday. 2005. *Mao: The Unknown Story*. London: Jonathan Cape.

Li, Peter Ping. 2005. 'The Puzzle of China's Township-Village Enterprises: The Paradox of Local Corporations in a Dual-Track Economic Transition', *Management and Organization Review*, 1(2): 197–224.

MacFarquhar, Roderick, and Michael Schoenhals. 2007. *Mao's Last Revolution*. Cambridge, MA: Belknap Press.

Meyer, Marshall, and Xiaohui Lu. 2005. 'Managing Indefinite Boundaries: The Strategy and Structure of a Chinese Business Firm', *Management and Organization Review*, 1(1): 57–86.

Naughton, Barry. 2007. *The Chinese Economy*. Cambridge, MA: MIT Press.

Nee, Victor. 1992. 'Organizational Dynamics of Market Transition: Hybrid Forms, Property Rights, and Mixed Economy in China', *Administrative Science Quarterly*, 37(1): 1–27.

Oi, Jean C. 1999. *Rural China Takes Off: Institutional Foundations of Economic Reform*. Berkeley, CA: University of California Press.

Wederman, Andrew. 2004. 'Great Disorder under Heaven: Endemic Corruption and Rapid Growth in Contemporary China', *The China Review*, 4(2): 1–32.

8

The Private Sector

Forms of privately owned business developed in China a long time ago, and there are many historical accounts giving a vivid picture of the traditional commercial life. For much of the last millennium, such accounts usually depict a context in which dense populations create highly competitive local markets with the help of—for the time—advanced transport systems and sophisticated institutions to handle trading agreements, investments, and associations. Much was concentrated in microenterprises based in households, as with the early 'putting-out' system of industrializing Europe. A national system of waterway connections, and the overall scrutiny of business affairs by government officials, provided some capacity for markets in certain goods to go beyond the local, although the main industries involved in this such as silk, cotton, salt, and ceramics were, for most of this long traditional period, controlled by the state.

This economy of mainly small businesses, many intermediaries, and much trading, took its character from the agricultural base of most people's livelihoods. It was in the main preindustrial, and entailed such work as food processing, small-scale craft-based manufacturing for local consumption, and services such as transport, moneylending, bookkeeping, and retailing, that went with it. The regular markets, structured to occur on fixed days of the week around a circuit of towns in a region, would bring together goods needing no more than a day's transport. The accumulation of capital by business owners could not be achieved without the co-opting of official support, as wealth attracted attention. Taxation was also unpredictable and to a degree negotiable. Following the inheritance traditions, family wealth would be continually divided at each generation, so that long dynasties were difficult to sustain—the contrast here with Japan being clear.

There were some forms of ownership that could last generations, but there were no laws which dealt with the business company until they came in from the West in the early twentieth century, so there was no incorporation. Instead, lineage (i.e. surname) groups would hold property and rights in common, and much business behavior would rest on the ritual and patronage that went with such groupings of people with a common ancestor. Typically in such structures, although there was book-keeping, there was no capital accounting, a tradition lasting well into the twentieth century in small business practices. The tradition did however prepare many Chinese people for the ideas of shared ownership, and cooperation within the clan. There was no national goal of progress via economic growth, and meeting the needs of the mushrooming popula-tion was itself an achievement for the state.

There were two features of special significance as legacies to the future. First, the traditional Chinese economy was highly fragmented. The weav-ing of cotton fabric took place in three-quarters of all Chinese counties until the twentieth century. Although this may well be accounted for in large measure by the sheer size and internal geographic variety of the country, it may also be partly due to the second feature. This was the absence of scale in the nonstate organizations, and a related absence of capital accumulation in the typical enterprise. In the private sector the building of large complex organizations, and the necessary managerial systems to go with them, seems to have been inhibited. This did not however result in a weak economy. For its time, purposes, and circum-stances, the economy was vibrant and effective. It is just that it contained a bias against growth of the enterprise as such. Mark Elvin once observed of this condition that commerce substituted for management. Other observers have seen it similarly as an economy of merchants rather than industrialists.

The entrepreneurial and competitive behaviors, and the instinct for social bonding in the face of high uncertainty, are modern-day reflections of the centuries of learning and, as Barry Naughton has observed, the rapid growth after 1978 is due in no small part to behaviors nourished at earlier times and remembered, such that 'China's contemporary economy includes a rediscovery of the traditional'.[1] As 80 percent of the workforce now works for the private sector (albeit 47 percent in farming), and as many people return to their traditional roots while the Communist ideal fades, it is not surprising that China's private sector—new though

---

[1] Naughton 2007, p. 52.

its current form may be, and learning fast from wherever it can—still reflects in many ways its distinct origins. Dominant among the historical influences is the fact that the state has not provided, or encouraged, the autonomous growth of an infrastructure of institutions to support reliable, predictable, stable exchange between people who do not know each other. Accountants, business lawyers, professionals such as valuers, actuaries, surveyors, and all the supporting specialist staff that go with them, are in short supply, or are simply components of a government bureaucracy not renowned for its efficiency, neutrality, or speed. Although now being strengthened, this infrastructure of institutional trust is still weak. Reliable information, the basis for risk assessment and credit references, is in short supply. So, to fill the vacuum, and make transactions work efficiently, the necessary glue holding business dealings stable has to come from personal connections and networks. It works, but by different rules than those of the advanced economies. China runs by *personal* trust rather than by *institutional* trust. Nor should we forget the negative implications of the resulting personalistic bonding for per capita income. It inhibits scale, and with that the investment in machinery and capital goods to help each worker's productivity. So per capita incomes in advanced countries are running between $30,000 and $40,000, and that of China—after a quarter of a century of stunning growth—is still at about a tenth of that. The capacity for handling scale does make a difference to the efficient use of resources seen at the national level, and it is likely to become China's most challenging testing ground.

To analyse the private sector business system of China is a convenience that temporarily treats it as a separate phenomenon from the other two main business systems—those of the state and the local corporates. We acknowledge at the outset that this distinction is made to permit some useful focusing, but that in the end, the three systems coexist and interpenetrate. The main qualitative difference lies in the workings of the psychology of ownership under conditions of both uncertainty and opportunity, and here the private sector exhibits a powerful flow of deep instincts held back in earlier decades and still regaining legitimacy.

We will use the business systems framework outlined earlier as the basis for the explanation (see Figure 8.1), and so build up a picture of how the culture connects with the institutions and in turn with the business system, the total predisposing this part of the economy to be good at certain forms of industry. We do so in the context that about two-thirds of the economy is now in this category, and that it is likely to expand further. Two surrounding features affect this positive view: firstly the

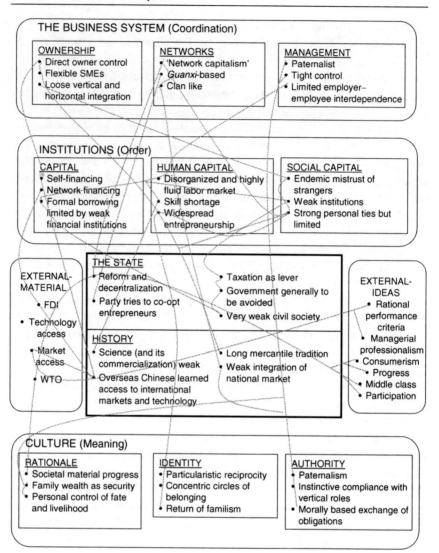

Figure 8.1. The private sector of the Chinese economy seen as a complex adaptive system

arrival of foreign banks used to commercial lending at high standards and the reforms of the indigenous banking and financing systems will together make it much more attractive for entrepreneurs to seek rationally allocated funding from a capital market; the second particular influence is the continuing decline of the state sector, as the remaining slack within it is taken out and it levels off with just the strategic industries remaining under state control.

Culture: Rationale

The answer to the question 'What does it *mean* to be running a private company in China today?' contains a cluster of associated aspects of how to make sense of the role of owner–manager. These might be labeled (*a*) the personal rationale; (*b*) the core ideals and perceived ends for economic behavior; and (*c*) the means seen as legitimate for achieving those ends, in the context.

The personal rationale is essentially built around two large features in the mindscapes of most Chinese entrepreneurs. The first, and dominant, one of these is family. The reason why the Chinese social fabric has survived the ravages of war, Maoist experimentation, famine, geographical uprooting, the implicit recanting of ideology, and years of grinding poverty is that its most ancient social architecture is robust in the extreme. As the historian W. F. Jenner has observed:

From the wreckage of twentieth century history, the one institution that has emerged stronger than all the others is the patrilineal Chinese family.

The family was the basis of the Confucian state for millennia, and the major part of the Chinese cultural legacy celebrates its centrality and significance. Much of the society's moral fabric is designed around it. China is a society in which people are socialized into clearly defined role behavior, much of this process occurring in childhood and in relation to family, and the system is self-perpetuating. Without a moral sense of reciprocal obligation, and especially a sense of duty toward parents, a Chinese person is uncivilized. The resulting possibility of becoming an outcast is deeply threatening. Without parents urging their children to prosper, their own long-term welfare is in danger, and so too is the society. The core moral virtues of the society are defined in such a way that the families take responsibility for much of the social order, and the policing of it, as well as of their own fates. It is an elegant and humanistic formula and has provided much of the psychological support needed under often-harsh conditions and authoritarian control.

The end result of this legacy is that most business owners are running their companies in order to accumulate family wealth, and to secure the perpetuation of the family's respectable reputation—what they commonly refer to as 'the family name.' The perspective is very long term and many families keep records over centuries detailing their lineage. There is also a wide perspective to membership and the family is seen with all its elaborate linkages and across up to five generations at any one time. In China today, these ancient ways of thinking and behaving are inhibited by two influences: the one-child policy that reduces the size of the grouping; and the weakening of the earlier ideals during the years of experimentation after 1950. For many, there is a sense of anomie, and a felt need to restore morality and to escape from the extreme pragmatism adopted in the recent times of opportunity when the competitive scramble licensed disreputable conduct.

A second major feature of the entrepreneurs' mindscapes is that of the return of pride in being Chinese. This had never disappeared but recent economic success has fostered a sense that the rebuilding of the nation's position in the world is a real and legitimate focus of 'face' and attention, even if it is never a subject of open discussion. Mao was responding to this when he told the Chinese people in 1949 that they had finally 'stood up.' The importance of this feature lies in its value for building cooperation between the worlds of business and government. They share a goal, a superordinate purpose. Unlike Russia, falling apart in a scramble for benefits, and with business and government at odds with each other (or in improper collusion), China has remained stable, and its government still respected. There were, of course, serious incidents of improper collusion, and there are visible now both excessive wealth and continuing poverty, but the overall scene is one of a massive lifting of people out of poverty, a steady progression of wealth, and a sense that the achievement is appropriately shared between the politicians and the world of the economy.

To what ends should the Chinese economy work? What are the core ideals? Most of these stem from the long-standing beliefs about the conduct of life. A US national would talk of individual freedom, equality, and opportunity as core ideals. Chinese owner–managers do not. Instead they talk about social harmony, hierarchical order, respect for knowledge, family collectivism, personalism and its obligations, and the need to gain control of one's fate in conditions of surrounding insecurity. This latter is in many cases accompanied by a sense that golden opportunities in the current era of radical change must be taken, even if there might be some bending of the formal rules. Dependence on the state is now out of date, and the solidarity of the communes has disintegrated, to be replaced by the family and civic virtues that preceded Communism. It is also to be acknowledged that many party officials and administrators are respected for their asceticism and dedication to the public good. Without this the remarkable Chinese capacity for cooperation with specific others would have been eroded.

The means seen by entrepreneurs as appropriate in building the economy are reflections of those aims. First among them is the idea that a business needs to be under the control of people trusted in personal terms. This means either family or partnership with close friends, and the funding of start-ups comes mainly from these two sources. This is also reflected in the assignment of key roles. It is common on visiting a private-sector firm to discover that the owner's spouse is the director of finance, or of personnel, and that children, nieces, and nephews are having their foreign education supported in the hope of their return with useable knowledge.

A second strong belief is in the need for an extensive network of trusted contacts—the regularly described *guanxi*. This is to help with the garnering of reliable and early information, to build partnerships for the taking of opportunity, to extend connections toward unknown people with whom business might be conducted, to gain official support if needed, and above all to cement the ties between those involved in everyday transactions within their overlapping networks. When the latter works well it drives down the need for lawyers, formal contracts, quality control structures, and debt recovery. The resulting transaction cost efficiency is a large part of the reason for China's dominance in global manufacturing of certain kinds of goods.

There are supporting beliefs about means that surround the core principles of familism and networking. Among these, the most crucial is the belief that status is acquired by wealth, a feature made stronger in its effects by the years of state economic control and the starving of opportunity. There is a powerful sense of wanting to make up for lost time, except that among the newer generation the bad days are simply in the family lore, and those born since 1980 have only ever known the race to succeed and have observed its gathering momentum.

Two final core beliefs are strongly developed in this culture. The first is the thirst for learning, and especially for the absorption of knowledge related to the business. Most knowledge acquisition is driven by personal motivation and the belief that the right knowledge will lead to social and financial success. There is strong societal support for the acquisition of technical knowledge, a feature common among Confucian societies, with their 'this-worldly' pragmatism, but markedly absent in, for example, present-day Islam. A final key ideal is that of secrecy about business dealings and performance. In a world where government intervention has been unpredictable and often costly, and where useful information is often strategic, this guideline has a long history.

Culture: Identity

The business owner, or a hired professional executive, is now a member of a respected new class in China. Recent surveys show Communist Party membership of between 15 and 34 percent among entrepreneurs, varying by region and sample. The highest ranks of the government are now accepting business people among them. The old days are gone, and the sin of being bourgeois long forgotten. In place of that there is its opposite and among the favorite readings now are the stories of the richest people. The bookshops are full of biographies of the successful, and the society's role models—at least for the aspiring young—are wealthy.

This means that identity as a businessperson is itself an ideal. In particular, ownership of the business is a key to respect. The old idea that 'it is better to be the head of a chicken than the backside of an ox' has not disappeared. If you own your business, you control your fate, and can fulfill your duties. For the competent, being an employee is a temporary condition prior to breaking out on your own. Stan Shih, the founder of Acer, once said that he employed thirty thousand people, of whom twenty thousand wanted to start their own businesses. We shall come later to the implications of this when we consider management.

Beyond the concentric circles of identity that a Chinese person lives in is a potentially hostile world. This is an environment populated by competitors and unpredictable regulators, and—in many industries—affected by rapid technical change and market volatility. The *guanxi* networks serve to reduce the uncertainties and to allow some counteracting of the limitations of small scale in the enterprises themselves. The effects on mistrust will be discussed shortly under the topic of the institutions of Social Capital.

Culture: Authority

China is an essentially totalist society as we explained in Chapter 4. Throughout there are stable vertical structures and an instinctive sense of hierarchy and order. This would not work efficiently if power were abused, and to avoid such abuse, an ethical system underpins the structure, and can be labeled paternalism. The person at the top is able to get people to cooperate with his or her intentions as long as—in return—the people are looked after adequately. He or she has a duty to protect. They have a duty to be obedient and diligent. It is understood that where authority is challenged, discipline may be imposed to restore order. In practice discipline is a clear feature of many organizations. So too is the abuse of power in situations where workers can be easily replaced, or when the boss has no ethical sensitivities. At the same time there are many factories where the ideal of the 'iron rice bowl'—the guarantee that workers will be protected—remains a first principle.

New forces and ideas are now changing these traditions, and we will consider them further in a later section on the institutions of human capital, but suffice it to say here that the meaning of work is slowly changing in China, as the government slowly adds legislation to shift relations in hierarchies from dependence and personalism toward performance-based reward and legally protected rights. The encouragement of some forms of grassroots democracy, visible in local politics, is now entering the economy.

Key Historical Events and the Role of Government

Before considering the institutions of Capital, Human Capital, and Social Capital, it is necessary to acknowledge certain formative historical influences on the emerging private-sector business system in China. These are features that have helped to shape the way business works, and without adding them the explanation is incomplete.

In such a state-dominated society, most of the influences here will be reflections of government policy and action. They may be classified as positive or negative in their effects, and we begin with the positives. The Chinese government has displayed an unusual degree of pragmatism in the period since 1978. The Deng Xiaoping reforms were themselves a massive turning point in Chinese history. The subsequent policies of gradual adjustment and experimentation have been the foundation of the success, and noteworthy among these has been the creation of the SEZ as test beds for cooperation with outsiders. In this latter context the availability of huge stimulus from the regional ethnic Chinese has already been pointed to for its significance. More recently, the transferring of decision power (albeit overseen) from the center to the local administrations has seen a releasing of energy and initiative that perhaps equals the 1980 reforms in longer term importance. Lastly the willingness of the state to participate in taking economic risk, especially via the banking system, is noteworthy, even though efficient use of that capital remains a major outstanding issue.

Formative influences of a less positive nature are mainly associated with the political dilemma, for the state, of fulfilling its sacred duty to maintain order and in consequence to keep control over much of the society's behavior. Clearly less totalitarian than it has been previously, and under challenge from new forms of communication such as the Internet as well as ideas pouring in from outside, China walks a tightrope as far as political freedom is concerned. As a potentially demanding *bourgeoisie*, the class of private-sector business people holds much of the influence over how the society will shape itself as it continues to modernize. In this context one feature is missing. China's civil society is essentially local, consisting of clan associations, and informally gathered groupings of business people, often alumni groups. But there is no structure of national bodies like professional associations independent of government, no freestanding bodies such as stock-market boards of governance, or cities with their own ordinances. The groups of business people congregating regularly in so many of the cities are still coordinated within the state system, and are unlikely to turn into revolutionary cells. It is perhaps another symbol of the gradualism succeeding in the world of business and has made its voice heard over a long period in bodies such as the Chinese People's Political Consultative Councils.

Two other significant historical facts need to be acknowledged here for their influence on the growth and probable future of the Chinese private sector, and they concern relations with the outside world. The first is the providing of access to their markets by the countries of the developed world. This was by no means assured at the outset of reforms but it has been retained, leading to a close and beneficial interpenetration of economic systems. Without the demand there would be no supply and the workshop might not be that of the world.

Closely related to that process of exchanging has been the tolerance displayed toward Taiwan and Hong Kong. This is such as to effectively eliminate borders as far as business transacting is concerned. As an illustration, one of the authors was teaching an executive MBA class in a coastal city in south China, and returning from a lunch break found the class in an uproar of argument about Mao. A group of six sitting together at the back of the class had been critical of the Great Helmsman, and was involved in a heated exchange with the others. They were 'the Taiwan boys' and they came across every week from Taipei, landing at an airstrip on an offshore island close by, then taking a small ferry to the city. For them, and for the university that accepted them, the border was not an issue.

Institutions: Capital

The savings rate within families in China is currently running at about 32 percent of household disposable income, according to the IMF, and amounts to about 17 percent of GDP. It is not surprising then that studies of where small businesses get their start-up capital indicate two main sources, the dominant one of which is family and extended family. The second source is friends. Formal sources such as banks, investors, government loans, tend to be not yet in extensive use.

The reasons why a formally organized national system of capital allocation is still in its infancy are complex, and connected with the government's long-standing control of the economy, and its consequent hesitation about letting loose the full dynamism of a freewheeling capitalism. Releasing the full logics of economic rationality is also a politically sensitive question of an unfamiliar source of societal power. At present the institutions needed to manage capital sourcing and allocation are too fragile and too new to take the strain of an immediate leap into one of the advanced country modes. There is also the perverse fact that the private sector has done very well so far without going outside its own cash flow for capital. We speculate that when capital becomes more readily accessible, it is the private sector that may prove the most efficient in using it. Stage 1 of its growth between the 1980s and now has been spectacular, but Stage 2 may well prove even more astonishing. Perhaps 'we ain't seen nothing yet.' The fusing of entrepreneurship with the close oversight and lending discipline of well-run banks was the foundation for Hong Kong's explosive postwar growth, in a closely parallel social and industrial context. Strict lending discipline is new to postwar China, but is now being injected forcibly both by government and by the arriving foreign banks. It is also worth recording that it was only in 2000 that the state opened all fields (except that of national security and the big state monopolies) to the private sector. Even though this final opening might have appeared late in the day, it was nonetheless done in an encouraging way, with the publishing of a detailed official guide to getting started in business.

The power of the private sector's money is conveyed both in its accumulating weight and its current use. In 1990 private-sector capital flows were $8 billion. By 2003 the figure had risen to $60 billion. Shanghai's new infrastructure is now being funded 50 percent privately, and Beijing's new investments in housing are 60 percent private.

When considering the sources of capital for the private sector, it must also be noted that a flourishing market exists in 'back-alley' banking. This system of informal credit is expensive to use, but it is also relatively easy to access. Many business people resort to it as a fallback, especially in microenterprises, and for short-term capital needs it serves a purpose. As more organized and competitive banking continues to penetrate the world of small business, the kerb-side lenders are likely to fade slowly from the scene, along with the pawnshops and the tontines.

Institutions: Human Capital

Generalizations are risky about the way in which China's private-sector companies relate to the country's stock of human capital, but allowing for some elasticity in reality there are nevertheless certain definable features that mark the scene. There is an enormous mass of low-cost labor. Advanced skills are in short supply. Many people move geographically to where the work is, stay a few years, and then move back home. Unions play an insignificant part in this sector. The state sector has shed about forty million workers over the last decade, and the private sector has been crucial in absorbing them. There is a market in labor and people move around a lot to improve their rewards, although the volatility of this changes with the fluctuations in the economy. Welfare is unevenly distributed, with migrant workers discriminated against. Basic education is very sound and literacy high, but provision gets scarce at higher levels, as does quality. Most firms are run by owners and paternalism is normal, but for many this brings quite severe discipline and often abuse. The best employees are often motivated by a wish to start their own businesses.

In March 2007, after fourteen years of wrangling behind closed doors between diehards and reformists, the Party Congress approved new laws protecting individual property rights, and although the effects will be spread over time, this property-rights revolution is likely to prove highly significant in shaping China's future economy and society. China's labor force is still heavily involved in agriculture, and used inefficiently by common standards, with low levels of per capita investment as a hangover from the traditional high-level equilibrium trap. Labor is so low in cost that capital investment in labor saving does not make sense. As the pull toward the higher pay packets in manufacturing takes people off the land, this old logic will break down and farming will reform itself. In the meantime about one-half of the labor force is based in household farms, although an increasing portion of this number have some kind of off-farm work in local industry. As investment in farming technology rises, with the new incentives of ownership, the workforce that is then released as redundant will feed into the manufacturing and service economies, in an almost endless stream unmatchable by any other country except India. If, at some future date the stream begins to dry up, all the government needs to do would be to relax the one-child policy.

The primary set of institutions shaping the quantity and quality of human capital are those of education and training. In 1993 the state announced a target to spend 4 percent of GDP on education but has not yet achieved that level, hoping now to do so by 2010. The actual level stayed close to 3 percent throughout the 1990s. Figures for other countries are 5 percent for the United States, 4.6 percent for Germany, 4.6 percent for Brazil, and 5.9 percent for France, although large countries with low average incomes tend to have low expenditures, such as Indonesia at 1.4 percent or India at 3.2 percent. An important leftover from the 1970s and 1980s affecting many older workers was the very low incentive to become educated. Investing in a year's extra learning in those years would have had almost zero effect on income and so the incentive to acquire knowledge and skill was absent. As a result many older workers are unskilled except for what they have learned in their jobs.

In recent years, the extra income derived from extra learning has increased greatly as the labor market rewards work performance, and the index is now running at just above the world average. In line with this there has grown a strong incentive for parents to invest family money in their children's education, and they do so. In higher education, there has been a recent explosion of investment, especially in the teaching of the sciences and engineering. Tertiary enrollment has increased threefold in seven years to its current level of 15 million and is expected to grow to about 25 million by 2010. Some caution must, however, be applied when making international comparisons, as—not surprisingly in the face of such urgent expansion—quality standards are still catching up. In a recent McKinsey study it was found that eighty-three HR professionals hiring staff for multinationals in China thought that less than 10 percent of graduate applicants would be valid candidates. There is much commentary about the much larger number of engineering graduates being produced in China compared to the United States; a detailed study of this by Vivek Wadhwa, Gary Gereffi, Ben Rissing, and Ryan Ong[2] reveals that the real figures are 137,000 per year for the United States, 139,000 for India, and 351,000 for China, but with the caveat that the China figures conceal a large proportion whose qualifications are nearer to those of mechanics, not engineers. A 2005 McKinsey study concluded that the Chinese engineering talent pool was no larger than that of the United Kingdom.

The higher education bias toward the sciences and engineering, while serving the pragmatic needs of the factories of China, has left unattended the development of critical and enquiring minds, a feature regularly complained of by foreign recruiters. Only 16 percent of graduates are in arts and humanities and half of those are studying languages. There is an obvious need for business graduates, and especially MBAs able to take roles of professional managers. Current output here is around 20,000 per year, but the McKinsey estimate of annual need by 2010 is 75,000. Again, the quality issue applies. The thirst for education, and family investment in it, lie behind the persistent brain drain that sees around 100,000 young people a year going abroad for their degrees and about 25,000 returning.

China's real strength in education is at the primary level, where local administrations are under pressure to provide nine years of schooling for all, to eliminate illiteracy, and to provide universal free primary education for all by 2010. In all this two groups have remained disadvantaged: female children in the rural areas; and the children of migrants to the cities. But attention is now turning to these gaps.

In the private sector, with its myriad small and medium enterprises, the training available is usually minimal. It normally consists of what is needed to do the work, handle the machines, meet the quality standards, and reach the speed of production. It does not usually provide wider learning, as would for instance a course in marketing, or a evening class in furniture design. The individual acquires these himself or herself as part of the accumulation of marketable skills.

In most societal systems of human capital, there are structures such as unions or class systems that affect the disposition of human talent into the economy. In China unions are virtually irrelevant in the private sector. Those that may exist would be left over from the political bodies of earlier days that represented the Party's concerns with welfare, and fostered downwards communication of the ideology. There are no unions

---

[2] Wadhwa et al. 2007.

militantly representing workers' rights to better rewards, and challenging the hierarchy of the organization.

The typical owner–manager in the private sector is faced with a human-capital context in which at most times in recent years there has been a buyer's market for labor. Factories would pay the minimum the market would bear, buy in skills rather than train people, hire and fire in line with market fluctuations, and reward key people enough for them to remain on board. Deep labor skills do not grow in such circumstances, nor do long-term commitments for the majority. At the same time this economy has been capable of very high responsiveness to changing market and technical conditions, and it says much for the adaptiveness of China's labor force that industrial change and growth has been so unhampered by human capital limitations. We shall consider in a later chapter how that scenario fits with the larger one of choosing the right industries in which such logics might be made to work.

Institutions: Social Capital

China's private sector firms in most cases are small or medium in size, and work in networks, collaborating to construct value chains where in other economies larger integrated organizations might dominate. The glue holding the structures together is interpersonal reciprocal obligation between the owner–managers of the autonomous units. This is network capitalism. It produces the miracle of efficiency and responsiveness that has allowed China to dominate the world's supplies of household goods, toys, apparel, electronic components, and a further wide array of consumer and industrial merchandise. As we have argued earlier, its being adapted to the modern world and being connected into the global centers of high demand through intermediaries, owes much to the experience of the 'Overseas Chinese,' especially in Hong Kong and Taiwan, as these two small countries grew in the later decades of the twentieth century into industrial powerhouses.

The Chinese instinct for cooperativeness lying deep in the cultural heritage is on display in the institutions that now carry trust, but it is circumscribed and needs to be understood for its limitations as well as its strengths. As we have said, economies work with two forms of trust to hold together the stable patterns of cooperation needed if people are to do business efficiently with each other. *Institutional trust* is made to work by laws, regulations backed by government or professional control, good quality and available information, and compliance with publicly understood standards. Using this the society underwrites the risks of uncertainty and provides certain guarantees, to a point where people can trust strangers. This overarching superstructure comes at a cost. *Interpersonal trust* is much cheaper, but it does not stretch nearly as far. In fact it is limited in its extent to a person's own network of accumulated obligations. But for certain kinds of economic behavior that is enough, especially when limitations of scale can be got around by networking, and when transaction costs are very low, given the absence of lawyers, of compliance procedures, of extensive record-keeping, and of reporting using executive time.

China's business environment is information-poor. Reliable data about companies, markets, prices, investment opportunities, competitor behavior, technology developments, government policy changes can only be obtained via personal networks. Such information—given it is often of strategic significance to a firm—is kept confidential and within the network. This is another reason why such networks have become a primary structure in this business system, and why they remain strong. Without a network it is hard for a business owner to function.

The usual way in which the networks function for export manufacturing is that a business owner will run a company specializing in a particular field—either an entire simple product at a low level of technology, such as underwear—or a component item or process fitting into the production chain for a more complex product. Examples of the latter might be shirt collars, or the extruding of plastic toy components, or the making of the heads for reading computer discs. To get the final product made requires much coordination within a web of connected companies, tight enough to ensure deadlines are met and quality controlled, but flexible enough to cope with changes in demand. These latter, as well as the design specifications, arrive into the web from intermediaries, usually trading houses, that handle the interface with the market and the global supply-chain logistics.

The social capital being used in such structures is that of interpersonal trust, based on the ethics of reciprocity. It leads directly to efficiency in transaction costs, as connections within the web are managed with low formality. It also leads to high managerial concentration on meeting required standards, as owners ensure their own livelihoods by compliance. And it also delivers flexibility of response, as owners tend to work with multiple connections to avoid dependence on one customer or supplier.

Business System: Ownership

The private sector displays a wide range of ownership patterns, but with one common feature: single-owner dominance or a high level of personal connection between the owners. They may be relatives, friends, partners in earlier ventures, people with local influence, but they know each other well. Missing here in most cases is the objective, external voice of the distant investor. By this means the person in the driving seat is likely to feel in control—a common need in a culture providing such high levels of surrounding insecurity and opacity. In the largest number of cases, there is one clear owner managing the firm.

Private firms in China are mainly small or medium. According to OECD's 2005 report, there were three million domestic private enterprises and twenty-four million sole proprietorships in the nonfarm sector in 2003. The 2001 industrial census gave a figure for the average number of employees in private-sector firms as eighteen. Only 5 percent of such firms had more than 500 employees. Almost always starting small these firms typically grow at 9 percent, comparing favorably with European experience, and they fund their growth through savings, retained earnings, and informal credit. According to a 3000-firm national survey reported by OECD, expansion is limited by the difficulty in finding 'trusted' managers.

Total factor productivity in this sector has been running at double that for the state sector, with almost a quarter of such firms earning a 25 percent rate of return, and almost 30 percent free of debt. Significantly there is also evidence that performance by firms owned within China is better that in firms owned outside the mainland, at least in the small-scale sector. It is then, not surprising that two-thirds of China's value-added is now coming from this adventurous and entrepreneurial sector.

Our concern in studying the ownership component of the business system is to understand its ramifications for the workings of the larger system, and by extension its effects on choice of industry. Here we see a system of small to medium enterprise usually focused on one field, such as component manufacture, low-tech production, or specific service. Because of the trust limitations noted earlier, there is an inhibition over the large-scale deployment of professional managers and in any case a shortage in the society of such skills. This puts a limit on organizational scale, unless the industry in question can continue as a machine bureaucracy with all strategic decisions in the head of the presiding owner, the *lao ban*. In consequence firm growth tends to be by diversification, in which the newly created unit can be in an unrelated field and often is, in order to hedge risk or to take opportunity. Diversification from socks to eel-farming, from food processing to jewellery (even in an extreme Taiwanese case from fast food to helicopters) are regularly reported, and a widespread hedging into property investment revives an ancient tendency common in societies with only partial and uncertain property rights.

The end result is that tightly owned, and tightly managed, small or medium organizations flourish in sectors where such features are virtues, the workshop of the world being such a typically hospitable field. But before analyzing what those virtues amount to it is necessary to add in the other two aspects of how economic action is coordinated—the networking across the economy, and the generating inside firms of efficient combinations of resources.

Business System: Networks

All economic systems have to be able to link their components efficiently. One specialist maker of parts has to connect with others. Marketing has to work with production. Design has to fit what can be made and what customers want. Money has to be sourced and put to work in various places efficiently. Some societies do this by putting many such activities inside large organizational envelopes, some others by creating large brotherhoods of organizations, and still others by leaving small organizations to make networks among themselves to the extent needed, leaving the individual units to stand alone as legal entities. The Chinese private sector fits into the third case.

We have described earlier, under Social Capital, the way in which the networks have evolved. Institutional trust is limited by a shortage of information, by an unpredictable top-down political system, and by having only limited protective legislation standardizing business conduct. Interpersonal trust, although powerful and efficient, is only so in limited circles. It is within such circles that one searches for the keys to what works best.

These keys are that (*a*) transaction costs between the circle members are very low; (*b*) flexibility of the network to incorporate changes to the shared product is very high; and (*c*) efficient use of assets is assisted by intense managerial focus within each small unit—an owner tends to look after his or her own money better than anyone else. The network is one answer to the problem of scale limitations faced in each unit, but it is an answer with conditions attached, in other words it will only work in certain kinds of industry. Before analyzing that larger point, we will need to consider the third aspect of coordination, that of management itself within the firm.

Business System: Management

If you consider where in the firm responsibility and action lie for (a) managing the efficient use of resources; (b) learning about what needs to change; and (c) adjustment of the organization as it adapts to such change, you find a variation in formulae, as we noted earlier. In simple terms, the flagship US enterprise handles these three challenges—which are themselves the essence of management—by giving the job to a cadre of professional managers trained to deal with them. The workforce (except in the Silicon Valley response) is generally not involved except as people carrying out the resulting decisions. In the Japanese and German cases the three questions are dealt with by a fusion of managerial and (usually highly informed) worker views, and decisions emerge by consensus. We regularly discuss this with audiences of Chinese managers, and the overwhelmingly dominant response to the question of who manages these three issues is for them to point to the ceiling and say 'the big boss'. While this response is entirely predictable and appropriate for most small firms, it is remarkable in China how many managers in the public sector and the large-firm hybrid sector also give the same reply. This suggests that there is something 'Chinese' here as well as something organizational, and it brings to mind the hierarchical societal power structure discussed earlier under Authority.

A significant outcome for the workings of the system is that the concentration of power that contributes so much to the network efficiency, by placing total discretion to commit resources in the hands of the networking owners, has a downside. In the typical organization the centralization of power will restrict the contribution of employees to doing their prescribed work. Innovation and change is not in their minds. Intermediate managers are likely to be transmitters and interpreters of commands downwards. The organization at scale is likely to divide into 'silos,' and horizontal communication is likely to be stifled. Vertical communication upwards is likely to be very limited if it challenges the status quo. An absence of mutual dependence between managers and workers flows from this. The workforce is relatively passive, can be hired and fired, trained and retrained easily, and only the key technical supervisors are crucial.

There are undoubtedly changes afoot in China as different ideas penetrate, often brought in by foreign companies. A westernized Chinese friend of one of the authors, now running a services outsourcing company in Guangzhou supplying the US market, and aware of 'modern' forms of human resource management, asked one of his workers recently whether she liked her job. She looked dumbfounded and said 'I am fifty and nobody has ever asked me that before!' He reported his company becoming a magnet in the labor market with very low staff turnover. Many studies of Chinese worker attitudes report a preference for employment in foreign firms. Management education is also slowly introducing new techniques for engaging the commitment of staff. Even so, the penetration of such ideas is limited, and the much more normal still is the tightly disciplined workforce under paternalistic control—benevolent or autocratic, depending on the personality of the boss.

The Changing Private Sector

The private sector has been a runaway success story since restrictions to it began to be lifted in the early 1980s. Private firms have become more profitable, shown themselves capable of organizational growth toward what may be natural limits within the type, absorbed all the massive labor displacements caused by the cleaning up of the state-sector companies, and have been capable of keeping up with technical and product changes in globally relevant product fields—without necessarily initiating such changes. The government, for its part, has adjusted both its ideology and its administration, in order to foster this huge positive force.

It is unconventional in analyzing China to see the government in a supporting—as opposed to a dominant—role, but that is perhaps the best reading of its adjustments to the new reality of rampant entrepreneurship. It is manifest in three principal deep changes. First, the acquiring of the state's assets held under local control in the old communes, and the turning of their use toward market-driven efficiency was done while the government stood back. It allowed this to happen, with the result that—put simply—those assets are now being used at twice the efficiency they would have had if left alone. The second of the government's crucial responses was the recognition that business people could join the Party. This provision of access to higher policy councils injected new perspectives into the debates over the future shape and purposes of the society. Its aftereffects are visible in the rising public acceptance of business leaders as societal role models, so visible on the newsstands and in the bookshops. The third, and perhaps in the end the most seismic, of the changes is the protection of property rights in the March 2007 law. This is likely to release an acquisitive energy never seen before even in China's long history, and its main beneficiaries will be the rising bourgeoisie, and especially within that the owners of firms.

Such a list is not exhaustive. Additional stimuli to private enterprise should include at least the SEZs, the openness to FDI, the investments in education and in infrastructure, and the thousands of new laws aimed at improving the condition of societal order. Permitting foreign banks has already been signaled as potentially very significant for the rational sourcing, allocation, and use of capital, and the private sector—relatively starved of banking capital so far—is the most likely sector to show the advantages of such discipline.

It is reasonable to conclude that the government, and the society as a whole, have embraced the idea of a flourishing private sector as the core of the economy from now on. It already contributes two-thirds of value-added, and this figure is likely to rise toward perhaps three-quarters over the next ten years. But questions remain as to how its preponderance will be maintained and such expansion achieved. In what kinds of industry, with what kinds of firms, will this growth take place?

Let us begin to answer these questions with a summary of the competences embedded in this network capitalism with its small and medium-sized base units. They are:

1. Efficiency in coordinating within the network, and so to transcend (to a degree) the limitations of small size.
2. Flexibility of response in making a value chain work.
3. Close managerial supervision of semiskilled, very low-cost workforces.
4. Workforce diligence and flexibility.
5. Entrepreneurial opportunity seeking and learning.
6. Operating efficiency in use of assets.
7. Cultivated connections into sources of technical know-how and market knowledge, particularly including foreign sources.

Let us now consider the nature of the sectors in which such competences are especially advantageous or otherwise. The first point to note is the high dependence of the system on other organizations for the provision

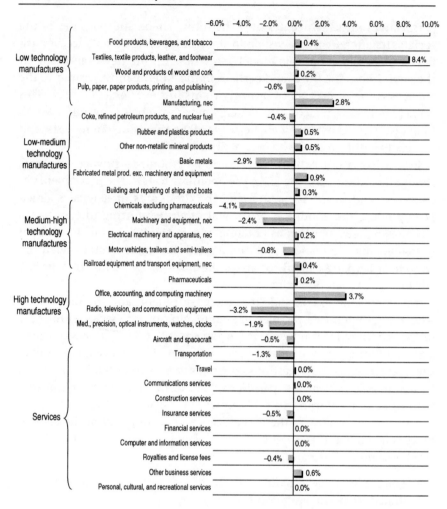

Figure 8.2. Mainland Chinese comparative advantage by industries, 2003 (Comtrade, UNCTAD Handbook of Statistics Online, own calculations). See next chapter and Appendix for details.

Note: nec = not elsewhere classified.

of (*a*) detailed market knowledge; (*b*) design; (*c*) supply-chain logistics into the market; and (*d*) branding and marketing. If these features can be supplied into the system (and they are by a multitude of intermediary agencies), the resulting complex hybrid structure is overall a world-beating formula in certain fields, notably low to mid technology consumer goods and industrial components, as illustrated in Figure 8.2. This figure will lead us to a discussion of comparative advantage in the next chapter.

It must also be acknowledged that the private-sector category in China's statistics normally includes foreign firms, and that they contribute very significantly to export success, accounting for about 55 percent of exports overall. One of the unknowns is how much of such foreign-owned production depends on locally obtained components and services, but as the industries concerned are largely in manufacturing, this contribution may well be large, and the classification 'foreign' not entirely accurate as it conceals the contribution of subcontractors within the industrial process. It is also necessary to note that foreign-owned in this context means primarily Taiwan and Hong Kong owned, and so still essentially Chinese. Putting the indigenous and foreign private sectors together and taking total exports, China now stands third in the world behind the United States and Germany. The OECD considers it likely to replace Germany as number two by 2008, and to be capable by 2010 of representing 10 percent of world trade in goods and services. But in what fields does the indigenous private sector come into its own?

These fields are textiles, garments, leather products, footwear, basic metal products, plastics, and office, accounting, and computing machinery. More tangibly, one might think of the world's toys, clothes, computers, and a wide range of consumer goods, and the materials that go into making them.

In the majority of these sectors the industrial structure is one in which large foreign firms specializing in mass marketing in advanced country markets either control brands such as Nike, Gap, Mattel, or control advanced systems of distribution, such as Wal-Mart, Sears Roebuck, C & A, and Littlewoods Mail Order. They source their supplies either through their own buying agencies or through intermediary agencies. Such agencies act as the interface between the market and the manufacturers, and through them pass the designs, the responses to market demand, and the supply logistics. The key needs are for low cost, reliable quality, and flexibility of production in the face of consumer response. Much of the value-added is captured by the intermediators. For instance, Ralph Lauren shirts retailing in the United States for about $30 are reported to be sourced in China at $3.50. Garden furniture retailing in France at €950 is eventually sourced out of a Hangzhou factory at about €50. Competition for orders among manufacturers is fierce and prices remain low as a result.

In such a structure, the manufacturing firm acts as the production department would in a larger integrated enterprise. It concentrates on what it is good at. It is not concerned with brand creation. It does not do R & D or product development—although it may well work scientifically to improve the production process itself. It does not normally go abroad and sell directly into foreign markets, unless it acquires scale and aspires to be multinational, but such instances are very rare. In essence the *workshop* of the world is exactly that. It is where things are made.

The concentration on production implied here becomes a strength only when it is allied to the other components. To understand this phenomenon is to understand the dependencies within the total. Without the design and the branding and the distribution logistics the Chinese private sector might well be trivial. Equally, without the flexible, reliable, and efficient manufacturing offered by China the global marketing would be far less effective. The system's power is a tribute to the distinctly high level of local and international cooperation achieved in this context. And that, in our opinion, is at least in some measure a result of a special Chinese genius for beneficial connecting.

Key References

Farrell, Diana, and A. J. Grant. 2005. 'China's looming talent shortage', *McKinsey Quarterly*, 2005–4.

OECD. 2005. Economic Surveys: China.

Pistrui, David, W. Huang, D. Oksoy, Zhao Jing, and H. Welsch. 2001. 'Entrepreneurship in China: characteristics, attributes, and family forces shaping the emerging private sector', *Family Business Review*, XIV (2): 141–52.

Redding, Gordon. 2002. 'The capitalist business system of China and its rationale', *Asia-Pacific Journal of Management*, 19: 221–49.

Rothman, Andy. 2006. 'Reinventing China: in search of an innovative economy', CLSA report, Sept 2006.

Rothman, Andy, C. Liu, and J. Zhu. 2005. 'China's capitalists; entrepreneurs attack', Special report, CLSA, Sept 2005.

Wadhwa, Vivek, G. Gereffi, B. Rissing, and R. Ong. 2007. 'Seeing through the preconceptions: a deeper look at China and India', *Issues in Science and Technology*, 23 (3): 1–15.

9

Introduction to the Comparative Chapters

So far, our discussion has focused mostly on China. This is hardly surprising for a book intended to shed light on the future evolution of Chinese capitalism. However, in the next five chapters, we change tack and explore the forms of capitalism in four other contexts: the United States, Japan, Germany, and South Korea. For each of these cases, we offer a concise description of the business system and its key themes, discuss in what industries the respective system produces a comparative advantage, and explore the implications for the future evolution of capitalism in China.

At this point, one may wonder why we would do this, and why it might be worth the time spent reading through these chapters. After all, in all probability, one picked up this book to know more about China, not all those other places.

There are two key reasons that not only justify the inclusion of a strong comparative element in this book, but even necessitate it. First, humans have an inherent tendency to make sense of the world around them by means of comparison and contrast with reference points taken as 'normal.' To call a person tall means that he or she is tall relative to the expectations we have formed about people's height, which are typically anchored on the population average. Someone of average height in Scandinavia will tend to appear as tall to most Japanese.

These mechanisms are also at work in the world of business. Unconsciously, we accept the characteristics of our own business system as 'normal.' Native residents are socialized into the rules of the game from childhood on, and they play by them without much thought. The tacit and implicit character of these rules is easy to demonstrate: One only has to ask people who have never worked abroad or traveled much to explain to an outsider how business is done in their home country. Most people will struggle. It is typically much more informative to ask a foreigner with extensive experience with the given country, because the process of growing accustomed to an alien environment involves making explicit in one's mind the differences between home and the new context. It is no coincidence that many of the leading scholars about given countries are not native to these countries, or study their native countries only after having accumulated extensive international experience.

Our objective in including explorations of other leading types of capitalist systems is to help make the comparative process explicit. We encourage you to read especially the chapter about the country that seems to be closest in character to your own. Making explicit the key differences between your own country and the Chinese context is likely to lead to new insights about China and Chinese business.

The second key reason for including brief explorations of four other contexts is to help answer the question of what kind of capitalism is likely to evolve in China. While every context is different, it is possible that some aspects of their evolutionary trajectories may be similar. To the extent this is the case, understanding these similarities may open up new insights into the future course of Chinese capitalism. In addition, looking abroad for models to emulate is common practice in government and business.

While conventional wisdom maintains that there is such a thing as universal best practice, the reality is that things that work well in one context may not function at all in another. A prominent example is Japanese production methods in the automobile industry. These are so heavily contingent on the Japanese societal context that transfer to other contexts, even relatively similar ones such as Germany, has been possible only with considerable adjustments. As a result, Japanese car-makers continue to be leading the world in terms of productivity, unaffected by their practice of giving foreign competitors unfettered access for studying their production methods. For each context, we will thus explore whether its core features and key themes could actually fit into the Chinese context.

The four contexts we have picked are—by dint of importance in the world economy, geographical proximity, history, or a combination of these—leading candidates for Chinese attention, in addition to the business system of the regional ethnic Chinese, whose influence we have already discussed in an earlier chapter. They are also clear examples of four of the six leading types of capitalism[1] scholarly research has identified. To the extent key themes and core characteristics are similar across countries with the same type of capitalism, we can thus also gain some leverage on possible shared evolutionary trajectories with, and Chinese learning from, other capitalist countries not explicitly included here.

Some Remarks on Comparative Advantage

Despite our image of the world as a globalized marketplace, location continues to play an important role in the economic activity of firms. Recent research by Rugman and Verbeke shows that on the front end, most sales of firms tend to be generated close to headquarters. Only nine of the Fortune 500 firms are global in the sense of having at least 20 percent of sales in each of the three major regions—Asia, Europe, North America—but no more than 50 percent in any one of them. The effect of globalization seems stronger at the back end, especially in terms of global sourcing of materials or components.

Productive activity and the underlying comparative advantages, however, still remain strikingly localized. As Porter and Wayland point out, '[T]he world's leading competitors in a wide variety of industries are all based in one or two countries.'[2] The world's leading carmakers are German or Japanese; same goes for mechanical engineering; the world's four largest chemicals firms come from Germany and the United States; the world's most successful electronics companies are Japanese and South Korean; and so forth.

Economists have traditionally linked variation in comparative advantage to differences in endowments in the production factors of land, labor, and capital. Countries were taken to specialize, and trade more, in industries drawing on factors that were relatively abundant. For instance, the United States would be expected to trade heavily in food products because of its large endowment in sparsely populated, arable land. In reality, however, revealed comparative advantage does not necessarily follow endowment patterns. As we will show in Chapter 10, the United States shows no revealed comparative advantage in food products, nor in

---

[1] See Whitley 1999. Besides the four types represented by the United States, Japan, Germany, and South Korea, there is a type exemplified by the regional ethnic Chinese (already discused in Chapter 5), and another type prevalent in European industrial districts. This latter form of industrial district-based capitalism so closely resembles the kind of capitalism found in Germany that for the purposes of this book, it can be subsumed in the Germany chapter.

[2] Porter and Wayland 1995, p. 63.

any of the other industries reliant on land mass, with a small exception in pulp, paper, paper products, printing, and publishing. Instead, it excels in high technology and especially service industries, whose comparative advantage is difficult to explain through endowments.

In a landmark study, Michael Porter in 1990 linked the competitiveness of nations to what he called a 'diamond model' with four vertices: (1) firm strategy, structure, and rivalry, which relates to the competitive dynamics among firms; (2) demand conditions, which concerns especially the extent to which customers are demanding; (3) related and supporting industries, whose spatial proximity may facilitate information exchange and innovation; and (4) factor conditions, with competitiveness building on created, rather than inherited, production factors such as skilled labor, capital, or infrastructure. Government plays a key role in this model as a facilitator of the formation of these four components.

Porter's model has received much praise and remains on the required reading list for most economic policymakers. At the same time, it has also attracted considerable criticism. Of immediate relevance to this work are especially three points. First, although Porter's analysis of company capabilities reflects decades of work in the economics of industrial organization, the societal and cultural roots of the factor and demand conditions remain mostly out of the picture. Second, firms are treated as black boxes, with their inside dynamics left unspecified. Third, perhaps because the framework was derived from a study of developed nations and not subsequently subjected to testing on a different set of nations, the diamond model has been diagnosed as most appropriate for the advanced industrial world. It does not travel well to the developing world, thus being unintendedly ethnocentric.

In later works, Porter has acknowledged the significance of social features, especially culture, but he does so from a declared position that he is updating the economics of Ricardo by the addition of technology, factor quality, and methods of competing. His position is that an economic culture is shaped by an economy, except for beliefs, attitudes, and values derived from purely social or moral choices. He sees the two sources as being difficult to disentangle. The agenda for him, however, is to modify economic culture in order to enhance national competitiveness, such modification being 'one of the greatest challenges'. This is to ensure that hard work, initiative, education, and saving are encouraged in line with a newly emerging international economic culture. At the same time, in an acknowledged paradox, the preservation of local sources of competitive advantage, such as special supplier or customer relationships, is becoming increasingly important and decisive in a globalizing world. Both for established and new industries,

The world's leading competitors in a wide variety of industries are all based in one or two countries, especially if industries are defined narrowly in ways that are meaningful for setting strategy, and cases where government heavily distorts competition are eliminated. Within companies, global firms have indeed dispersed activities to many countries, but they concentrate a critical mass of their most important activities for competing in each business, in one location.

(Porter and Wayland 1995: 64)

If, as Porter notes, 'the home base for a particular business is where comparative advantage ultimately resides' (ibid: 64), the global strategies become ways of leveraging it. We would argue that they might also include understanding, protecting, and fostering, the sources of comparative advantage attached to the home base.

Throughout this book, including in the chapters that follow, we build on Porter's later insights and recent scholarly research suggesting that comparative advantage may at least partially be a result of the structure of society and the business system. For each context, we identify the industries with the greatest comparative advantage (and, where appropriate, disadvantage), and we point out how the structure of the business system supports (or discourages) productive activity in these industries. Our focus will be on more knowledge- and skills-intensive industries, as we expect to see there the greatest impact of societally distinct 'ways of doing things'. By contrast, comparative advantage in low-technology industries is often almost entirely a function of developmental stage and the associated levels of labor costs.

We use the OECD's 'contribution to the trade balance' measure[3] to identify comparative advantage and disadvantage. The measure compares the actual trade balance produced by each industry with the trade balance one would expect if no comparative advantage were present. It takes into account both exports and imports, as large exports in a given industry may be heavily dependent on imports in the same industry. To allow for international comparison, the contribution value is expressed as a percentage of the respective country's total trade. A positive value indicates a revealed comparative advantage, while a negative value suggests a revealed comparative disadvantage. By construction, the sum of values over all industries is zero.

---

[3] OECD 2003, p. 150.

The revealed comparative advantage numbers published by the OECD exclude service industries, even though services in advanced industrial nations typically account for more than 60 percent of GDP. We have consequently recalculated the revealed comparative advantage measure to include services, using the OECD's own statistics on trade in services. We give further details in the Appendix.

Key References

Hall, Peter A., and David Soskice, eds. 2001. *Varieties of Capitalism: The Institutional Foundations of Comparative Advantage*. Oxford: Oxford University Press.

OECD. 2003. *OECD Science, Technology and Industry Scoreboard*. Paris: OECD.

Porter, Michael E. 1990. *The Competitive Advantage of Nations*. New York: Free Press.

Porter, Michael E., and Rebecca E. Wayland. 1995. 'Global Competition and the Localization of Competitive Advantage', *Advances in Strategic Management*, 11(A): 63–105.

Ragin, Charles C. 1987. *The Comparative Method*. Berkeley, CA: University of California Press.

Rugman, Alan M., and Alain Verbeke. 2004. 'A Perspective on Regional and Global Strategies of Multinational Enterprises', *Journal of International Business Studies*, 35(1): 3–18.

Streeck, Wolfgang. 1996. 'Lean Production in the German Automobile Industry: A Test Case for Convergence Theory', in S. Berger and R. P. Dore (eds.), *National Diversity and Global Capitalism*. Ithaca, NY: Cornell University Press.

Whitley, Richard. 1999. *Divergent Capitalisms: The Social Structuring and Change of Business Systems*. Oxford: Oxford University Press.

10

United States

In this chapter, we describe US-style capitalism. With some differences in detail, similar forms of capitalism can be found throughout the Anglo-Saxon countries. Key themes in this type of capitalism (summarized in Figure 10.1) are shareholder value, professional management, application of science, competition, organization, and adaptability. It produces comparative advantages predominantly in professional services and science-driven industries. We conclude that the applicability of this type of capitalism to the Chinese context is highly limited.

The Business System

Culture

Most US firms see their raison d'être in the creation of shareholder value. Shareholder value is perceived as the vehicle of wealth transmission from the corporate entity to the individual, and its salience is considered central to the rationality, discipline, and dynamism of the economic system. Other stakeholders in the firm are, in the words of a senior US executive, 'to be conscious of—as long as there is some benefit to the bottom line'.

The emphasis on shareholder value is tied to the famous right to the 'pursuit of happiness' enshrined in the Declaration of Independence, which relates to individual fulfillment and the desire to attain liberty through financial independence. Given the immigrant origin of the United States, equality of opportunity is an important corollary of these objectives. Competition, market discipline, scientific progress, and minimal state intervention other than to maintain a level playing field are key means toward these ends.

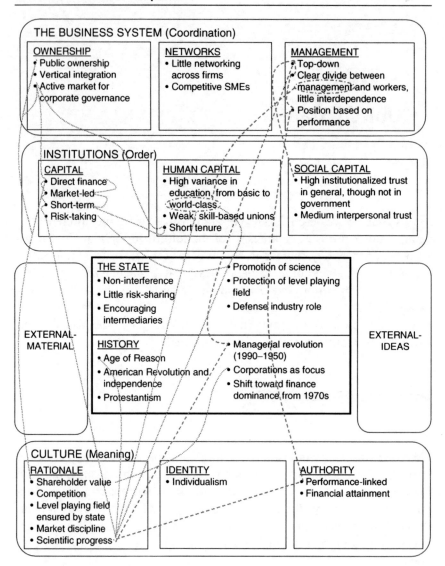

Figure 10.1. Key aspects of the US business system. The dotted lines indicate linkages supporting R&D and high tech industries, the dashed lines professions-based industry. For the sake of simplicity, only the main linkages are shown.

Reflected in the desire for freedom and self-fulfillment is a strong sense of individualism. Comparative studies generally diagnose the United States as a highly individualistic society, though there are regional variations. Farmers in the Midwest, for instance, are likely to have a more communitarian bent to themselves than New Yorkers. Still, the sense of community seems to be relatively weakly developed in what is sometimes termed a 'transactional' society, that is, one that is bonded by pragmatic, convenient, and temporary connections rather than communal ties. This is evident, among others, in the losing battle fought over 'family values', which stands in contrast with the reality of dysfunctional families evident in the world's highest divorce rates and common estrangement between parents and their children. Apart from the self, salient sources of identity includes school ties and the professions.

Authority relations are quite egalitarian. The respect and fear of superiors, also known as 'power distance,' is somewhat higher than in the northern European nations, including Germany, but less than in the other countries studied in this book. The emphasis on individual liberty tends to endow Americans with a strong sense that they are at least 'as good' as anyone else, which precludes the formation of strong hierarchical relations. The concomitant challenge to legitimate authority is likely to be a contributing factor to the breakdown of families and communities that is so apparent in the United States.

A key dimension for earning social respect is successful 'pursuit of happiness,' as expressed in financial success. In line with the ideal of a level playing field for all, this respect is largely independent of other attributes, such as education or age. Old World societies would look down upon individuals who are rich but uneducated; the New World applauds them. Perhaps more than in most other developed countries, the way to the top is linked directly to performance. That said, recent evidence shows that the actual ability to perform seems increasingly dependent on family background and quality of education.

Government

The US government is relatively little interventionist. It sees its main objective as ensuring free and fair competition. It seeks to do so by providing and enforcing a regulatory framework that spells out the rules and regulations deemed necessary for the market to function, such as antitrust and securities regulations. Intervention to save firms from bankruptcy is shunned, though not unheard of. In some areas, however, government intervention can be quite far-reaching. It provides some social security benefits, though at a low level compared with European nations. In addition, government promotes science strongly. Especially the funding of high-technology R & D through the Pentagon sometimes takes on characteristics reminiscent of industrial policy as seen in Japan. Free and fair competition also reaches its limits where domestic firms are on the losing end of globalization. 'Dumping,' for instance, is defined in US law in a manner that disallows any foreign firms from possessing a competitive advantage over US firms. Where lower cost competition emerges, trade barriers are a relatively frequent response.

Policy-making mirrors the ideal of fair chance for all. In principle, any stakeholders in an issue can lobby government to follow their view. De facto, successful lobbying is a function not only of quality of argument, but also of money, expertise, and access to policy-makers.

Institutions

The US financial system is predominantly geared toward direct finance, that is, provision of funds directly through the capital markets. Almost 60 percent of the funding requirements of US firms are met by the equity or debt markets. Financial resources are almost exclusively allocated by market criteria on the basis of quarterly results, personal relations have limited influence. The availability of capital is mostly for the short term. The significance of these capital markets is indicated in their size relative to GDP. In the cases of the United States and the United Kingdom, they reach about 160 percent. Almost all other major economies are around 60 percent or lower.

The public education system is comparatively well developed. Education is universal, though quality of output varies considerably by financial strength of the respective state and school district. Universities similarly exhibit wide variation in quality, ranging from community colleges offering remedial classes, to the world's very best. The latter tend to be private institutions, with few exceptions such as the University of California at Berkeley or the University of Michigan. While tuition fees for private schooling can be astronomical, many private schools, especially at the college and university level, seek to preserve some equality of opportunity by offering substantial financial aid packages based on academic performance. Public vocational training occurs at a relatively low-skills level, but is highly flexible and readily available. Given median job tenures in the 1990s of about four years—less than one-third that in Japan—many US firms are reluctant to invest much in training workers.

Unions play a relatively minor role in the US business system. The socialist movement of the nineteenth and twentieth centuries that legitimized unions in continental Europe failed to gather similar momentum in the United States, in part because of successful government measures to suppress it. The ideals of socialism are seen with deep suspicion, just as the ideals of liberalism are seen with deep suspicion in a country like France. Unionization levels are at about 12 percent of the working population, lower than in any other OECD country. Ironically, however, the United States loses many more working days to strikes than more unionized states such as Germany and Japan. The ILO suggests that from 2000 through 2002, the United States on average lost 6,576,925 working days per year to strikes. The numbers for Germany and Japan are 127,760 and 25,471, respectively.

Social capital is high in terms of institutional trust, less so in terms of interpersonal trust. Institutional trust in the fairness of the overall economic system and the legal system is quite high. Americans by and large do seem to believe that they live in the land of opportunity where talent and hard work will be fairly rewarded, and they eagerly turn to the legal system to settle disputes (though ironically lawyers are as much reviled as respected in the United States). Trust in government, by contrast, is relatively low, which is linked to fact that the founding fathers and many immigrants saw the United States as a refuge from oppressive government elsewhere in the world. Interpersonal trust appears to be at medium levels. There is neither an a priori assumption that others will act opportunistically, nor much upfront trust, though trust levels tend to be higher in the more rural areas of the country and lower along the coastlines. Associations are generally numerous. However, owing not least to the ideal of free competition, the number of business associations, standardized by population, is only about two-thirds that in Germany and half that in Japan.

Business System

Major US firms tend to be publicly held corporations. Share ownership by other corporations and financial institutions other than pension funds is virtually nonexistent, though firms do show a propensity for integrating their supply chains. Firms are consequently fully exposed to the forces of the financial markets, which also play an important role in corporate governance. From 1990 through 2004, there were 335 hostile takeover attempts in the United States, 75 of which were successful.

As already indicated by the relatively low number of business associations, networking among US firms is very weakly developed. Strict antitrust laws make many forms of networking illegal or at least risky, as even the exchange of market information or R & D results could be interpreted as collusive behavior. US firms are deliberately ring-fenced so that their performance can be measured and controlled unequivocally. The most common forms of networking are collaborative research in R & D consortia, legal only since the 1980s, and interlocking directorates among noncompeting firms. The poaching of employees from competitors, a common practice facilitated by low staff loyalty, can be seen as a partial substitute for information exchange through networking.

US management tends to be relatively top-down and technocratic. It is anchored in the ideal of management as a science, and formal business education in the form of an MBA is the typical prerequisite for joining the ranks of management. The perception of management as a science, combined with the short job tenures already noted, tends to work against high levels of delegation and interdependence between management and workers. Advancement is more directly related to raw performance than in many other countries and is often accomplished in the context of changing employers.

Key Themes

Shareholder Value

The dominance of shareholder value as an ideology allows its proponents (directors, professional managers, analysts, financial service providers) to lay claim to rewards and influence, and so to perpetuate that ideology. The growth of the economy has legitimated this power shift within the society since the 1970s and ensures that it dominates in much senior management decision-making and public discussion of performance.

These tendencies are supported within the institutional fabric by the growth of widespread share ownership via funds and pension plans, by a very active market in corporate control, and by a powerful driving rationality that very publicly calculates and reports on company performance.

In this context, key actors are senior managers, boards, fund managers, and analysts, and the pressure placed on professional managers gives the system its strong dynamic tension. The role of the government is traditionally hands-off, except for the setting of rules for the competitive game.

The thinking about the design of such a society and economy can be traced to the birth of the state, and so to the Age of Reason and the emergence of a form of democracy. Ideals about freedom and the acceptance of individual responsibility are also supportive. The Protestant ethic arguably played a key part in setting the ideals into institutions. An important part of the rationale continues to be the drive to consume, acting as a stimulus to the pursuit of economic growth.

Professional Management

The growth of management as a profession in the United States, visible in the significance there of the MBA, and of management theory, would normally be examined as an aspect of Human Capital, but a number of complementary features can be identified within the institutional workings of Capital.

Because share ownership is widespread, even though often clustered via fund managers, firms need to be managed by professionals as agents of owners, the managerial revolution having started early in the US (arguably a century before that of France, for instance). Shareholder value creation is then stimulated by a coldly rational concentration on performance, led by portfolio managers. Firm strategies are not constrained by adherence to a single sector. Strong competition policy is exercised by the separation of firms from each other into discrete compartments, designed to facilitate performance measurement, discipline, and reward. A related feature within processes of management is the strong control and decision power exercised by managers (compared with that in other capitalist systems).

This system is supported by the high significance of equity-market funding, and the related strength and sophistication of venture-capital funding, these in turn resting upon a base of publicly accessible reliable information of great density and reach. A connection exists here with the rich fabric of civil society institutions, and especially the professions such as accounting, which (as aspects of Social Capital) provide a high level of comfort that information is reliable, qualifications have meaning, and regulations will be adhered to. This contribution to the maintaining of order in society is a crucial component in the architecture of decentralization and market freedom. The strength of identity with a profession, for many individuals, is a valuable counterweight to the increasing weakness of identity with corporations, as the risks of being fired increase, such labor market mobility being a response to the strategic adaptiveness demanded under the drive for shareholder value.

Applying Science

The innovative strength of the US economy lies largely in its ability to bridge scientific inventiveness and commercial application. It is most clearly visible in Silicon Valley, Route 128, and the Raleigh–Durham triangle, but such inventiveness is not restricted to the hard sciences. It is equally visible in financial services and consultancy.

This may be traced to a chain of supporting features. The highly developed venture-capital system has grown alongside a system of education and of government support for scientific research, which together foster close links between science and its application. Scientific research per se rests on a strong ideological heritage. Reason, order, foresight are all cardinal virtues stemming from the Age of Reason, and they still legitimize the allocation of scientific resources that produces the world's second highest innovation index score, and the sixth highest percentage of GDP spent on R & D. Incentives for risk-taking, and especially the accumulation of wealth (e.g. property rights, patents, IPOs), are also well provided for in the institutional fabric.

Competitive Intensity

An essential aspect of the US system of capitalism, and one that distinguishes it from many others, is the enforcing of competition between firms via the outlawing of cartels, monopolies, and other forms of collaborating against the market. The interlocking networks of Germany and Japan are absent here, and US firms operate in compartments separate from one another. They rarely collaborate in R & D, education, or shared investment. Contracts are normally arm's length. They stand on their own feet, and are held to account by the public (via the analysts), not by their peer companies. They live and die by the discipline of the market.

A complex cluster of features supports the implementation of this ideal of competitiveness. We see here the full flowering of the 'specific and peculiar rationality' of Western cultures identified by Weber. Respect for the scientific method, for calculation, for economic logic, for accounting are all manifest in the highly elaborated legal and financial frameworks. So too does the codification and diffusion of information reach unusually high levels, both of penetration and of reliability, allowing the market, in large measure, to run itself. Objectivity, neutrality, bureaucracy are natural corollaries.

The government stands back from direct intervention and is strongly influenced by the corporate interest group in formulating and applying regulation. The legal and financial systems work in support of the overall ideal, and in doing so are biased toward the protection of owners.

Within the culture, competitiveness as legitimate behavior may be traced to ideals of freedom, material progress, and respect for winning. These also serve to strengthen the legitimacy of the private sphere in the economy and so to keep government influence under control (in strong contrast to many other systems in Europe and Asia). Supporting cultural ideals include individualism and self-responsibility, the generally low context nature of society, and a strong belief that status should be based on measured achievement.

Organization

The institutions of Capital in the US make only a partial contribution to the nature of economic organization. The institutions of Human and Social Capital need also to be factored in. But, staying with Capital, it is possible to discern connections between the priorities determined in the process of capital sourcing and allocation, and the way these come to be interpreted in the managing of organizations.

Managers are under pressure to perform. This comes from the rationality and discipline applied in the pursuit of shareholder value, and the consequent response of allocating power to managers to enable the delivery of performance. The transparency and related detailed judgment of performance raise the significance of managerial action, and enhance its power and status, compared for instance with that of labor. This enhancement is furthered by the tendency of firms not to build strong bonds of interdependence with labor (as occurs, e.g., in Germany and Japan). Labor is dispensable in a mobile labor market, and strategic dependence on the accumulation of high levels of labor skill is not common. Instead, there is high task fragmentation and standardization, leading to further reliance on managerial control. Rather than crucial knowledge being vested in a 'permanently' employed group of workers, it comes to reside within the managerial hierarchy. This concentration of decision power, combined with the all-pervasive rationality, and the ideals of bureaucracy, and supplemented by the objectivity and professionalism of the hired manager (as opposed to the owner–manager), leads to high capacities for coordinating complex organization. The efficient stitching together of elaborate firms, although not unique to this system of capitalism, provides it with certain inbuilt competences relevant to firm growth. These competences remain grounded in the system itself, and are expressed in a distinct organizational style.

Adaptability

The US business system is highly adaptable to changing conditions, such as technological progress. Levels of regulation are relatively low, and economic actors such as individuals and firms retain high degrees of freedom for changing behaviors and routines without formal or informal coordination with other actors. In most cases, responses to rapid technological advances or other developments that may require new production and work processes can be relatively quick. Because of the absence of coordination among firms across the economy, different kinds of adaptation responses appear. Only over time, as the superiority of one or few responses becomes obvious, does the variety get whittled down to the winners.

Comparative Advantage

The United States is the only country examined in this book with strong comparative advantages in several service sectors (see Figure 10.2). The institutional structure of the business system has relatively little to do with the comparative advantage in some services, such as that in travel (+2.2 percent), an industry that is heavily dependent on endowments such as natural beauty and attractive cities.

Many of the other service industries, however, benefit from the shape of the US business system, and specifically its ability to create and sustain highly skilled and mobile professionals. This is most clearly visible in the context of the creation of intellectual property through R & D, as reflected in the 'royalties and license fees' category (+1.8 percent).[1] The 2005 OECD *Factbook* indicates that among OECD countries, the United States occupies rank six in terms of R & D expenditures relative to GDP, rank seven

---

[1] Payments for other intellectual property such as movies, music, and books are included in 'personal, cultural, and recreational services.'

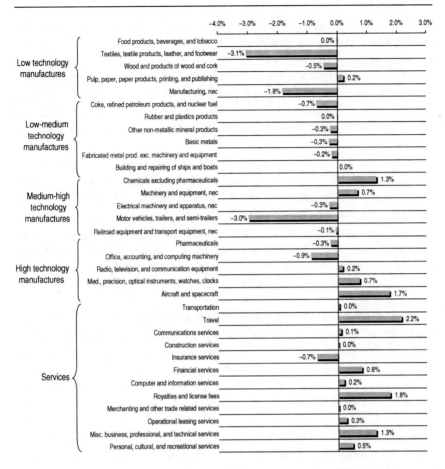

Figure 10.2. US comparative advantage by industries, 2003 (OECD, own calculations). See appendix for details and also next chapter

in terms of patents[2] per million population, and rank four in terms of number of researchers per thousand employed. However, the large size of the United States both in terms of population and GDP means that more new knowledge is created there than anywhere else in the world.

[2] This refers to the 'triadic patent family' measure employed by the OECD in its annual *Factbook*. The measure standardizes for varying patenting practices in the various OECD countries by counting only those patented in all three parts of the Triad: Europe, Japan, and the United States.

This is expressed, among others, in the fact that more than one-third of all OECD[3] patents originate in the United States. Knowledge creation is facilitated by world-class research universities such as Harvard, MIT, and Stanford, plentiful research resources especially in high-technology fields with potential military applications, and a strong venture-business culture that encourages the commercialization of research. Foreign producers may then gain access to new technologies by purchasing licenses.

The strength in professional services is further visible especially in the categories relating to financial services such as investment banks as well as in the other 'miscellaneous business, professional, and technical services' category comprising service providers such as accounting firms, consultancies, and international law firms. As in science, many of the world leaders in these service industries are based in, and often originate from, the United States. The management consulting industry, for instance, is said to have come into being with the founding of McKinsey in Chicago in 1926.

The ability of the United States to apply technology developed by its scientists is visible in the comparative advantages in high-technology industries, which tend to involve rapid innovation, improvement, and change. Largest comparative advantage in these industries is in aircraft and spacecraft (+1.9 percent). The main exponent of this industry is Boeing, which is one of the world's two large producers of civilian aircraft and a maker of virtually anything of military value that can fly. In appealing to its international customers, the company can point to the sophisticated technology especially of its military equipment. This natural appeal may be further amplified by the possibility for other governments of closer military ties with the United States as a reward for buying US machines, and the fact that aircraft and military equipment purchases from Boeing are a relatively easy way especially for Asian governments to reduce their trade surpluses with the United States.

What US capitalism is not good at is industries where high levels of dependence on labor skills, or on close permanent customer links, are strategic necessities. In the former case, the need for constant improvement and technical upgrading in stable industries such as automobiles, consumer durables, and consumer electronics has not been met, and such industrial dominance as the US had in the 1960s has now been lost to Japan and Germany.

[3] Cf. fn. 2.

Applicability to China

Transferability of the US formula to the Chinese context seems highly limited. Of the six key themes we have identified for the United States, only two—competitive intensity and adaptability—fit the Chinese context, though for different reasons and with different institutional underpinnings.

Convergence on shareholder-value-oriented management seems unlikely for the foreseeable future. While many major SOEs are publicly listed, most remain under the control of the Chinese state, which views them as instruments of industrial policy for developing China rather than a tool of creating wealth for shareholders. Local corporates and enterprises in the private sector are typically closely held. For those that are listed, our expectation is that they will continue to focus on the interests of the original founders or families, rather than on all shareholders equally—some shareholders are likely to be more equal than others. This kind of varied treatment is in line with the interpersonal character of social capital, which implies that nothing is owed to anyone not included in the concentric circles of trust. The absence of well-designed and strictly implemented corporate governance codes combined with weak legal infrastructure give minority shareholders little recourse.

As previously discussed, professionalization of management is only beginning to occur in present-day China. One major issue is the relative absence of skills. Though professional training programs have multiplied rapidly over recent years, the numbers are still small compared with the need, and the quality of education at all but the best local programs is questionable. A second issue—relevant mostly for local corporates and the private sector—is the blending of control and ownership in the same hands. Major decisions are made by the *lao ban* or a small handful of leaders and, to a lesser degree, their confidantes, who often include family members. Personnel outside this exclusive circle, even if highly qualified, are reduced to recipients of orders from above, rather than trusted stewards of the business on behalf of its owners. In part, this is related to the absence of the institutional underpinnings that would allow owners to keep managers honest. The most likely arena for professionalization of management among native Chinese firms would thus, prima facie, seem to be the large SOEs intended to be grown into national champions. Even here, however, we routinely see strong leaders emerge as de facto *lao ban*. In addition, these firms are vulnerable to management interference by their controlling owner, the state.

As elaborated earlier, China has had a poor record of applying scientific advances in everyday economic life. At present, the system faces major challenges. China has yet to build a strong R & D capability. Efforts are afoot in this direction, often aided by the patriotism of Chinese trained abroad and ethnic Chinese from outside the mainland. Much progress remains to be made, however. The number of triadic patents registered by China in 2002, the latest year for which data are available, was 144. This compares with a number of 18,324 for the United States, with a population one-fourth the size. Researchers and engineers that could contribute to raising the number of Chinese patents and putting them to practical use are in scarcer supply than commonly believed. For instance, a 2005 McKinsey study estimates that out of a pool of 1.6 million young engineers, only around 160,000 are sufficiently qualified to work for multinational enterprises. In other words, the engineering talent pool in China is no larger than that of the United Kingdom, which managed to produce 2,045 triadic patents in 2002. To further complicate matters, the institutional infrastructure necessary for venture capital to aid the transfer from laboratory to factory remains underdeveloped, though it is noteworthy that Western venture capitalists have made valiant efforts to establish themselves in the Chinese market.

Obstacles further remain in the organizational realm. As noted earlier, many Chinese firms tend to be run by one or several persons occupying the role of owner–manager, thus preventing professionalization of management. This concentration of power in the hands of few implies a reduced capacity for organizational complexity, as relatively few tasks are delegated to lower levels of management. The fate of businesses is thus closely dependent on their top leaders. Unwise decisions will remain unchallenged. The death of the leader will often kill the company as well, unless a suitable successor has been groomed in time.

China superficially does share with the United States high levels of competitive intensity and adaptability. Yet where competitive intensity in the United States tends to be governed by sober calculation, a different kind of rationality seems to apply in the Chinese case. Underpinning US competition is a strong belief that competition produces the best outcomes for everyone, a notion that finds its expression in legislation designed explicitly to maximize competition. At the same time, the need to make profits places a natural limit on the extent of competition. In China, by contrast, competition often seems to be motivated by the desire to outlast other competitors, in the hope of eventually being able to enjoy a profitable position. A limiting factor tends to be not the imperative of profits, but the availability of finance to keep the concern afloat.

Counter to conventional wisdom, much of the adaptation process in China is as decentralized as in the United States. In line with the principle of 'groping for stones to cross the river,' regional institutional variations serve as models for national-level reforms, just as they often do in the United States. In both cases, the state tends to give citizens relatively generous space to devise their own solutions to new problems. The key difference, however, is that in the United States, this process tends to be subject to constraint both by social values and a reasonably reliable legal system. In China, these constraining elements apply only sporadically, and a sense of social responsibility in economic activity is frequently absent. All too often, anything goes, it seems, as long as it generates profits, in an oversimplified, single-minded interpretation of Deng's maxim that 'to get rich is glorious.' Salient expression of this tendency are recent findings of fake baby formula without any nutritional value and fake medication, increasingly engineered with great care to give the impression of being genuine. Recent reports indicate that more than half of the antimalarials in Southeast Asia are fake, with most of them coming from China. The absence of reliable social and legal constraints means that adaptation processes in China are likely to show a greater divergence from what is socially desirable than is evident in the United States.

Key References

Berger, Suzanne, and Ronald Philip Dore, eds. 1996. *National Diversity and Global Capitalism*. Ithaca, NY: Cornell University Press.

Dore, Ronald Philip. 2000. *Stock Market Capitalism: Welfare Capitalism: Japan and Germany Versus the Anglo-Saxons*. Oxford: Oxford University Press.

Hall, Peter A., and David Soskice, eds. 2001. *Varieties of Capitalism: The Institutional Foundations of Comparative Advantage*. Oxford: Oxford University Press.

Redding, Gordon. 2005. 'The Thick Description and Comparison of Societal Systems of Capitalism', *Journal of International Business Studies*, 36(2): 123–55.

Redding, Gordon, and Michael A. Witt. 2004. 'The Role of Executive Rationale in the Comparison of Capitalisms: Some Preliminary Findings', *INSEAD EAC Working Paper Series*. Fontainebleau, France.

Whitley, Richard. 1999. *Divergent Capitalisms: The Social Structuring and Change of Business Systems*. Oxford: Oxford University Press.

Witt, Michael A. 2006. *Changing Japanese Capitalism: Societal Coordination and Institutional Adjustment*. Cambridge: Cambridge University Press.

11

Japan

The Japanese business system represents the one known example of what the literature calls 'coordinated capitalism,' although it has a close cousin in the collaborative form of capitalism typical of much of European business. Key themes summarized in Figure 11.1 are employee-centric stakeholder value, delegation, and interdependence within the enterprise, firm-specific skills, as well as societal coordination and structural inertia. Japanese capitalism produces comparative advantages mainly in industries requiring incremental innovation. It is difficult to see how any of the key themes of the Japanese business system might work in the Mainland Chinese context.

Business System

Culture

Japanese firms exist foremost for the sake of their own employees. In the words of a Japanese executive interviewed for this project, 'If I were to say for what the company exists, it is to make the employees it is embracing happy.' Important is also a sense of duty toward society as a whole, both in Japan and, in the case of large, multinational corporations, also in the host nation. Shareholders, by contrast, have only recently gained recognition. However, this does not mean shareholder value. Rather, the attainment of the primary objectives—contribution to society within and outside the firm—is now seen as subject to the new constraint of satisfying shareholders' demands for returns. Accordingly, the executive quoted earlier continues his explanation saying, 'To maintain that happiness, we have to give a return to the shareholders from whom we have received the money.'

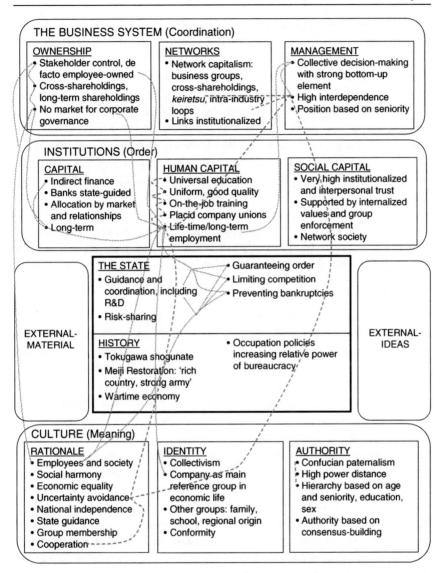

Figure 11.1. Key aspects of the Japanese business system. The dotted lines indicate linkages supporting incremental innovation, the dashed lines, standardization and high product quality. For the sake of simplicity, only the main linkages are shown.

The notion of responsibility toward the community grows out of, and interacts with, central elements in the Japanese mental landscape such as social harmony (*wa*), economic equality, protection against insecurity, and, through the economic growth implied by the latter two, independence as a nation. State guidance, group membership, and collaborative efforts represent accepted means toward these ends.

Reflected in the accepted ends and means is a relatively collective sense of identity espoused by most Japanese. Though not as strong as in China and Korea, the view that the interests of the collective supersede those of the individual persists. An implication is that social deviance is frowned upon, as expressed in the Japanese proverb that 'the nail that sticks out gets hammered in.' While family matters in Japan, the defining community, or 'in-group,' for most Japanese is the company. This is to be seen in the context that employment tends to be long-term or even for a lifetime, and employees typically spend many more hours a week at work than with their families. Besides the company and the family, school ties represent an important source of identity.

Authority relations are fairly hierarchical and structured along Confucian lines. The respect and fear of superiors, also known as 'power distance,' is higher than in most northern European countries, but about on par with Korea and much of southern Europe and lower than in Chinese environments. The paternalistic element of Confucianism, a trade-off of obedience for benevolence, interacts with the strong sense of community and desire for harmony and is augmented by an element of consensual decision-making. Superiors typically refrain from imposing their views, but engage their subordinates in an effort to create a consensus.

Well preserved are the Confucian criteria by which hierarchy is established: age and education as well as predominance of the male sex. A one-year difference in age is sufficient to define a hierarchy, typically expressed in the terms *sempai* and *kohai* (senior and junior). Once this kind of relationship is defined—by graduating class in school, for instance—the hierarchy will persist one's entire life. The importance of education derives from the Confucian notion that position in society should be linked to education attainment. Confucius advocated a universal education system with state examinations. The Japanese education system still fundamentally functions that way, and one's career perspectives in essence depend on which university one has graduated from, which in turn depends on the quality of one's high school, middle school, and all the way down to kindergarten, some of which have entrance examinations.

Government

The role of the Japanese government in the economy is to guide and stabilize. The Japanese have interpreted the free interplay of market forces as inimical to these objectives, resulting in a fairly interventionist state that relies on industrial policies to counter and supplement market forces. Since firms are seen as living organisms, a key objective is to give enough room to each firm to live. One role of government is thus limiting competition through formal rules and regulations and informal agreements. Where bankruptcies do occur in large firms, Japanese government routinely engineers bailouts or distress mergers, as evident in the Japanese banking industry during the past few years.

This conservative role is supplemented by a forward-looking one, in which government seeks to induce firms to develop and adopt new technologies. R & D consortia represent a commonly used tool toward this end. In these consortia, government assembles on average about twenty firms for some 6–10 years of collaborative research on new technologies. The collective nature of the effort reduces the associated risk for firms, as does government funding covering part of the costs. For instance, the ten-year micromachine technology consortium of twenty-three firms received about $250 million in government support.

In all these efforts, government guidance typically occurs through reciprocal consent between business and government. Numerous mechanisms exist for bureaucrats to exchange opinions and forge a consensus with business representatives. These include deliberation councils *(shingikai)* within each ministry as well as thousands of industry associations, many of which employ retired bureaucrats as managing directors.

Institutions

Japan's financial capital system relies to a large extent on indirect finance, that is, bank loans. Two-thirds of the external funding needs of Japanese firms continue to be covered by bank loans. Loans are typically for the long term, and where the capital markets would withdraw funds from ailing firms, Japanese banks often extend new credit in order to keep the company afloat. One element explaining this behavior is human relationships that form between banks and their customers over the years. These imply a sense of obligation to help. Another is the role of government, which still continues to play an important role in the business of Japanese banks. Banks used to be a government tool of industrial policy, with limited discretion for their lending business. As a result, Japanese banks know relatively little about running their business, and many major bank decisions still seem to be made, informally, by the government bureaucracy.

The public education system is well developed, with the exception of vocational training, which occurs almost entirely within firms. Education is universal through high school. Both public and private schools and universities exist, but private education does not necessarily imply higher status. On the contrary, the universities held in the highest esteem, for instance, the University of Tokyo and the University of Kyoto; both are public. Control over the curriculum in public schools is highly centralized. The Ministry of Education determines the curriculum for the entire country, and it is said that if one could manage to be in two classrooms of the same grade level at opposite ends of the country at the same time, one could witness precisely the same material being taught.

The rules of the game are basically similar for both public and private schools: admission requires passing entrance examinations. In order to prevent failure, parents of children studying in both public and private schools tend to spend considerable amounts of money to send their children to cram schools in the late afternoon and evening.

Unions are organized along company lines and are usually very placid. Their strength is difficult to gauge because their interests are typically aligned with those of the company, with the result that strikes are a rarity. Collective action is mostly confined to the ritual of the 'spring offensive' (*shuntou*), during which employees may stop work for a few hours in support of the annual wage-bargaining process. Management sees the unions as partners in administering the firm, and it is not rare for lower level managers to be union members.

Similar to financial capital, the availability of human capital is long-term. Despite claims in the press that lifetime employment in Japan was dead, the evidence suggests the opposite. Average tenure for male employees has risen from 10.8 years in 1980 to 12.5 years in 1990 and 13.3 years in 2000. Long-term or lifetime employment is typically not available to women. They would normally join a company after graduation to work for a few years, quit when they get married, and possibly reenter the workforce on a part-time basis once the children have graduated high school or college. Career women are still relatively rare.

Social capital, interpreted as trust, is relatively high in Japanese society. This is especially true for institutional trust, and opportunism is rare. A striking expression of this trust is that many Japanese employees do not have written employment contracts. Hand in hand with high levels of trust goes a strong propensity to engage in social networking. One indicator is the number of business associations, which, standardized by population size, is twice as high in Japan as in the United States and some 50 percent higher than in Germany.

Business System

Most large Japanese firms are corporations in name, but de facto employee-owned. Shareholders matter little, and corporate governance remains weakly developed. According to one estimate in 2001, about a tenth of Japan's 3,500 listed companies had breakup values more than twice their market capitalization. A market for corporate governance through hostile takeovers or buyouts is virtually nonexistent. From 1990 through the end of 2004, only four hostile takeovers were attempted in Japan, three of which were completed.

Pressure for change has been emanating from a rising share of foreign ownership, which in 2004 reached about 20 percent of outstanding stock. One accompanying effect has been a decline in cross-shareholdings and long-term shareholdings. Cross-shareholding in the general market is down to less than half the levels seen in 1990 at about 7 percent. Long-term shareholding has also declined, down about 40 percent from levels in 1990 to now around 27 percent.

The pervasiveness of networks in Japanese society also extends to the business system. Most prominent of the networks in Japanese business are the business groups, also known as (horizontal) *keiretsu*. There are six major groups: Daiichi, Fuyo, Mitsubishi, Mitsui, Sanwa, and Sumitomo. These groups in 1999 accounted for 13.2 percent of capital, 11.2 percent of assets, and 10.8 percent of sales in the Japanese economy. The early 2000s have seen a series of mergers of firms across formerly impregnable business-group boundaries. It is not yet clear whether this is a sign of the decay of the business groups, or of their reconfiguration into larger entities. Japanese firms also tend to maintain dense networks with suppliers and distributors (vertical *keiretsu*) and with competitors within the same industry (intra-industry loops). The large number of industry associations, previously mentioned, facilitates the latter networks.

Japanese management is collective and bottom-up. A review of company strategy, for instance, will typically involve extensive meetings and consensus building across departments and hierarchical levels, and all constituents will give their input. The formalized proposal will be

173

circulated to all concerned, who indicate their consent by putting their chops on the document (signatures are rarely used).

Hierarchy in management is a function mostly of seniority. Contrary to reports in the press that seniority was giving way to performance-based promotions, there is again no statistical evidence that the seniority principle has been weakening. A major reason is that performance always did matter in Japanese firms. Seniority merely means that in general, no one will hold a higher position in the company than others with longer job tenure.

Key Themes

Employee-centric Stakeholder Value

Key to understanding the Japanese business system is the realization that firms do not exist to generate profits for shareholders. Their main purpose is to generate sufficient value to keep as many employees as possible on the roster. This is reflected in both public opinion and the thinking of executives. According to the 2000 World Values Survey, public opinion favors stakeholder value over shareholder value by 44 percent versus 32 percent. Similarly, the executives we interviewed about their view of the purpose of their firms tended to support the stakeholder view, as expressed in the statement quoted earlier. There was widespread recognition of the increased importance of shareholders and the institutional infrastructure accompanying it, though this tended to be considered an unavoidable consequence of globalization rather than a desirable feature.

In clarifying relations with shareholders, one executive compared his company to a child, and his shareholders to the child's parents, in the sense that the shareholders were the ones to put up the capital to make the foundation of the firm possible. Just as a child owed gratitude to his or her parents that is to be expressed as filial piety, he explained, the firm owed gratitude to shareholders, expressed in form of dividends. But just as a child at some point began to lead a life of its own, free from parental control, so the firm's existence was to be free of interference from shareholders.

The survival of this norm is supported by a number of mechanisms insulating firms from shareholder pressures. The indirect nature of the Japanese financial system means that firms have limited need to obtain funds from the markets. The withholding of funds from firms not pursuing shareholder value is thus not a viable pressure tactic for disgruntled shareholders.

Nor can shareholders count on corporate governance mechanisms. There have been recent changes in corporate governance regulations in Japan, allowing firms to restructure their board along more Western lines. However, only a small minority of firms has taken up the opportunity, mostly in response to foreign majority ownership. Hostile takeovers as the ultimate tool of corporate governance, however, remain exceedingly rare and difficult. Cross-shareholdings and long-term shareholdings by other firms are an important contributor to this difficulty. As of 2003, some 56 percent of outstanding stock was still in the hands of firms and financial institutions, which suggests cross- or long-term shareholdings. The discrepancy with the official statistics, which suggest combined cross-shareholdings and long-term holdings at some 34 percent, is likely to be an artifact of recent reshufflings of portfolios as a consequence of the Japanese banking crisis of the 1990s.

Delegation and Interdependence

Japanese organizations exhibit very high levels of delegation and of employer–employee interdependence. While leadership is not alien to Japanese firms, decision-making is typically consensus-driven and involves a strong bottom-up element. Enabling this approach is the long-term character of employment, which ensures a high degree of alignment between the interest of employee and employer. The average job tenure of more than thirteen years suggests that most males may change jobs before retirement at 55–60 years of age about two times. Most of these changes tend to occur among younger employees, who may decide to return to the entry level in exchange for a company that is more prestigious or seems like a better fit. The labor market for older workers is very small.

The long-term character of employment is closely linked with the view of the firm as a community and source of identity, and of course with the stakeholder rationale of the firm. A critical enabling factor is the long-term availability of funding. Since Japanese banks tend not to recall their credit lines even for firms in distress, firms are well insulated from short-term pressures to lay off workers in large numbers when business is in a downswing. Labor force reductions may occur by other means, such as voluntary retirements and transfers to subsidiaries, but outright layoffs are rare and closely circumscribed by regulations and legal practice.

Firm-specific Skills

Most vocational training in Japanese firms occurs within the firm. This means that many of the skills acquired are firm specific. In marked contrast with the United States, in which employees have an incentive to develop general skills that are transferable to different employers, the long-term nature of Japanese employment and the virtual absence of a secondary labor market increase the willingness of employees to invest in firm-specific skills. Conversely, the fact that employees will stay for the long-term tends to increase the willingness of Japanese employers to offer training.

Further elements of the business system lend additional support to the acquisition and further development of firm-specific skills. The consultative mode of management allows production-line workers to come together in regular meetings to discuss optimization potential in the production process; strong identification with the company and its products and the fear of disappointing the group's trust motivates employees to give their best; and extensive networks with suppliers and competitors facilitate the setting of strict standards for components and machinery used in the manufacturing process.

Coordination and Structural Inertia

The Japanese business system shows very high levels of coordination across issue areas. These include company strategies as well as changes in the formal and informal rules of the game, including those undertaken under government auspices. For instance, competing firms often announce similar projects or investment decisions almost simultaneously. Through extensive social networks with their competitors, but also with suppliers, customers, bureaucrats, academics, bankers, and the press, firms are typically well apprised of what their competitors do. In an informal iterative process, an industry will thus move to a consensus on what steps to take next, culminating in the same decisions and actions. Scholars of corporate strategy have consequently attested that Japanese firms are devoid of strategy, as strategy in their view requires differentiation. The same networks also serve as conduits of pressure to conform to business norms, rules, and regulations, and they are used to build consensus to change these rules of the game. The desire for coordination is linked to high levels of risk aversion in Japanese firms, which itself is a function of high risk aversion in Japanese society in general and the imperative the stakeholder rationale puts on firm survival.

The tendency toward coordination implies that changes to the business system typically require extensive deliberations and information exchange among the various affected firms, organizations, and agencies. This takes time, and structural inertia is consequently high.

Comparative Advantage

Japan shows a very strong comparative advantage in automobiles, followed by machinery and equipment as well as radio, television, and communication equipment (see Figure 11.2). The biggest disadvantage outside the primary industries is in travel (−2.8 percent), which is related to the fact that many more Japanese travel abroad than foreigners find their way to Japan.

The Japanese automobile industry registers the largest comparative advantage found in any country examined in this book (+8.4 percent). The well-known protagonists in this industry are Toyota, which is about to surpass General Motors to become the world's largest car producer, as well as Honda, Nissan, Mazda, and a number of smaller producers. The main competitive strength of Japanese cars lies in quality and reliability at competitive prices. Especially Toyota is famous for its zero-defects policy, reinforced through strict quality controls by each individual worker and team-based continuous improvement of product and production process. In customer-satisfaction surveys and vehicle-breakdown statistics, Japanese cars typically receive top scores.

Comparative advantage in machinery and equipment is also considerable (+4.1 percent). This is a highly heterodox category, covering general-purpose machinery such as engines and turbines, pumps, bearings and gears, and compressors; special-purpose machinery such as agricultural, mining, construction, food processing, and textile manufacturing equipment as well as machine tools; and domestic appliances such as refrigerators and dishwashers. Among the many firms active in this category, major players are Hitachi, Mitsubishi Heavy Industries, and Komatsu. Hitachi is not only the world's second-largest electronics and electrical equipment producer, but also a major producer of power and industrial systems—such as industrial machinery, construction equipment, and elevators—as well as home appliances.

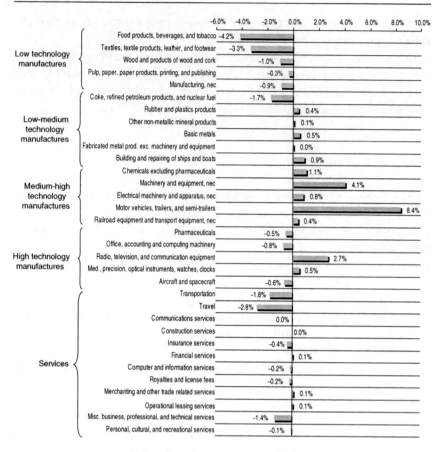

Figure 11.2. Japanese comparative advantage by industries, 2003 (OECD own calculations). See appendix for details.

Note: nec = not elsewhere classified.

Mitsubishi Heavy is the world's third-largest producer of industrial and farm equipment by revenue. Power systems and mass and medium-lot manufactured machinery account for more than half of the company's revenue. Komatsu is a leading manufacturer of construction and mining equipment, with about two-thirds of its sales volume overseas. As in the case of the automobile industry, quality paired with competitive prices is the basis of the comparative advantage in this industry.

Japan further possesses significant comparative advantage in radio, television, and communication equipment (+2.7 percent). Leading producers in the field are Matsushita and Sony, the numbers one and two in the consumer electronics world. Matsushita, known through its National, Panasonic, Technics, Quasar, and JVC brands, is the world's largest producer of audio-visual equipment. Sony is slightly smaller, but more internationalized in the distribution of its sales: While Matsushita generates about half of its revenues in Japan, Sony does almost three-quarters of its business outside its home market. In addition to these big two, major Japanese producers of audio-visual equipment include Hitachi, Mitsubishi Electric, Sanyo, Sharp, and Toshiba. High quality at reasonable prices and rapid innovation have been the core ingredients of Japanese success in this industry.

All these industries share the characteristic that innovation tends to be incremental rather than radical. New features keep being added to the same products. The emphasis on firm-specific skills and their continuous upgrading supports this kind of strategy. As we have seen, the ability and willingness of workers to invest in these skills is dependent on long-term employment, which in turn is enabled by long-term finance and the employee-centric type of stakeholder value. Further reinforcing the tendency toward stepwise innovation is the risk aversion of firms growing out of their concern for maintaining employment.

By implication, the Japanese business system is less suitable for radical innovation. Radical innovation requires the availability of risk capital as well as the ability to redeploy capital and labor rapidly. Banks cannot provide much risk capital without putting their viability at stake, and the venture-capital infrastructure in Japan is weak. Government has attempted to mitigate some of these problems by providing seed money in the context of public R & D consortia, but the bureaucratic policymaking process is too slow for radical developments, and the available funds are relatively small. The very rigidity in the labor markets that enables firm-specific skills and continuous improvement is an obstacle to rapid redeployment of human capital to new industries. In addition, the tendency of firms to coordinate and high structural inertia make it difficult for Japanese firms to engage in radically different forms of activity even if they tried.

All three industries further benefit from the standardization of parts and processes that allows for very high product quality. This mode of production is enabled by uncertainty avoidance, the integration of shop-floor workers in improving and monitoring quality, as well as in the close cooperation within supplier networks. By contrast, the Japanese business system is less suited for nonstandardized processes. These processes are hampered by the need for autonomous decision-making they imply.

Nonstandard situations do not jibe well with uncertainty avoidance and the perceived desirability of uniformity within the in-group, and the typical Japanese response is consultation with the group on how to handle the situation. This takes more time than most nonstandardized situations can bear.

The Japanese business system further tends to perform less well where industries for one reason or another can support only one or perhaps two players, such as the commercial aircraft industry. If no firm naturally emerges, the logical course of action may be for government to select one national champion or to forge an alliance from several firms. Neither is feasible, as the former violates Japanese norms of equitable treatment, and the latter tends to run foul of the centrifugal forces resulting from the competitive rivalries of Japanese firms.

Applicability to China

It is difficult to see how the key themes of the Japanese business system could apply to the Chinese context. Chinese firms used to subscribe to the objective of taking care of their employees, as symbolized by the notion of the 'iron rice bowl.' This objective has in many cases given way to others, such as the acquisition of personal wealth and the building of world-competitive multinational corporations. Where state-owned enterprises show concern for maintaining employment levels high, this is typically related to political concerns about possible social unrest growing out of mass unemployment rather than interest in the personal well-being of the employees.

As we have discussed in Chapter 10 on the United States, top management in China shows considerable resistance to delegation even within managerial ranks. Emulating the Japanese way of business would require China to go one step further still by permitting delegation throughout the organization, including shop-floor workers. This would represent so radical a departure from the historical and present mode of running a firm that we expect the likelihood of it occurring to be virtually zero.

The decline of long-term employment especially among qualified workers has reinforced the reluctance to build an interdependent relationship with employees. It also acts as a break on employees' willingness to invest in firm-specific skills, and on employers' willingness to expend resources for training employees. Of course, some individual employees, typically those falling within the circles of trust of the leadership, may stay for the long term and acquire a deep knowledge of the firms' processes. The key difference is that in Japanese firms this outcome is the norm rather than the exception.

The capacity for coordination in China is low. This is partially by design, as the leadership in Beijing has encouraged locally independent development as part of its 'crossing the river by groping for the stones' development strategy. This strategy provides experiential information about the feasibility of new approaches to doing business and thus the direction of central government policy. In addition, it ensures that institutional change toward a market system progresses even in the absence of consensus on how to proceed at the center. Coordination of the kind evident in Japan would not fit into this scenario.

But even in the absence of this strategy, coordination capacity would probably remain relatively low, both under state leadership and in voluntary form at the industry level. The Japanese state has had a relatively high capacity for monitoring and enforcing compliance in the private sector. It is not clear whether the Chinese state has this capacity, or indeed whether it ever had. Especially in parts of China distant from the capital, deviations from central government policy have historically been common, even in the heyday of Mao—as the proverb has it, 'the heavens are high, and the emperor is far away.' At the industry level, the state penetration of business associations in China is likely to limit the capacity of associations to act as trusted intermediaries enabling coordination, which is a routine function in many Japanese associations.

Key References

Dore, Ronald Philip. 2000. *Stock Market Capitalism: Welfare Capitalism: Japan and Germany Versus the Anglo-Saxons*. Oxford: Oxford University Press.

Economist. 2001. 'Japanese Corporate Raiders: Ever So Polite', *The Economist*, 15 February 2001.

Hall, Peter A., and David Soskice, eds. 2001. *Varieties of Capitalism: The Institutional Foundations of Comparative Advantage*. Oxford: Oxford University Press.

Redding, Gordon and Michael A. Witt. 2004. 'The Role of Executive Rationale in the Comparison of Capitalisms: Some Preliminary Findings', *INSEAD EAC Working Paper Series*. Fontainebleau, France.

Whitley, Richard. 1999. *Divergent Capitalisms: The Social Structuring and Change of Business Systems*. Oxford: Oxford University Press.

Witt, Michael A. 2006. *Changing Japanese Capitalism: Societal Coordination and Institutional Adjustment*. Cambridge: Cambridge University Press.

12

Germany

The German business system is the clearest and strongest example of the collaborative capitalism commonly found in continental Europe, especially in the northern countries. Key themes (see Figure 12.1) include stakeholder value, coordination and structural inertia, delegation and interdependence, firm-specific skills, profession and vocation, and dual structure. While there are differences in the details, the German business system shares with Japan the propensity for incremental innovation. In addition, German firms tend to be strong in industries requiring extensive professional or vocational training. Some aspects of the German training system as well as the dual structure seem to be applicable and relevant to the Chinese context.

Business System

Culture

German firms exist to produce economic value for the benefit of multiple stakeholders. Stakeholders in the mind-set of German executives typically include customers, employees, shareholders, society at large, and suppliers. As one executive summarized it:

[Our firm] is certainly driven by the vision ... that we can make a contribution to society, to our employees.... We do not only see the shareholder value, but we put more emphasis on the stakeholders, that is, all participants in firm activity, be those customers, suppliers, or our employees. Naturally not least also the investors.

No clear sense of priority of one group of stakeholders emerges. By implication, shareholders do not occupy a privileged position in the German

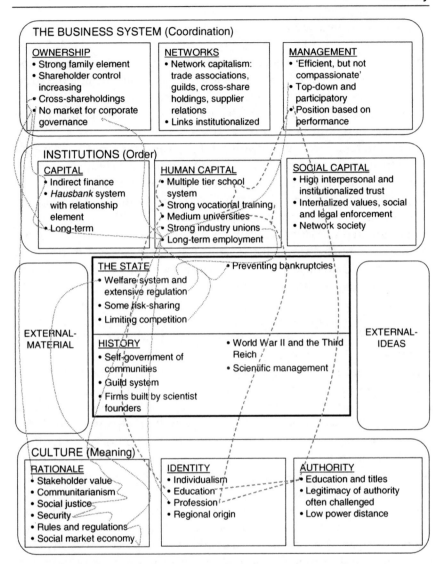

Figure 12.1. Key aspects of the German business system. The dotted lines indicate linkages supportive of incremental innovation, the dashed line, of industries requiring highly qualified personnel. For the sake of simplicity, only the main linkages are shown

mindset. Many of the senior executives we interviewed gave no special precedence to the concept of shareholder value. Instead, they tended to emphasize creation of economic value, which can then be distributed among the various stakeholders.

This is consistent with the communitarian underpinnings of German society. Deeply embedded in this mind-set is the concept of social justice, which is construed of as equality of outcomes, and a desire for protection against insecurity. Important means toward these ends include the structuring of society and life through rules and regulations and the ideal of the 'social market economy', which entails a strong social security system and redistribution of wealth from rich to poor.

Communitarian values notwithstanding, Germans tend to have an individualistic sense of identity, although comparative studies show Germans to be somewhat less individualistic than their Anglo-Saxon counterparts. The apparent contradiction between communitarianism and individualism is at least partially resolved through the institutionalization of communitarian solidarity. Solidarity is not expressed on an interpersonal level, but channeled through the state. The perceived need to maintain interpersonal harmony, which is crucial in group-based cultures, is low. Open exchange of ideas and criticism is welcomed and encouraged, in part because conformity is seen to have played a major role in sustaining and enabling the horrors of the Third Reich. Leading sources of identity are profession, educational and professional attainment as expressed in titles and positions, and geographic region of origin.

Authority relations are highly egalitarian. The respect and fear of superiors, also known as 'power distance,' is roughly on par with that found in northern European countries, the most egalitarian cluster of cultures. This reversal of historical conditioning represents a response to the Third Reich experience and is linked to egalitarian, nonconformist education that seeks to inculcate children against strong, nonconsensual leadership. As a consequence now, even legitimate authority relations can be difficult to establish and maintain.

A key dimension for establishing authority relations remains formal qualifications and titles. Especially academic titles instill respect, and a doctorate degree was long seen as a prerequisite for success both in public office and in the corporate world. Of the eight postwar chancellors, five earned at least a doctorate, and of the seventeen German executives interviewed for this project, only five—all active in finance—had no doctorate degree. Other formal qualifications, such as the vocational title of 'Meister' (master), also command respect, though to a lesser extent.

Government

The German state is fairly interventionist. The desire for stability and predictability in German society finds its expression in a multitude of rules and regulations in the economy that even Germans sometimes find cumbersome. For example, existing laws regulate how long shops are allowed to remain open and prohibit bakers from starting their work too early in the morning. Much of this intervention is related to the ideal of the social market economy and the desire to reduce volatility in economic life. Intervention further includes cartels, which are used to minimize the risk of bankruptcies, with about 400 approved cartels in existence in 2003. Where large-scale bankruptcies loom, the state often helps engineer a rescue package.

Despite this interventionist bent, the German state itself does not play a strong role in guiding the development of the economy. Even if it wanted to, it could not. The main reason for this inability is the federal structure of the state, which distributes the competences for economic policy between the federal and the state level. What was designed as a safeguard against a repeat of the strong state seen during the 1930s also makes strong economic leadership impossible, not least because state and federal governments often come from opposing parties. The picture is further complicated by the need to craft societal consensus. Economic policymaking requires extensive negotiations with representative organizations such as unions, guilds, and business associations.

Institutions

The German financial system is predominantly one of indirect finance, that is, based on bank loans. About 95 percent of the external funding of German firms comes in the form of loans, which tend to be long-term in nature. Loan decisions especially for SMEs, which form the industrial backbone of the German economy, have historically depended not only on creditworthiness, but also on the relationship between a firm and its main bank, or '*Hausbank*.' However, recent changes in regulations have forced banks to take a more market-based view of their lending relations. This may either lead a larger number of firms to raise funds in the still little developed equity market, or cause the atrophy of the SME sector by starving it of cash.

The public education system is generally well developed. Education is universal until the age of eighteen. Private schools and universities are rare and not seen as offering an inherently superior education. Responsibility for education lies predominantly in the hands of the individual states. The result is considerable variance in curricula and academic standards. International studies suggest that the further south one goes in

Germany, the higher the quality of the education system. The universities show some clusters of excellence, but are generally no longer among the world's best.

A special feature of the German education system that has survived especially in the south is the early sequestration of students into academic and vocational tracks. Starting as early as grade 5, high-potential students are separated and placed into *Gymnasium*, a form of university preparatory school. A middle layer is later moved to *Realschule* in preparation for commercial and administrative positions, and the remainder stays on to complete a basic education in *Hauptschule* (main school) until grade 9. Almost anyone not attending university will undergo an additional two to four years of vocational training, alternating between an apprenticeship in a firm and attending a vocational school. Selection criterion for the different tracks is academic attainment, as measured by grade-point average.

Unions are organized along industrial lines. They occupy a privileged position as an integral part of Germany's political landscape. In addition to their traditional role in collective bargaining, they have a say in most matters of economic policy, including the organization of the vocational training system and the administration of unemployment benefits. In addition, the German system of codetermination in firms gives them half of the seats on the supervisory board of corporations. Despite these privileges, union strength has been waning in recent years.

Similar to financial capital, the availability of human capital is long term. Average job tenures exceed eleven years, which jibes well with the desire for stability. Women tend to have shorter job tenures, both for family reasons and because German firms still tend to assume that men are the family breadwinners when deciding redundancies.

Social capital is relatively high. Germans have traditionally organized in groups such as associations and guilds, which provide an environment for building trust through repeated interaction. The number of business associations, standardized by population size, is about 50 percent higher than in the United States, though about 25 percent lower than in Japan. Along with this goes a propensity for networking. Institutional trust is still high, but dropping. Restructuring by firms and resultant high unemployment are seen as a sign that firms are no longer willing to play their part in society. The inability of the state to reduce significantly unemployment and limit its economic repercussions is undermining public confidence in the efficacy of the state.

Business System

Most large German firms are listed companies. Shareholders are viewed as important stakeholders, though their interests must be balanced against those of other stakeholders. The weight of shareholders in this equation has increased over the past decades as a consequence of financial globalization, but also because the political need to appease labor diminished with the end of the Cold War and the discrediting of socialism. Cross-shareholding is extensive. In addition, a number of large concerns, like Bertelsmann, BMW, and Porsche, continue to be fully or partially family-owned.

Cross-shareholdings and family ownership contribute to the virtual absence of a market for corporate control through hostile takeovers or buyouts. From 1990 through the end of 2004, only seven hostile takeovers were attempted in Germany, four of which were completed.

The German governance structure is unusual in that it features a two-tier board system. The management board is in charge of daily operations. Each of its members is individually responsible to the supervisory board. Under the principle of codetermination, unions receive half of the seats on the supervisory board for firms with more than 2,000 employees. The other half goes to representatives of capital, who are typically drawn from retired management board members of the company as well as representatives of banks and other firms holding a stake in the firm.

Germany is a network society, a feature that is facilitated by high social capital. Cross-shareholdings and interlocking directorates are common, even among competitors. Allianz, for example, holds shares in Deutsche Bank, but is also sole owner of Dresdner Bank, Germany's third largest private bank and thus a direct competitor of Deutsche. Many large firms also appear to maintain long-term relationships with suppliers.

Informal networking within and across industries is common and facilitated by the employers' associations. Since these are firmly established as the representatives of capital in Germany's political structure, membership takes on an almost compulsory nature, which gives associations an important role as network hubs. Chambers of commerce, guilds, and professional associations play an equivalent role for smaller businesses.

German management has been described as 'low on compassion, high on performance' (Brodbeck 2002). Error-free, competent performance is the standard against which employees will be judged. Performance issues are taken up directly and bluntly, in line with the low perceived need to maintain interpersonal harmony. Advancement and hierarchy are mostly contingent on performance and technical skills.

Decision-making involves a mixture of top-down and participatory elements. Firms are required by law to involve employee representatives in many management decisions such as redundancies under the principle of codetermination. The input of individual employees, however, is often limited to the election of the representatives and consultation with them. Similarly, management decisions are normally well deliberated in groups and consensual.

Key Themes

Stakeholder Value

Despite recent moves toward shareholder value, the main objective of the German firm continues to be the creation of economic value for the sake of all stakeholders. The 1997 World Values Survey shows that 63 percent of Germans favor the stakeholder-value view, as opposed to 29 percent in support of shareholder value. Most senior executives we interviewed seem to share this opinion.

This emphasis on serving no particular group, but all interested parties, can be traced to the concept of social justice as well as the desire to keep relations between labor and capital nonconflictual. This latter factor is also evident in other structural features of the business system, such as the principle of codetermination in corporate governance and the formal inclusion of unions in many aspects of economic and corporate decision-making. Stakeholder value also jibes with the need of German firms to build commitment among the workforce in order to encourage the formation of firm-specific skills that enable the production of highly specialized goods at high levels of quality.

Firms were historically able to emphasize stakeholder over shareholder value because the structure of the German financial and governance systems insulated them from the capital markets. High levels of cross- and long-term shareholding centered on the financial institutions such as Allianz, Munich Re, Deutsche Bank, and Dresdner Bank meant that long-term investors held a high proportion of shares. Firms have reportedly been selling off some of these holdings in recent years, but even today, other firms hold about 20 percent of outstanding shares. Indirect finance means that firms are little dependent on raising funds in the capital markets. And the requirement to staff half of the supervisory board with labor representatives places a limit on the influence of shareholders on corporate strategy.

Overall, however, stakeholder value has increasingly come under attack in Germany. There are three main reasons for this development. First, with the demise of the Soviet Union and the discrediting of the socialist models, capital has seen less of a reason to appease labor. Second, financial globalization has increased the influence of Anglo-Saxon investors, who have been more assertive in demanding returns to shareholders. Third, internationalization of the economy has enabled firms to put pressure on the unions by threatening to move production abroad. While it seems unlikely that German firms will abandon stakeholder value altogether, the weight of shareholders in the equation is undoubtedly on the rise.

Coordination and Structural Inertia

The German business system is highly coordinated and as a consequence generally very slow to change. Decisions on matters such as economic policymaking, restructuring of the business system, changes in rules and regulations, setting of wage levels, determining industrial standards, or deciding redundancies are almost always negotiated among associations representing the various stakeholders in the issue. For instance, a change in the law regulating opening hours of retail shops may entail formal and informal bargaining among state agencies, employers' associations, associations representing small shop-owners, unions, and the churches— the latter because of their interest in keeping shops closed on Sundays. The formation of bargaining positions within the various constituencies is facilitated by the encompassing membership of the representative associations, but also by the extensive social networks permeating society and the business world.

Decisions are typically not made until a consensus emerges that satisfies all stakeholders in the issue, which can take a very considerable time. Unlike in Japan, where consensus constitutes a tool of mitigating uncertainty and risk, the emphasis on consensus in the German system is a function of the political culture. Consensus-seeking is seen as an integral part of democratic processes and represents a tool for reducing political friction, especially between capital and labor. It also is an expression of the postwar German dislike for strong leadership exerted by any one part of society.

Delegation, Interdependence, Firm-specific Skills

German organizations show relatively high levels of delegation and inter-dependence, though to a lower extent than their Japanese counterparts. Underlying this theme are essentially the same structural features seen in the Japanese case, especially the tendency toward long-term employment.

As in the Japanese case, long-term employment tends to encourage employees to develop firm-specific skills. However, in contrast with Japan, where employees acquire virtually all their relevant skills in on-the-job training, qualified German employees enter after having undergone years of vocational, academic, or professional training. The result is dedication to the line of business of the company, though with a strong under-current of professional pride. So while Japanese engineers may strive to produce the best products needed by their firms in order to compete, German engineers have a tendency to seek to build the best product possible without necessarily taking into consideration their firms' market position. The consequences are a German propensity for overengineering and not adding features desired by customers. For example, Daimler-Benz engineers used to refuse to fit Mercedes cars with the cup holders US customers demanded, on the grounds that these were inappropriate in a proper vehicle.

Profession and Vocation

Profession and vocation are taken extremely seriously in the German business system. The German term, *Beruf*, is etymologically linked to *Berufung*, which translates to 'calling' and suggests divine intervention and preordainment (as does the Latin root of the English term 'vocation'). This is linked to the medieval guild structure, in which professional association was passed on from generation to generation and thus de facto preordained by birth. While the free choice of profession is guaranteed in the German constitution, elements of the medieval apprenticeship structure survive in the present-day vocational training system. A key advantage of the professional system as practiced in Germany is that those certified as members of a profession are typically very well qualified in their craft. A concern is that this system introduces considerable rigidity into the business system. For individuals, their profession is often a source of personal identity, and many are averse to changing profession even at the pain of long-term unemployment. Firms typically offer employment even for simple tasks only to those with the proper professional certification, and in many professions, only a *Meister* (master) may start his or her own business.

Dual Structure

The German economy is built on a mixture of large multinational corporations as well as a plenitude of SMEs known collectively as *Mittelstand*. What is unusual about the German case is that *Mittelstand* firms tend to be highly competitive and export oriented. The German machine-tool industry, for instance, consists almost entirely of SMEs. *Mittelstand* firms are heavily concentrated in the southern states of Germany, especially Baden-Württemberg. They tend to be family-run and deeply embedded in the communities in which they are located. Features of the German economy such as stakeholder value and long termism, especially in employment, are typically much more pronounced in these firms. Commitment from the workforce is consequently high, which enables these firms to pursue a strategy of high-quality, highly specialized, and highly flexible production in small lot sizes. This system is critically dependent on the availability of long-term finance at low costs of capital. Both are under threat, the former by new banking regulations, and the latter by the relatively high interest rates accompanying the European currency union.

Comparative Advantage

Germany's comparative advantage is strongest in medium–high technology manufacturing industries (see Figure 12.2), especially motor vehicles, machinery and equipment, and chemicals. Its greatest area of comparative disadvantage, travel, is explained by the high propensity of Germans to spend their six weeks of vacations outside Germany, especially in the more reliably clement climes of southern Europe.

Germany's largest comparative advantage is in motor vehicles, at +4.1 percent of overall trade. Leading manufacturers are Volkswagen (including Audi and a whole series of other brands), DaimlerChrysler, BMW, and Porsche, as well as truck manufacturer MAN. Most German carmakers focus on building premium cars, which cater to the drive to offer the best engineering possible. In addition, both Ford and General Motors have large manufacturing facilities for the European market in Germany, and Germany is home to strong parts-suppliers such

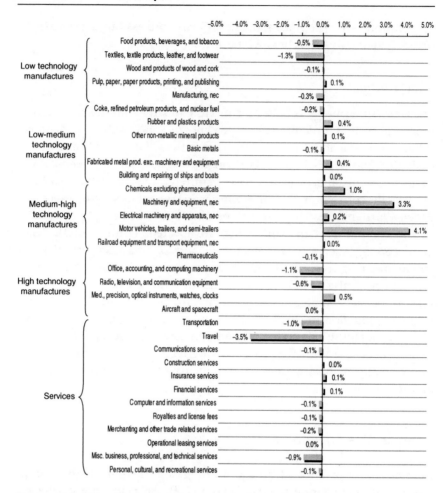

Figure 12.2. German comparative advantage by industries, 2003 (OECD own calculations). See appendix for details.

as Robert Bosch. Key competitive strengths of German cars have been prestige, performance, and reliability. While the ability of the industry to deliver on performance has been strong continuously, reliability has only recently returned to levels competitive with those offered by Japanese manufacturers.

The second largest comparative advantage of German industry is in machinery and equipment (+3.3 percent). Products counted toward this industry include general-purpose machinery such as engines and turbines, pumps, bearings and gears, and compressors; special-purpose machinery such as agricultural, mining, construction, food processing, and textile manufacturing equipment as well as machine tools; and domestic appliances such as refrigerators and dishwashers. Many of Germany's producers of machinery and machine tools are *Mittelstand* firms with fewer than 500 employees. Large players include Robert Bosch, ThyssenKrupp, and MAN. Robert Bosch is not only a major producer of automotive parts, it is also active in the manufacture of industrial technology such as packaging equipment and, through a joint venture with Siemens, household appliances. ThyssenKrupp is known for its involvement in steel production, but it also active in mechanical engineering and the production of elevators. MAN, finally, makes not only commercial vehicles, but also printing systems, industrial equipment and systems, diesel engines, and turbo machines such as industrial turbines. All these firms derive far more revenue from foreign markets than from Germany. The major selling point of German machinery is quality and precision.

A third, though relatively smaller, area of comparative advantage is in chemicals (+1.0 percent). Leading players are BASF and Bayer, by revenue the world's numbers one and three in the chemicals business and very heavily involved outside Germany. Both firms trace their origin to an entrepreneurial boom in organic dyes in the late nineteenth century. Supported by strong ties to leading German researchers, German firms such as BASF, Bayer, and Hoechst quickly became world market leaders. German domination of the chemicals industry was such that until the 1970s, chemistry reference works worldwide were published in German. While this dominance has since been challenged by the likes of Dow Chemical and DuPont, German chemical firms continue to derive part of their competitive strength from their ability to draw on highly qualified chemists, engineers, and related personnel in the German market.

Especially the motor vehicles and machinery industries benefit from German strength in incremental innovation. The foundations of this tendency are the same as we have seen for the Japanese case: long-term finance enabling long-term employment, which in turn gives an incentive to invest in firm-specific skills. This combines with a strong undercurrent of general skills acquired in training before joining the firm, which makes it possible for smaller firms that may not have the resources to train employees themselves to compete at world-class levels. As in the Japanese case, firms tend to be risk averse and thus prefer taking small steps, which is linked to the German desire for protection against insecurity.

German firms also tend to perform well in industries requiring high levels of vocational or professional training. Engineering and chemistry are leading pockets of excellence at German universities, and strong public vocational training systems are in place to feed qualified labor to these industries.

The German system is less geared toward radical innovation. Long-term finance and employment reduce the ability of firms to redeploy resources quickly, as does the tendency not to employ people outside the profession or vocation in which they received formal training. Bank-led finance limits the ability of firms to take risk, and venture capital still tends to be relatively underdeveloped. Coordination and structural inertia limit the ability to produce rapid institutional change in response to technological progress.

The German business system further tends to be weak in marketing-driven industries. In line with professional pride, firms have had a tendency to focus on building the best product possible, in the conviction that customers will appreciate the engineering prowess displayed. German industry has only relatively recently begun to discover that customers' notions of what represents the ideal product may diverge from those held by engineers.

Applicability to China

For reasons that we have already elaborated in the chapter on Japan, it is unlikely that the themes of stakeholder value, societal coordination, delegation and interdependence, as well as firm-specific skills will play a major role in the evolution of the Chinese business system.

While the German pride in profession and vocation are cultural characteristics not easily transferable to China, parts of the underlying infrastructure can, and have been, adapted to the Chinese context. The present Chinese vocational training system, for instance, draws on the German system as one of its models. In addition, German firms active in China have collaborated with Chinese authorities in a number of localities to open German-style training centers, apparently with some success. Some of the details, however, are likely to be lost in translation. For instance, the setting of occupational standards in Germany is a coordinated process that depends heavily on input from employers, through their respective associations, and unions. Since both associations and unions in China are penetrated by the state, it is unlikely that the dynamics of adjusting standards to changing requirements will mirror those seen in Germany. This may be a good thing if the influence of the state accelerates the speed of adaptation and leads to more forward-looking certification standards. On the other hand, bureaucrats of any country are a notoriously bad source of business-related foresight.

China already possesses a dual structure with highly competitive SMEs. Whether it can sustain it over the long term is a different question. SMEs have been able to thrive in the private sector as providers of cheap labor. Over time, competitive pressure from other, less-developed nations is likely to push China up the value chain into more skill- and capital-intensive processes and industries. The problem, at least for now, is that neither skilled labor nor capital is available to SMEs in sufficient quantity; nor is professional management. Skilled labor will tend to work for foreign enterprises with higher wages, and even foreign firms complain of the talent pool being too small. The financial system continues to funnel capital to the large SOEs. SMEs have very limited access to bank loans, unlike their counterparts in Germany. Nor can they access the stock market, as might some of their US counterparts. The upshot is that unless policymakers recognize a vibrant dual structure as a competitive asset for the future, the SME sector may atrophy from a lack of human and financial capital.

Key References

Brodbeck, Felix C., Michael Frese, and Mansour Javidan. 2002. 'Leadership Made in Germany: Low on Compassion, High on Performance', *Academy of Management Executive*, 16(1): 13–5.

Dore, Ronald Philip. 2000. *Stock Market Capitalism: Welfare Capitalism: Japan and Germany Versus the Anglo-Saxons*. Oxford: Oxford University Press.

Hall, Peter A., and David Soskice, eds. 2001. *Varieties of Capitalism: The Institutional Foundations of Comparative Advantage*. Oxford: Oxford University Press.

Redding, Gordon, and Michael A. Witt. 2004. 'The Role of Executive Rationale in the Comparison of Capitalisms: Some Preliminary Findings', *INSEAD EAC Working Paper Series*. Fontainebleau, France.

Siebert, Horst. 2005. *The German Economy: Beyond the Social Market*. Princeton, NJ: Princeton University Press.

Streeck, Wolfgang. 1997. 'German Capitalism: Does It Exist? Can It Survive?', *New Political Economy*, 2(2): 237–56.

Whitley, Richard. 1999. *Divergent Capitalisms: The Social Structuring and Change of Business Systems*. Oxford: Oxford University Press.

Witt, Michael A. 2006. *Changing Japanese Capitalism: Societal Coordination and Institutional Adjustment*. Cambridge: Cambridge University Press.

13

South Korea

The South Korean business system is a classic example of state-led capitalism. Key themes are patriotism, the state and the *chaebol*, family control, and labor relations (see Figure 13.1). The system seems to be well suited for a strategy of close technology follower, especially in industries that do not require high skill levels on the shop floor. Much of what we see in South Korea could be applicable to the Chinese case.

South Korea

Culture

South Korea presents itself as a torn country in terms of the underlying rationale of business. Professional managers and many in the older generation of company owners tend to stress the importance of contributing to the country and to economic development as the reason for doing business. As one executive put it, 'I think job creation the most important. And then . . . [strengthening] the related industries. And make money, bring in the foreign currency.' This is linked to national pride, but also a collective sense of vulnerability related to centuries of aggression by China and Japan, most immediately expressed in occupation and colonization by Japan (1905–45), as well as the threat of war emanating from North Korea. In this mode of thinking, strong leadership by the state and collective effort are emphasized as appropriate responses.

By contrast, especially the younger generation of company owners tends to emphasize shareholder value. This schism seems to be an aftereffect of the 'IMF Crisis' of 1997–8, which interviewees consistently identify as a watershed in their thinking about firm and economy. In addition, many of the younger owner generation attended college or business

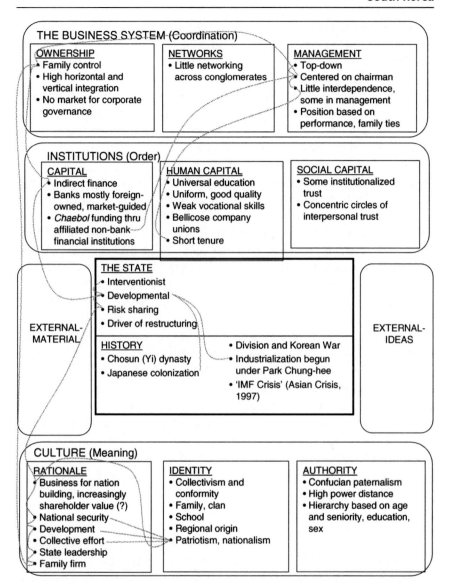

Figure 13.1. Key aspects of the South Korean business system. The dotted lines indicate linkages supporting a fast follower strategy. For the sake of simplicity, only the main linkages are shown.

school in the United States and returned inculcated with the idea of shareholder value. Actual behavior suggests that the concept in many minds seems to equate with creating the largest benefits possible for the founding family of the concern.

Korean society espouses a highly collective sense of identity. Comparative studies suggest that collectivism is more strongly developed in Korea than virtually anywhere else, though the scores for China tend to be close. Conformity levels are high, and deviance from social norms and expectations is frowned upon. There is an emphasis on preserving harmony in human relations, though Koreans are reputed to have somewhat shorter fuses than the Japanese. Korean sources of identity and affiliation mirror the model of concentric circles found in China. The most important sources of identity are the family and clan as well as school ties. There is also a very strong sense of national pride, bordering on nationalism, which can be linked to centuries of threat to the survival of the nation.

Authority relations are quite hierarchical and structured along Confucian lines. Power-distance scores are slightly higher than in Japan, but still a good deal lower than those observed in China. The paternalistic element of Confucianism is well preserved. Within the family, authority rests with the father, who in turn owes obedience to his father and elder brothers. This pattern is replicated in firms, with the company chairman in the position of ultimate authority. True to Confucian teaching, obedience is typically unconditional, and authority, rarely questioned. Well preserved are further the respect for age and educational attainment, whose expressions closely mirror those we discussed for Japan. At the same time, the authority of leaders is only legitimate if they, in turn, look after their people.

Government

The main role of Korean government in the economy is to promote economic development. Modern Korean governments have tended to be very strong, at times with near complete control of the economy. Economic policy aims to induce firms to move up the value chain to more capital- and technology-intensive industries with higher value-added. Firms entering new industries received, and to some extent still receive, protection from foreign competition in the domestic market, but are expected to compete in the world markets through exports. In the initial phases of development under President Park Chung-hee, firms failing to meet export quotas would be shut down.

Korean government follows Confucian notions, with a powerful president occupying the position of the emperor who is supported by an elite cadre of highly educated bureaucrats. Consistent with the Confucian model of government, the making and implementation of policy has tended to be a top-down process. The growth of the large conglomerates, the *chaebol*, has chipped away at the absolute hold on power enjoyed by earlier governments, but not eliminated it.

Institutions

The Korean financial system relies largely on indirect finance through bank loans. Banks used to be state owned, and loans used to be for the long-term and allocated according to government policy. Risk assessment did not play an important role in lending decisions, as indicated by average debt/equity ratios exceeding 500 percent in 1997, with some firms exceeding 3,000 percent. This picture changed radically following the IMF crisis. The major banks now tend to be majority owned by international banks and investors. The implication is that loan decisions and terms are now governed mostly by market conditions. The major conglomerates have responded to this development by founding nonbank financial institutions and sourcing part of their funds through them.

The public education system is well developed, with the exception of vocational training. In line with Confucian thought, education is highly prized. Education is universal through high school, and almost 80 percent of students move on to tertiary education. Both public and private schools exist, but as in Japan, private education does not automatically imply higher status. The university held in highest esteem, Seoul National University, is public, as is the Korean Advanced Institute of Science and Technology, the country's premier postgraduate institution. Control over the curriculum is highly centralized, and success is determined on the basis of entrance examinations for every level of schooling, sometimes including kindergarten. Many Korean parents spend a fortune on cram schools for their children in order to enhance their chances of passing these entrance examinations.

Unions are organized along company lines. They were suppressed for many years, and most companies still view them with hostility. Unions gained strength with democratization and the election victories of the pro-labor Presidents Kim Dae-jung and Rho Moo-hyun. Conditioned by autocratic management styles and low internal transparency, labor disputes tend to be frequent, drawn out, and violent. Korean executives unanimously view labor relations as the greatest problem of the Korean economy.

Labor has tended to be engaged on a short-term basis. Labor tenures are even shorter than those registered in the United States, especially for women. Most mobile seem to be blue-collar workers and highly trained personnel. The redundancies of the IMF Crisis, which revealed the promise of lifetime employment as hollow, further reduced loyalty to the firm.

Historically, the institutionalized form of social capital was relatively scarce in Korean society. Centuries of weak and often corrupt government created little trust in the ability of the state to provide for fair and equitable outcomes. Since the 1960s, however, the state has been able to provide a relatively predictable environment for economic growth. This has contributed to the accretion of institutionalized trust, though at levels that are still low relative to those in the other advanced industrial countries we have discussed. Trust at the personal level consequently remains important in Korean society. Similar to the Chinese system, this personal trust is laid out in concentric circles, weakening with distance from the center. At the core lies the family, followed by the larger clan, personal and school friends, and finally individuals from the same region. The opportunities for social networking across group boundaries are consequently relatively limited in Korean society, especially when compared to societies like Japan's or Germany's.

Business System

Most *chaebol* are widely held, but de facto controlled by the founding family and thus essentially family businesses. This resonates with the cultural trait of familism and the structure of social capital. Government has made considerable efforts in recent years to improve corporate governance. Before the Crisis, the board of directors used to be staffed almost exclusively with insiders, who exerted no effective control over the chairman. Shareholder-rights protection was weak. Since then, government has sought to introduce outside directors, strengthen shareholder rights, improve accounting and disclosure, and make takeovers easier. However, many of these reforms do not appear to be legally binding, and enforcement of the existing provisions seems to be toothless. No market in corporate control exists, with only two hostile takeovers attempted between 1990 and 2004, both of which were successful.

Networking with firms outside the same family of *chaebol* firms is weakly developed. The *chaebol* followed a growth strategy of vertical integration, which has made them relatively independent of outside suppliers. The size of the *chaebol* allows them to squeeze those outside suppliers that do exist, rather than to cooperate with them as in Japan. Though the founding families of the leading *chaebol* tend to be well acquainted on a personal level, a high sense of rivalry means that cooperation among *chaebol* is rare. This has important implications for collective action of any sort, including lobbying government and cooperation in R & D consortia.

Korean management practices tend to be top-down and authoritarian. This is related to the structure of authority in Korean society and may have been reinforced by compulsory military training for every Korean male. The role of subordinates seems to be largely limited to obeying their superiors, who do not necessarily show the benevolence for which Confucian teachings call. Delegation of tasks tends to be very limited, with high supervision of task performance. This is related to the very short job tenures of Korean employees.

Most major management decisions originate in the chairman's office. This allows for quick decision-making, but carries with it the known risks of centralized planning resulting from disregarding information known only to 'the man on the spot' (Hayek 1945). Firms have attempted to mitigate this risk by keeping large staff attached to the chairman's office for consultations. Samsung, in a deviation, has made it a point to build a strategic planning group staffed exclusively with foreign MBAs to increase the quality of its strategic decision-making.

Key Themes

Patriotism

A key driving force underlying Korean economic dynamism is a strong sense of patriotism and national identity. As a relatively small country situated between two large and not always friendly neighbors—China and Japan—Korea's historical position in northeast Asia was similar to that of Poland in Europe: constantly under threat. Japan is still resented for its colonization of Korea (1905–45), and especially for the attempt to assimilate the country fully by eradicating Korean culture. After World War II, North Korea and, by extension, China and the Soviet Union, replaced Japan as the dominant source of external threat. The North

Korean economy in the 1950s grew at about three times the pace of that in South Korea, prompting Park Chung-hee to assume power in a coup and initiate drastic economic reforms.

The traditional rationale for the existence of the firm, contributing to the building of South Korea, reflects this strong sense of patriotism and identification with the nation. Patriotism also underlies a striking willingness to make sacrifices. For instance, during the IMF Crisis, many citizens sold their stocks of gold, which is exchanged as a traditional gift, for won in order to help stabilize the currency.

The State and the Chaebol

The state played a central role in the rapid industrial development that commenced in 1963 under the auspices of President Park Chung-hee. Korean industrial policy mostly followed the Japanese template, though with some differences. For one, Park nationalized the banks. This assured that government had full control over directed lending that channeled funds to targeted industries, first to light, later to heavy industries. For the individual business, funding and other government services such as licenses and permits were conditional upon meeting export quotas set by the government as measures of economic performance. Businesses meeting these targets would receive further funds and permits to expand into new industries; those failing to make the cut would be shut down. Cooperation among firms, common in Japan, has been difficult to achieve in Korea because of the intense rivalry among *chaebol*, which is related to familism and the structure of social capital.

Also unlike postwar Japan, the targeted firms in Korea were family enterprises. Many leaders of these enterprises, the *chaebol*, had started their businesses under the Japanese colonial regime or under the notoriously corrupt government of President Syngman Rhee. The taint of collaboration and corruption, and of doing business in a society whose Confucian disdain of commerce made many averse to economic activity, increased government leverage over the *chaebol*. Park's government initially arrested business leaders on corruption charges, and only by pledging their full devotion to 'nation-building through industrialization' under Park's terms would they receive exemption from punishment. Unlike in Japan, where the relationship between business, business associations, and government was collaborative (though not equal), the relationship between state and business in Korea was clearly one-sided in favor of the state. Strong rivalries and the heavy hand of the state largely prevented Korean business from forming associations that could have served as a counterweight to state power.

Park's explicit aim was to create 'mammoth enterprises', and in the *chaebol*, he succeeded. The four largest *chaebol*—Samsung, Hyundai, LG, and SK—together have assets worth more than 40 percent of GDP and sales worth about two-thirds of GDP. While government retains ultimate power over the survival of the *chaebol*, it has to tread carefully in dealing with them so as not to kill the geese that lay golden eggs. One government means for signaling who is in charge seems to be the occasional singling out of one of the *chaebol* to make an example of it. Tax audits are a popular means, as is withdrawal or withholding of support. For instance, the refusal of government to prevent Daewoo's bankruptcy during the IMF Crisis can apparently be traced to bad relations between President Kim Dae-jung and Daewoo's chairman Kim Woo-jung.

Family Control

Founding families remain in control of the *chaebol*, even though in 2000, these families controlled on average only 4.5 percent of the total equity of the thirty largest *chaebol*. To retain control, the founding families augment their ownership by pyramidal or circular ownership patterns. In the former case, the founding family holds a controlling stake in one member firm of the *chaebol*, which in turn holds a controlling stake in other subsidiaries, and so on. The Lee family of Samsung, for instance, controls the conglomerate through its stake in Samsung Everland, an unlisted amusement park company serving as its de facto holding company. In the circular pattern formerly used, for example, by the Cheong family of Hyundai, firm A owns parts of firm B, which owns parts of firm C, which in turn owns parts of firm A. Through these mechanisms, the founding families of the thirty largest *chaebol* in 2000 de facto held around 43.4 percent of *chaebol* equity, enough for operational control. The effect of the Asian Crisis and government efforts at *chaebol* reform has been limited: direct ownership has halved, but an increase in the in-group ownership of shares has counterbalanced this development. Most *chaebol* thus continue to be run out of the chairman's office, with the chairman in most cases being a lineal descendent of the group founder.

Labor Relations

Relations between labor and management are highly conflictual. Per worker, Korea loses more working days to strikes than the other four industrialized countries considered in this book. An important cause lies in the top-down, nonparticipatory management structure typical of Korean firms. As a consequence, the motivations for management decisions affecting workers adversely are often ambiguous. For instance, if management claims that a wage freeze is necessary to respond to economic conditions, it is difficult for workers to verify independently whether management is telling the truth or trying to increase profits by squeezing labor. One of the key demands of Korean unions has thus been the introduction of German-style codetermination. Given strong resistance from management against codetermination and the culturally conditioned unwillingness to increase internal transparency through Japanese-style participatory management, pacification of Korean labor relations in the foreseeable future looks unlikely.

Comparative Advantage

South Korea's main areas of comparative advantage are in (1) motor vehicles; (2) office, accounting, and computing machinery as well as radio, television, and communications equipment; and (3) shipbuilding (see Figure 13.2).

The major comparative advantage of Korea is in the automobile sector (+4.1 percent). The single remaining large Korean producer is Hyundai Motor Company, which also owns Kia Motors Corporation. Foreign automobile firms acquired all other Korean manufacturers during or after the 1997–8 Asian financial crisis: General Motors snapped up Daewoo, and Renault acquired Samsung Motors. Hyundai Motors began producing cars in 1967, the same year as Honda, under license from Ford. As required by Korea's industrial policy, exports commenced almost immediately. Hyundai cars initially sold in international markets entirely on the basis of price. In recent years, the company has made much progress in terms of quality, not least by investing heavily in its engineering force. Success in this is expressed, among others, in strongly improving initial quality ratings by J. D. Power. The present basis of competitive strength for Hyundai is thus a combination of competitive pricing, which remains below the price point of Japanese manufacturers, and good and improving quality.

As a cautionary note, we should point out that the actual size of comparative advantage in automobiles is almost certainly smaller than

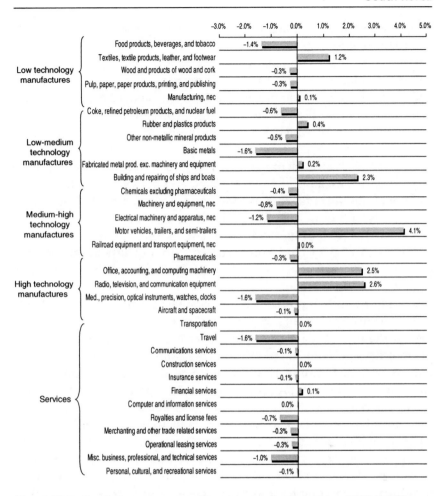

Figure 13.2. South Korean comparative advantage by industries, 2003 (OECD own calculations). See appendix for details.

our calculations show. The reason for this is strong import protection of the South Korean car market through government measures such as tariffs and tax audits of purchasers of foreign cars. As a result, foreign cars command a share of only about 3 percent in the South Korean market, which compares unfavorably even with the notoriously difficult Japanese car market, of which foreign brands have managed to capture about 5 percent. South Korean car-makers can thus charge higher prices in the domestic market and use the rents gained in this fashion to subsidize exports. The result is higher exports and lower imports than would otherwise be the case, though we cannot quantify the precise impact on comparative advantage.

The second largest comparative advantage is in office, accounting, and computing machinery and the closely related area of radio, television, and communications equipment (+2.5 percent and +2.6 percent). The main players in both areas are the same: Samsung Electronics and LG Electronics, both of which are among the world's top electronics and electrical-equipment producers and sell most of their products abroad. Both concerns share most of their areas of competitive strength, including displays and televisions, mobile handsets, and household appliances. In addition, Samsung ranks as one of the world's most competitive producers of memory chips, an area from which LG withdrew when it merged its semiconductor business with Hyundai's to form Hynix. Both makers derive much of their competitive strength from quality at competitive prices, though they continue to be heavily dependent on production equipment made in Japan.

South Korea further possesses a comparative advantage in shipbuilding (+2.3 percent). Korean shipbuilders are global market leaders, commanding a world market share exceeding 40 percent in 2003. Major players in the industry are Hyundai Heavy Industries, which is the world's number one, as well as Samsung Heavy Industries, and Daewoo Shipbuilding and Marine Engineering. All three are heavily export-oriented to a point where Daewoo sells almost all its products abroad. Their competitive strength is built on a cost advantage of about 10 percent compared with Japanese shipbuilders, their closest competitors. In the long term, the rise of Chinese shipyards is likely to threaten this area of Korean comparative advantage, though Korean shipyards have been trying to respond by focusing on more complex and technology-intensive vessels with higher value-added.

The Korean business system thus seems to show particular strength in areas requiring quick decision-making, quick deployment of labor, risk tolerance, and the long-term availability of large sums of capital. Significant also is an organizational capacity to coordinate complex activities at large scale. The top-down nature of decision-making in *chaebol* makes it possible to change course, or enter new industries, quickly. One *chaebol* owner pointed out that decisions that took Japanese firms months to reach could be fully implemented in his group within 3 days. This form of decision-making is risky, as it does not take all available information into account. At least for the large *chaebol* like Samsung, Hyundai, or

LG, this risk is mitigated by the fact that they are too big for the Korean government to allow them to fail.

Low labor loyalty and limited specialized technical expertise mean that redeployment of labor is relatively easy. At the same time, it tends to discourage the acquisition of deep firm-specific skills of the sort seen in Japanese and German firms. The relatively high comparative disadvantage in industries relying on labor skill, such as medical, precision and optical instruments, watches and clocks, and machinery in general is likely to be related to this characteristic. Hyundai seems to have addressed this issue at least partially in the context of automobiles, an industry that tends to benefit from incremental innovation, by investing massively in its engineering force. It remains to be seen, however, whether the company can thrive in the long term once the South Korean domestic market stops benefiting from the current protection from international competition.

Overall, the Korean business system seems to be predisposed for a strategy of close follower. Korean business can make up its mind quickly, and it can redeploy labor and capital at relatively high speeds at relatively low costs. However, its overall technological basis is still weak, as the dependence on foreign equipment shows. The dominant strategy for the *chaebol* may thus be to observe nascent industries until the period of foment has passed and then pounce, relying on competitive advantages in labor and capital costs. This is consistent with *chaebol* behavior in industries like memory chips, LCDs, or cellular phones, where Korean firms rolled up the market coming from behind. It is also in line with the promotion of venture capital by many *chaebol* families, for instance, through the society. It may be possible that their efforts to promote startups may represent a vehicle for the *chaebol* to reduce the risks associated with high technology while retaining the option of entering the industry if it proves successful.

Applicability to China

Many of the key characteristics and themes of the South Korean economy jibe quite well with the Chinese context. There are important differences in many details, but overall, China may develop over time a similar capacity as South Korea in areas requiring quick decision-making, quick deployment of labor, risk tolerance, and the long-term availability of large sums of capital. The essential challenge is how to take family-dominated business to very large scale—at world standards of efficiency—in the Chinese context.

Just as in Korea, economic development and business in general does carry patriotic connotations. This is especially true for the SOEs that the Chinese state intends to transform into world-beating multinational enterprises. It rings true, however, also for much private business, thanks to Deng Xiaoping's famous dictum that 'to get rich is glorious.' The connotation in the minds of Chinese entrepreneurs is that by enriching themselves, they are also serving the nation. Similar thoughts may be in the minds of the owner families of the South Korea *chaebol*.

Like the Korean state, the Chinese state actively intervenes in the economy to further economic development, and it engages in considerable risk-sharing with designated SOEs. On the other hand, its capacity to control and steer the economy is much less developed than in the Korean case. Part of this is, as we have seen, a result of design, such as decentralization in order to allow for local experimentation. Even if the Chinese state had wanted to, however, it would almost certainly not have been able to seize as tight control of the country as the Korean state managed to do. Not least because of China's size, there has always been considerable slack in the bureaucratic administration of the country. Korea, by contrast, inherited a strongly centralized and highly efficient bureaucratic machine from its Japanese colonizers.

In contrast with present Chinese government policy, South Korean policymakers saw family control, and if in name only, of the *chaebol* as an appropriate means of growing 'mammoth enterprises.' In doing so, of course, Korea explicitly followed the example of prewar Japan, where the major industrial conglomerates (Mitsubishi, Mitsui, Sumitomo, Yasuda) were all under control of a handful of major industrial families. The Korean policy of allowing only those *chaebol* with outstanding export performance to survive ensured that those individuals with the greatest entrepreneurial talent were at the helm of Korea's infant multinational enterprises. As we now know, the policy succeeded spectacularly—to such extent, in fact, that one of the most burning issues of Korean economic policy today is how to make the economy less dependent on the industrial dynasties it has bred.

With its strong tradition of family business, China would in principle be well positioned to take a page out of Korea's book. Instead, it has chosen to leave private entrepreneurs to their own devices and tries to reform its most promising SOEs into viable 'mammoth enterprises.' This raises the question of whether really those with the greatest business talent are running the firms that are supposed to be at the heart of the future Chinese economy. A halfway solution might be to allow private entrepreneurs to seize control of the key SOEs, subject to clear and strictly enforced performance criteria. However, even if suitable entrepreneurs could be persuaded to give up their own concerns in the private sector in order to run SOEs, it seems highly unlikely that the Chinese state will adopt so radical a measure for what it perceives to be the crown jewels in its industrial portfolio.

While no one of sound mind would want to emulate South Korean labor relations, there is a distinct possibility that China may inadvertently end up with a similar state of affairs. Just as in Korea, Chinese management is top-down and nonparticipative, and managerial motivations are opaque. And just as in South Korea before the 1980s, the Chinese government suppresses labor protests and independent labor organizations. Once the lid of government suppression comes off, as it did in South Korea in the 1980s, labor militancy is a distinct prospect.

Key References

Amsden, Alice H. 1989. *Asia's Next Giant: South Korea and Late Industrialization*. Oxford: Oxford University Press.

Hayek, Friedrich Anton. 1945. 'The Use of Knowledge in Society', *American Economic Review*, 35: 519–30.

OECD. 2005. *OECD Economic Surveys: Korea*. Paris: OECD.

Redding, Gordon, and Michael A. Witt. 2004. 'The Role of Executive Rationale in the Comparison of Capitalisms: Some Preliminary Findings', *INSEAD EAC Working Paper Series*. Fontainebleau, France.

Song, Byung-Nak. 2003. *The Rise of the Korean Economy*. Oxford: Oxford University Press.

Whitley, Richard. 1999. *Divergent Capitalisms: The Social Structuring and Change of Business Systems*. Oxford: Oxford University Press.

Witt, Michael A. 2003. 'From Last to Fast: Political and Economic Transformation in Korea, 1961', *INSEAD Case Study*. Singapore: INSEAD.

14

The Future of Chinese Capitalism

We have taken readers through a sequence of steps beginning with a posing of questions about the nature of economic 'miracles'. Why do some countries grow rich? To answer such questions requires a perspective wide enough to cover most of the key features of an explanation, and dynamic enough in its use to allow for the shifts and trends of history. Having presented such a framework, we then exercised it to show how China has various trajectories of industrial progress within it, and we presented the three main ones. We also introduced alternative systems of capitalism found in other countries to see what might be learned from them. We now move from what might be possible to what we think is likely to happen, and we do so in the context of the features of societal evolution used as a framework through the book.

More than any other large society China displays a history in which individuals exert immense influence. Without Mao Zedong, Deng Xiaoping, Zhu Rongji, and Jiang Zemin, China would have been very different indeed. As each of them took hold of power, the country was changing dramatically, and it was largely their personal vision that shaped its next phase. Although now the tendency for the elite to be technocrats is firmly established, with top positions of influence held by engineers, there is nonetheless always the chance of a return to dominance by a surrogate emperor. It is with this caveat that we proceed to read the tea leaves.

We began at the outset to consider how societies develop successfully. In doing so we identified four questions to be asked of any society as it moves toward the modern (or postmodern) condition of very high GDP per capita. These questions point to challenges to be dealt with, and whereas all societies face them, they do not deal with them in the same way. The questions are universal, the answers are specific to each country. The questions were about (*a*) horizontal order sponsoring exchange;

(b) the rational pursuit of legitimate purposes; (c) vertical order sponsoring appropriate motivation; and (d) incorporating innovation. Our focus of interest is the society's economic life, not its political evolution—although these are inextricably entwined with each other. Most of the understanding of how the economic challenges are met comes to rest upon the organization and management of firms. But that itself is not enough. The 'how' is multifaceted, and we will need to call upon all the boxes of the theory to describe those facets.

Trust and Mistrust

We have called trust 'social capital', and we have identified it with two main origins: the society's capacity to apply rationality to the organization of economic life, and the society's formulae for identity—where you belong—in the social fabric. This latter is the basis for the horizontal order across which trust needs to stretch. We have also noted the two main forms of trust: that deriving from institutions such as law and regulation, and the other deriving from networks of interpersonal obligation. In China the latter predominates by a wide margin. Institutional trust is still in its infancy and its growth is not aided by any collective memory of its existence in the past. It is a new phenomenon in the Chinese sociopolitical arena, and the immediate historical legacy from Mao is the experience of extreme, and often frightening, central control, the worst form of nursery for such a delicate plant. The apparatus for that control is still in place, although its abuse in the present era grows less likely as time passes and as success releases some of the tensions and fears that feed the obsession with control that has always marked Chinese governments. It should in this context be noted that control is also the expression of traditional ethical duty to preserve an orderly state, and is not just crude authoritarianism.

Our question was first stated as follows: How does the society build stable, widespread horizontal order of a kind that fosters efficient exchange between economic units across the society? On what basis does trust work and how? Put simply, can you trust a stranger? In China you cannot, so what are the implications?

China's most efficient response to this issue has been network capitalism. Small and medium firms escape from their scale limitations by becoming very specialized, and thus efficient, but linked with other equally specialized firms in stable but flexible networks. The circles of trust are small and limited by the individual capacities to cope with the social interactions and obligations involved. The efficiency of the resulting total system of production is based on two features: (*a*) low transaction costs between the units, a feature achieved by the use of interpersonal trust bonds and the absence of formalities like elaborate legal contracts and negotiations; and (*b*) high efficiency inside the units because of intense control of costs and performance by owner–managers. The flexibility of adjustment within the network, and the speed of response to changes in demand are further competitive advantages.

At a larger scale, another form of networking occurs in the case of the local corporates, known as 'clan capitalism.' The name refers to the presence of strong local networks stretching across the political and economic domains. Here networks of alliance are formed, usually in a urban or regional context, between local officials, entrepreneurs, and often foreign partners bringing technical or market knowledge. The scale of such firms is usually larger than in the SME networks, and they may well display more formality in procedures. They may also absorb more professionalism in administration. But of the cases that succeed, the majority are commanded by powerful charismatic individuals. This feature is addressed more specifically in answering the question on authority.

These clan systems are responses to the opportunity of pulling together the underutilized local state assets, the poorly invested state banking loan facilities, the local entrepreneurial skills, and the foreign know-how. It is a very successful response and has produced a number of firms with international potential as well as home-country dominance. Their future growth will depend on their capacity to adjust to the decentralization of decision power within them.

Institutions designed to foster more formal kinds of trust are being added to the society at a fast rate. The ability to trust information about the performance of firms is being boosted by a huge investment in the training of accountants. Laws are being created to allocate rights and responsibilities over more and more business fields, and a growing body of lawyers is emerging to make them work. Educational standards are being closely monitored to protect the value of degrees and other qualifications, and so to standardize and regulate the commodification of talent. The world of finance is seeing more stringent regulation in the interests of raising the low level of efficiency in the sourcing and allocation of capital. All these changes are moving the society to one in which institutional trust might take hold, but two barriers remain.

The first barrier is that government control remains paramount, and in consequence the forming of voluntary and independent citizen associations is very limited. Few societies have achieved widespread trust without the growth of civil society. What that means is that members of the society form systems to foster trust across the society and take responsibility themselves for its maintenance. The more people you have who are concerned with order, the denser and more complete becomes the order. Thus in dense-order societies the professions act independently of government to guarantee the quality of information and standards of behavior. The legal process becomes divorced from the political. The stock market is regulated mainly by its members. We see this development—which is in essence a Western formula resting on an individualist ethic—as being impossible for China to apply, at least in any presently conceivable future. In some subtle way the state is too big to take the risk, but neither do the ideals support it. For instance, strong familism is counter to civil society. For this reason alone, we consider that China's future economy will not rest on institutional trust.

The second barrier is the one just hinted at—the sheer scale of China. To dismantle a power structure with millennia of tradition behind it and replace it with a non-state alternative might be feasible as a concept, but in reality it would be an awesome risk. The moves in that direction that one sees in the rush to produce professionals are not necessarily designed to use them in the same way as might occur, for instance, in Europe. Their role is more likely to be that of ancillary technocrats rather than key power holders. So too is it necessary to see the enormous demand for such new talent, and the tiny nature of the supply, by developed country standards.

All this points to a conclusion that China's economy will remain essentially diffracted into units bonded in personalistic ties, at least in the sectors where efficiency reaches high levels. This is not to say that large firms will not emerge and escape from those limitations, becoming national players or even multinationals. It is to say that such firms will not do so on the basis of a managerial revolution whereby ownership and control separate out, and professionals take over the total running of the enterprise.

The Rational Pursuit of Purpose

It is not a trivial point that a bad society is not capable of fostering a good economy. There needs to be a societal agreement—usually built up slowly from a state of acquiescence—that economic behavior as it is structured and organized is acceptable to the majority, and preferably that it is not just acceptable, but desired. In the long-term evolution of this state of acceptance, various interest groups (labor, management, shareholders, communities, and government) battle to defend their standpoint in the political arena. If the process runs its normal course—in other words, if it does not get sidetracked by the imposition of special interests over others—what has happened historically in other countries is a gradual release of power from the political superstructure into the economy. Those in receipt of this power are the owners, managers, and professional specialists in the business organizations. They are permitted to act as deliverers of the societal good, on that society's terms. In Europe they became the *bourgeoisie* and the professionals, in Japan the salarymen, in Hong Kong the business owners. In the United States they are now the new financial aristocracy of the fund managers, the financial analysts, and the broader investment community.

Putting it simply, what these newly powerful people do is to apply a calculus to what they are supervising, and that calculus interprets the agreed ends into acceptable means. As Robert Heilbroner (1985: 97) in his analysis of the nature of capitalism has observed:

[T]he engineer who supervises the 'functional' organization of production is guided by the prevailing interest-system, which not only designates the ends for which he must plan his means but which also establishes the calculus— and beneath the calculus, the concepts—by which the rationality of the means themselves are established...capitalism imposes such a calculus in the form of profit considerations.

These calculi vary between systems. Serfdoms, aristocracies, theocracies, and economies subservient to political dogma, all have different calculi, as they have different rationales; they have different means serving different ends. Significantly also for our analysis, there are many shades of difference within the generic category of capitalism. Ends and means are not universally agreed. Each society has its own, as we have demonstrated in our earlier societal comparisons.

What we have seen in China in recent decades is an accelerating momentum toward a society in which the profit motive has become legitimate. The welfarism of the state is no longer a workable ideal for retaining dominance; using it, China was being left behind in the race for progress, and Deng Xiaoping and Zhao Ziyang could see that. The facts of the resulting transition are clear: the state sector has reduced itself down to the bare essentials of the strategic industries, and a struggle continues to prepare the 'national team' of large firms for their immersion in global competition; the local corporate firms, hybrids of local state interests and entrepreneurship, are highly active and expanding rapidly, having acquired much managerial and technical competence via alliances and foreign markets; and the private sector has exploded with growth, and continues its fierce pursuit of both foreign and home markets.

The dismantling of the political superstructure that would inevitably accompany such change is visible in three main shifts. First, the Party has opened its doors to the private-entrepreneur class, and not just by way of gesture, but by including the views of that interest group in its policy deliberations. Second, there has been massive decentralization (albeit still controlled) of financial, tax, and policy discretion to local authorities. Third, there has been an avalanche of legislation to increase both individual legal rights, and to ensure representation, especially in labor law. Government has thus shown a certain level of responsiveness to people's needs, though most scholars seem to doubt that this is a sign of a nascent development toward liberal democracy.

The question we now face has two components. First is the degree of rationality now being applied. In other words, how 'tight' and how efficient is the system in its connecting of means and ends? And second, how clear and legitimate are the ends being pursued? We will conclude that the connections are becoming efficient in many domains, but the ends are still cloudy and disputed. But we need to argue that, and consider the effects, rather than just state it.

The full question on this topic as we posed it in Chapter 1 was: How does the society make a tight set of connections between the purposes (of economic action) seen as legitimate by most people, and the rationally organized pursuit of those purposes? We would argue that in the United States there is little argument about the significance of the shareholder-value motive in making the system work, and widespread acceptance of the central institution of the stock market in making that motive active and efficient. All sorts of supporting elements in the fabric add to the rationale: widespread ownership of shares; strong belief in individualism and self-responsibility; competitiveness as an ideal; strong regulatory frameworks; and government standing back from the game itself. The distribution of benefits from the generation of added value is based on merit in contribution to work or in taking risk. The system of order reflects the system of meaning, and the elements are tightly coupled.

In other societies, we see different sets of priorities and different patterns of coupling between meaning and order. All firms need to make profit, but in Japan this purpose contends with keeping *people* employed as an ideal, in Korea it contends with *national development and pride*, in Germany it contends with the ideal of *service to the community*. For the regional ethnic Chinese it contends with duty to *family*. What does it contend with in China?

Why do firms exist? In China, the answer growing in weight and significance is private wealth, and that is connected to the ancient sense of duty to a family, and of pride in a family's reputation and 'name' in the community. This is the source of *status* that matters most, and the most respected are those who build that reputation. In many cases, given the powerful sense of family history going back centuries, it is a matter of *rebuilding the family pride.*

In the small and medium business sector, where entrepreneurs and small groups of business partners own shares in the company and are rewarded by its growth, the connections are straightforward. The ideal is family respectability; this is served by wealth; the wealth buys education and old age security, and, in case of a surplus being available, additional respect through contribution to community; firms are run by owners, and control of the firm is sacrosanct; hard work and care with money become instinctive; efficiency reaches high levels; and most ambitious people want to be owners, so as to fulfill their moral duties toward their families. The government is in the background, providing order.

China is not the only country with such a response, but it is one of the few countries with an originally Confucian system of ethics giving specific support to such an ideal. As in Jewish culture, the family is the centerpiece of the social structure, and in both cases that principle is surrounded by literally millennia of socialization and the accretion of cultural support in religion, art, literature, history, and education.

In the state sector, this ideal of private wealth can only be met partially. Ownership of most assets is by the people as a whole, and although seen by many as a noble ideal (understandable given their sacrifices for it), it does not have the same immediacy, the same 'bite,' as having your own company. Working in the state sector tends to be a largely 'political' process, where meritocracy and professionalism are still to fully penetrate, so the connection there between effort and reward is weak. In compensation, there has been the reliability of steady, modest reward, and at times of uncertainty, that might well have been the best way of fulfilling the duties of a person to relatives. However, there are now alternatives that did not exist previously, and the pulls of state duty or of security are less attractive in a society full of new opportunities.

In the local corporate sector, by contrast, the injections of hard performance demands—as state companies, or parts of them, were taken to the market—have resulted in spectacular gains in productivity. This is where the richest pickings have been for those with an appetite for risk and a capacity for networking. Entrepreneurship in this arena is especially richly rewarded. Such drives typify so many Chinese that the growth of this sector comes as no surprise.

If it is now glorious to be rich as a valid interpretation of socialism, some new ideology has been formed in which egalitarianism has been airbrushed out of the Marxist conception, or its later interpretations. Certainly in interviews with Chinese owners, there is a widespread sense of duty to rebuild the society, an acknowledgment that community is central in the mind-set. And yet, in many of those same interviews, there is a sense of confusion about ideals, and a sense that the government is searching for a new platform as it abandons the simplistic faiths of Communism. Our conclusion is that China overall is still searching for a clear set of new ideals for the rebuilding of its society, and that while that goes on, the business owners are setting in place a new version, heavily influenced by the varying formulae of Hong Kong, Taiwan, and Singapore. In this version, pragmatism will return and replace social idealism, and paternalism will return as the moral glue holding things together. As pragmatism is perhaps the most appropriate and necessary of the range of government responses, and as its value has been so well proven in recent decades, this conclusion should be seen as more optimistic than pessimistic. If so, the retention of strong organizational control by owners will mark the industrial scene and will shape the nature of industry. It means also that personal control will continue to block the growth of professional management.

Legitimate, Motivating Authority

We asked the questions: How does authority in the society function effectively to channel the behavior of people in work? Where does legitimate, motivating authority come from? The answer is that the Chinese accept strong personal leadership, and allocate preponderant control to those in top positions. This is not to say that leaders do not have to argue with, or persuade, others about their intentions. It is to say that in most contexts, and especially in the economy, they argue and persuade from a very strong position.

To make this process work in the economic arena—that is, for the most part, in firms—this requires that the top position is secured by clear ownership. Control then follows automatically. The normal primary concern of business leaders is the securing of this dominance, without which the power system becomes fuzzy and may break down. The acquiescence of subordinates follows when the *lao ban* either behaves paternalistically, and thus by strong traditional ethical principles, or when the state of dependence of the subordinates is such as to leave them no countervailing power. In these latter cases—common where there is labor surplus and low-skill work—the more pragmatic response of labor abuse is common.

In organizations with this form of vertical order two outcomes are noticeable and have strong implications for the workings of companies and the kinds of industry in which they might succeed. The first outcome is that 'middle management' in larger companies and supervisors in smaller companies tend to act as conduits of downward communication and maintainers of disciplined control. They do not tend to act as colleagues in strategic discussions with the big boss, except perhaps in matters of technology or detailed control. This divides large organizations into 'stovepipes' and weakens coordination across the company, and across the value chain, the latter being only seen and thought of in its entirety by top management. Such centralized, tightly controlled systems are ideal in certain industries, as we shall conclude shortly. But they place heavy constraints in industries requiring organizations to address complexity with a response of integrated and coordinated variety. Such organizations can replicate a Chevrolet, but not create a Lexus, can reverse engineer a camera, but not create a new form of image reproduction.

The second outcome is that the state of interdependence between management and workers is weak. The workforce is far less 'strategic' than it is in, say, Japan or Germany. Its contribution is mainly to follow orders, to comply with established routines, and not to do the firm's thinking for it. In consequence, labor turnover can be high without seriously damaging a firm's competitiveness. The advantage of this is great responsiveness and adaptability in industries with low- to mid-tech production, and great efficiency stemming from the high specialization of tasks. But again, the type of industry for which this works well is limited. It is perfectly adapted to garments, or toys, or components, and it is a matter of fortuitous historical timing for China that the world's markets for consumer goods were opening up as this formula came into its own.

Innovation and Adaptation

We argued earlier that all organizations need to have three features available for use. They should be managed to a point where the maximum value is being squeezed out of the many resources at their disposal, and especially the resources of capital, human skill, and technology. They need to be capable of constant learning so as to respond to their changing environments. They need to be able to change internally, and do different things externally, to seek competitive advantage over others. We now return to an earlier question: How does innovation become part of the behavior of the economy, and with it the flexibility of the system and the organizations within it?

Much is made of China's innovativeness. There are science parks, R & D budgets, research universities, and venture capital. Some companies, such as Broad Airconditioning or Haier, are producing consumer goods that pay tribute to design and engineering flair. Doubtless in such a large economy some outstanding successes like these will always be evident. But the wider impression gained is one less of innovativeness than of opportunistic copying and borrowing. In high-tech industry, foreign firms dominate, and in international patent registration, China lags a long way behind many smaller countries. In 2002, China registered 144 'triadic' patents, that is, those that are registered in Europe, Japan, and the United States, and of whose innovative value one can consequently be fairly certain. This compares with 282 for Austria and 216 for Denmark, with total populations of about 8.3 million and 5.5 million, respectively. A recent study[1] for the UK government finds that as of 2005, 99 percent of Chinese firms have never registered a patent; about 50 percent of patent applications in China are submitted by foreign firms; and China's share of patents registered with the World Intellectual Property Organization is 1.4 percent. The same report also states that patent applications have been growing at an annual rate of 23 percent annually since 2000; if we assume heroically that this pace continues, that it translates into a 23 percent increase in triadic patents generated every year, and that patent registrations elsewhere keep growing at the same average rates they have shown from 1990 to 2002, China would catch up with Germany and Japan in 2027 and with the United States in 2032. Chance would still

[1] Wilsdon and Keeley 2007, p. 219.

be that many, if not most, of those patents would be owned by foreign firms.

So how does China meet the needs for innovation? As the patent numbers already show, most of China's manufacturing and product development in high-tech industry is due to the arrival of firms from abroad. Almost 90 percent of exports of electronic and IT products are produced in foreign-owned factories with only limited local connections into supply chains. Taiwanese companies hold around 80 percent of the world market in notebook computers, and manufacture three-quarters of that on the mainland, assembling with components sourced globally, and including software from the United States, screens from Korea, and hard drives from Japan. The depth of embeddedness of Taiwanese industry in Silicon Valley (and vice versa) is not something yet achievable by China, nor is it likely to be unless intellectual property rights protection on the mainland reaches global standards. Moves are beginning in that direction, but there is a long road ahead, and this is simply another aspect of the wider problem of societal order. In China the difficulty is made worse by the aggressive entrepreneurialism: it can produce growth, but at the same time it can cut corners without a conscience.

The institutional support needed to make innovation a core competence in industry and the basis for strategy, includes as well as strong property rights a set of strong domestic sources of technology supplies. Also needed is close collaboration with universities, a sophisticated venture-capital industry, and the ability to absorb and diffuse imported technology. These features are still in their infancy, and their evolution is handicapped by the secretiveness that is part of the managerial ideal in many companies. Even within a company, the diffusion of innovation is hindered by the stovepipe structures and the managerial inhibitions described earlier. The vertical nature of the socioeconomic system and the diffracted nature of the economy mean that collaborative innovation—as occurs in Germany and Japan—is weak.

It would appear that overall, China will continue with its high level of technical and scientific dependence on the economically rich economies, and that its absorption of those technologies will remain filtered and suppressed by its internal complexities. We do recognize the high capacity for learning China has exhibited, which implies the possibility that our expectations might be too pessimistic. On the basis of the available evidence, however, it seems that the arrival of radical scientific innovation indigenously, and the conversion of that into production and market advantages, seems a very long way away.

Implications for the Likely Evolution of the Chinese Business System

The implications of these conclusions are consistent with, and further underscore, our findings in Chapters 11 through 14, in which we explored the key characteristics of other major types of capitalist systems and their applicability to the Chinese context.

It clearly suggests that the probability of China's evolving a business system that resembles that of the United States is low, and that of developing a business system similar to those of Germany and Japan, virtually nil. Without relatively high levels of institutionalized social capital, the delegation of tasks that is so key in these systems is likely to remain exceptional in China. Owners will not trust management to be reliable stewards on their behalf; and managers will not trust blue-collar workers to show much commitment to the firm; labor will suspect that managers may take advantage of any commitment they may show; and so forth.

Delegation beyond a very limited circle of close confidantes requires institutionalized trust. In the United States, laws and regulations as well as professions are a key ingredient in creating this trust. According to one study,[2] about one fifth of the US workforce is involved in checking that others are doing their job properly. The required level of institutionalized trust in Germany and Japan is arguably greater still. The peaceful working together of labor and capital (the latter represented by management) requires a fundamental understanding that despite varying interests, neither side will take advantage of the other's cooperation. That this fundamental understanding is working well is visible in the low number of strike days in both countries compared with the situation in countries, such as the United States, in which no similar arrangement exists.

Institutionalized trust is also the foundation of another key characteristic of Japan and Germany; namely, high levels of societal coordination in the economy. Given that societal coordination has in recent years been a source of structural inertia and thus a brake on economic performance, it would seem unlikely that China would want to foster it. In fact, present policy in China stresses locally independent experimentation over coordinated approaches for finding the best steps forward. Yet even if, for whatever reason, societal coordination were to prove desirable, it is highly unlikely that we would witness much of it emerging. Societal coordination is contingent on high levels of institutionalized social capital, yet

---

[2] Gordon 1994

China remains a 'tray of loose sand,' to reiterate Sun Yat-sen's verdict. Perhaps over time some clumps will form in the sand; yet we should not expect it to coalesce into a monolithic piece of granite.

With the US, Japanese, and German systems out of reach, that leaves, for now, two basic possibilities, which are not necessarily mutually exclusive: further spread of the Hong Kong/Guangzhou personally owned and managed business model, and emulation of the South Korean *chaebol*. The former is already more a fact than a hypothetical scenario, as is clear from our discussion of the influence of the regional ethnic Chinese on developments in recent years. Indeed, a recent study of emerging managerial ideologies by David Ralston and his colleagues presents evidence suggesting that the Hong Kong/Guangzhou model may be set to make a clean sweep across China to establish itself as the dominant mode of doing business. By contrast, the Shanghai model favoring the idea of reforming SOEs that can compete in world markets seems to be on the defensive.

It is quite likely that a Chinese economy dominated by personally owned and run SMEs will continue to exhibit high levels of economic performance for a good number of years to come—especially if the Chinese state gives the private sector easier access to formal sources of financial capital. Yet China cannot rest content with this scenario, for two main reasons. First, the continued absence of institutionalized social capital limits the volume of transactions that can take place in China to those enabled by interpersonal trust. To the extent additional transactions may add further value, this implies an opportunity cost for society. Social networks and the Internet may be able to mitigate this effect partially, but these are ersatz coping mechanisms, no real substitutes for institutionalized trust.

Second, as we have discussed, the peculiarities of Chinese family businesses, and especially the reluctance to delegate, have important implications for the ability of firms to handle tasks involving high levels of complexity, as is typical of firm activities with high value-added. Network production can partially compensate for this, but this form of organization also has its limits, as the transaction costs of handling complexity through network ties grow prohibitively large. There is a reason why complex products tend to be handled by firms that in themselves are normally complex and large; yet the Hong Kong/Guangzhou model is unlikely to be able to sustain such firms.

Government policy is to groom a select group of SOEs into such large and complex operations. This policy has not been without success, and many of these firms are now reported to be profitable. Yet while there is no doubt that progress has been made, we believe that the effort will by and large prove very difficult, if not futile. For example, Lenovo, a Chinese poster child in the computing business, is reported to be held together almost entirely by the US talent retained after the acquisition of IBM's personal computing business. Much time and effort is reportedly required for training Chinese middle management to become actual managers rather than mere conduits for orders from the top. Even if this effort succeeds, it raises the question of how other reformed SOEs are supposed to develop the requisite organizational capabilities for being world-beaters. Not all of them will be able to acquire well-run firms abroad, and those SOEs that manage to do so will no doubt find confirmed what Western companies such as DaimlerChrysler have long realized: that it is difficult to make international mergers and acquisitions work, and even harder to transfer tacit knowledge across organizational and business system boundaries.

The prospect of the emergence of a large number of world-beating Chinese MNEs thus seems rather bleak. A glimmer of hope is provided, albeit faintly, by the South Korean experience. No one expected South Korea to be able to develop MNEs, and yet it has. And as we have discussed before, many of the key features of the South Korean business system seem to be quite compatible with the Chinese context. The Korean approach of growing—as opposed to throwing independent companies together to form business groups, as happened under China's 1992 Group Company System—family-controlled 'mammoth enterprises' would thus seem to be the least unrealistic non-Chinese model China could choose for its own development.

Yet, even there, major obstacles remain. First, the international political context has changed tremendously. Few perceived South Korea as a potential threat, be it economic or military. On the contrary, up until the end of the Cold War, the country was a key component in the US strategy of containment of communism. If running a trade deficit was the price of strengthening an important ally in this effort, the United States was willing to pay it. Obviously, China's situation is different, in that many already see it as an economic and increasingly also a military threat, and in that it is no frontline state in the containment of communism, but in itself nominally at least socialist. One should thus not expect a great deal of patience among China's trading partners, and especially the United States, for an export-led development strategy. Recent trade sanctions imposed by the United States may well be only the beginning of massive trade frictions that could dwarf anything we saw between Japan and the United States in the 1980s and 1990s.

Second, though South Korea's levels of institutionalized social capital at the start of its rapid development in the 1960s were relatively low, it still seems to have had a head start compared with present-day levels in China. Since then, institutionalized trust seems to have strengthened, most likely as a consequence of government policy starting under Park Chung-hee in 1961. Not all aspects of Park's rule are praiseworthy, but he did introduce into government policy one clear objective—economic development of the nation through the creation of family-owned 'mammoth enterprise'— backed by clear incentives and uncompromising enforcement. Park used export quotas as measures of firm success. Entrepreneurs meeting them would receive state help and new licenses to grow their businesses, while those falling short would find themselves out of business. In a 1976 poll, 94.8 percent of businessmen reported that government policy under Park was always or almost always implemented without change; for policies under his immediate predecessor, Syngman Rhee, the percentage was 20.5 percent. The effect was that entrepreneurs could be relatively sure of what outcomes to expect from the state under what conditions, giving them an incentive to grow their firms in accordance with government policy. Workers, in turn, saw that unsuccessful entrepreneurs would be taken to task by the state, which created a level of certainty about the objectives of the state and also of the goals entrepreneurs were likely to pursue for their firms and, by implication, their workers. Increasing the predictability of the system may thus have helped raise levels of institutionalized social capital to the point of enabling South Korean firms to handle the complexity levels common in present-day MNEs.

Third, and related to the last point, is the question of the strength of government in terms of creating a predictable environment geared toward development. Conventional wisdom regards the Chinese central government as supremely powerful; the truth is that many of its directives never seem to leave the walls of Zhongnanhai, the compound housing the CCP's headquarters. And even when they do, decentralization of the state means that many orders and directives are observed mostly in the breach. Postwar South Korea, by contrast, has been a strong, centralized state with a well-functioning national bureaucracy. The relatively higher administrative capacity of the Korean state is linked to the small size of the country, but very likely also to a historic event that cannot (and should not) be repeated, namely, Japanese control and colonization (1905–45) and the attendant imposition of

Japanese bureaucratic structures.[3] South Korea has thus been in a much better position to implement policies firmly and consistently than China.

On this latter point, intriguing parallels can be drawn with the other 'Chinese' economies in the region: Hong Kong, Singapore, and Taiwan. All three of them have been economically highly successful. And all three entities feature highly effective administrative structures, aided by small size of the territory and population to be administered and almost certainly also the influence of heavy injections of efficacious and stable institutional structures from outside: Taiwan under Japanese rule (1895–1945), and Hong Kong as well as Singapore as British colonies. To the extent strong (Singapore, Taiwan) or at least highly competent (all three) government is a contributor to economic development, these economies almost certainly had an advantage relative to present-day China.

Fourth, the Chinese central government may be reluctant to be seen as promoting the personal wealth of private entrepreneurs through industrial policy, as the Korean government did. Income disparities are already a highly sensitive issue, and a government policy producing more of it would be a heavy political liability.

One possible solution to most—but not all—of these issues could be for local governments to step into the breach. Locally confined Korean-style industrial policy is much less likely to be seen as a threat by international trading partners, yet could still be significant given the large population sizes of each of the provinces; local governments are relatively close to the firms they oversee, especially the local corporates, which may enable government to be firm in implementation; and concerns about income inequalities may be less pronounced in some regions than in others. It would still be a long shot, because the question of institutionalized social capital remains unresolved. We suggested earlier that consistent and predictable government policy might, over time, help build such institutionalized capital. Yet can local governments provide the consistency and predictability of South Korean industrial policy, especially with interference from the central government always looming?

---

[3] This being a sensitive issue, we hasten to add that this does obviously not provide a justification or excuse for Japan's colonization of Korea. The same goes for the cases of British and Japanese colonialism in Hong Kong, Singapore, and Taiwan, treated in the following paragraph.

Practical Implications

Our discussion has important implications for business in and with China. First, for firms looking at China as a place of business, our findings provide additional insight into what is possible, and what is not. As for the latter, our discussion suggests foremost that the lack of institutionalized trust and the attendant managerial vacuum will make it extremely difficult to build from scratch large organizations capable of handling high levels of complexity. Similarly, it would be naïve to expect to thrive in China in industries in which worker creativity or high levels of labor skills are key, or in industries relying on high levels of active coordination in the creation of standardized processes.

What we do expect to work well is approaches in which outsiders provide organizational templates designed in such detail that they can be implemented in China as a machine bureaucracy, with a handful of expatriate managers ensuring proper operation. In other words, foreign firms should do well if they succeed in breaking down complex tasks to a point at which the individual worker has a clearly defined task that requires no personal initiative and only limited organizational capacity for spontaneous coordination. For example, Ikea or Wal-Mart have the capacity to handle extremely complex supply-chain systems. To the extent they can implement the required processes as a machine bureaucracy supervised by expatriate managers, this should be a source of competitive advantage in the Chinese market, as Chinese competitors are unlikely to be able to build and operate their own templates. Similarly, international automobile manufacturers may find that they have a competitive advantage over Chinese carmakers in their ability to reach sophisticated integration across multiple functions, such as marketing, design, R & D, and production engineering. Other areas combining high levels of complexity with the potential for machine bureaucratization include retail banking, insurance, and distribution (including fast food).

Foreign firms may also enjoy sustained competitive advantage if their core competence is built on a professional bureaucracy capable of handling large complexity. This may be the case in businesses such as merchant banking, consulting, architecture, or high-level accounting. These firms usually rely on a relatively small core of highly trained professionals. McKinsey, for instance, is reported to employ no more than 7,500 consultants worldwide. In the Chinese context, key positions in professional firms are likely to be occupied by heavy hitters who are non-Chinese, or ethnic Chinese raised in the West, and who have proved their mettle in other locations. To the extent Chinese nationals are on the staff, they are normally foreign educated and thus inculcated with Western professional values, an effect continuously reinforced by the strong corporate cultures present in most professional firms.

Foreign firms can also still expect to have an advantage if their line of business involves high levels of technical competency, especially if part of this competency is in the form of tacit knowledge embedded in the labor force. This includes automobiles, but especially also machine tools and capital equipment. To be sure, Chinese copies of machine tools and capital goods have emerged. At the same time, highly sophisticated equipment is still beyond reach. For instance, Bao Steel, a leading Chinese producer of steel, relies heavily on Japanese equipment on its production lines. If this equipment were easily reengineered, a company like Bao Steel should be a prime candidate for rejecting Japanese equipment and buying locally.

For foreign businesses interested in sourcing, our discussion suggests that China is likely to remain, for the foreseeable future, the assembly workshop of the world. In particular its private businesses represent an extremely competitive system of sources of supply that can be tapped into through intermediaries such as agents or internal purchasing departments. This system is very flexible and produces at very low costs. At the same time, the system cannot handle highly complex assembly tasks if these need to be coordinated with design, market trends, and new science. It is also almost entirely dependent on its customers for design and marketing as well as the provision of sophisticated components and subassemblies. OEM manufacturing—or more specifically, assembly—is its outstanding strength.

This picture is actually good news for many non-Chinese firms: The fact that China has become the assembly workshop of the world does not mean that all other such companies elsewhere are doomed. Of all the steps in a firm's value chain, assembly tends to contribute relatively little to overall value-added. By contrast, exactly those parts of the value chain with high value-added—such as design, marketing and brand management, distribution, and supply-chain logistics—Chinese firms have been unable to handle. Of course, this has not escaped Chinese firms and policymakers, but because these high value-added tasks also tend to be fairly complex, they are likely to be beyond the organizational capabilities of mainland Chinese firms.

This has important implications for the strategy of non-Chinese firms. First, non-Chinese firms that focus on manufacturing only, and especially relatively simple assembly, ought to consider ways to use the China

227

advantage in manufacturing, but develop the rest of their value chain in design, marketing, supply logistics, and alliances; the likely alternative is to succumb to Chinese competition. Second, it may improve firm prospects to move the assembly process to China while retaining control of the other steps of the value chain. This, of course, has political ramifications, as it is likely to involve manufacturing-job losses outside China and thus the possibility of a public backlash against firms pursuing this strategy as well as a risk of increased trade protection as a general response. From the perspective of the individual firm, however, the logic of moving at least the assembly of its products to China is often inexorable. It can take various forms, including outsourcing of assembly work, assembly in a wholly owned subsidiary, or the formation of an alliance with a Chinese firm. The sine qua non of these approaches, it bears repeating, is that the non-Chinese firm must not be a pure manufacturer, but have control over further steps in the value chain.

For firms choosing the alliance option, our discussion strongly suggests not to forget about the personal aspect of alliances. Especially in the West, but also in Japan, alliances are perceived to be existing at the organizational level, independent of the presence or absence of specific individuals. People may come and go; the alliance will persist until strategic priorities change and render it obsolete. In China, the importance of personal ties suggests almost the opposite picture: strategic priorities may come and go, the alliance will persist until the key people in it change. Interpersonal trust—friendship—is thus an element in alliances with Chinese firms that is not to be underestimated. In a case known to us, a Western entrepreneur with a long-standing relationship with a Chinese supplier received permission to use the firm's offices to receive another Western business partner. When the latter remarked that this generosity was a sure sign of a good business relationship, the responsible Chinese manager protested, 'No, it's not a business relationship! It's a friendship!' The emphasis on interpersonal trust in the Chinese context thus implies a need for outside alliance partners to foster ties that are interpersonal, rather than institutionalized.

For non-Chinese MNEs fearing the specter of Chinese MNEs doing to them as Chinese private enterprise has done to the manufacturers of the world, the picture emerging from our discussion suggests that the prospect is remote. Today's MNEs are not only large; the vast majority of them are also highly complex organizations capable of handling highly complex tasks. This is in good part the result of developments in the last fifteen years. The end of the Cold War created an environment in which global capitalism can flourish; gone is the perception that the forces of capitalism need restraining for fear that dislocations, especially in the workforce, caused by market forces could increase the support of communism in the affected countries. This move toward globalization has coincided with rapid technological development, especially in the field of IT. The combination of these factors has opened up new opportunities for MNEs. However, it has also ratcheted up the intensity of international competition to unprecedented levels. With firms under immense pressure to find efficient adaptive responses to the new environment, rapid organizational innovation has ensued, as evident in the rise of decentralized organizations, web-based structures, virtual organizations, the meta-national enterprise, and project-based organizations. Each successful innovation, in turn, increases the pressure on everyone else to devise new efficient organizational forms. In the academic field of coevolution, which studies how organizations and their environments evolve together, this is known as the 'Red Queen Phenomenon': one must run ever faster to stay in the same place. Not all firms have managed to keep up with the pace, but those that did made a quantum leap in organizational complexity in areas such as R & D, brand management, global distribution, supply-chain logistics, production logistics, and the organizational integration of decentralized structures.

It is not clear that the Chinese government and its would-be MNEs recognize the magnitude of the challenge. The strategy of reforming large SOEs into world-beating MNEs was formulated in the 1990s, and is seems possible that perceptions of what it takes to become a successful MNE have not been updated sufficiently to take account of what is a fundamental shift in the nature of the game. Even in the 1990s, the challenge was formidable, as non-Chinese MNEs loomed so large in world markets—in terms of size, but also technological sophistication—that breaking into their phalanx would not have been easy and only possible through the commitment of massive state resources. However, the last fifteen years have added to this a rapid escalation in organizational complexity. No amount of state resources will help Chinese firms tackle this issue, because the capability to do so is rooted in the structure of society. Chinese society itself would need to change, and in light of the South Korean experience with industrial policy already discussed, this would very likely also imply a need for Chinese political governance to adjust—not necessarily to a democratic system, but at least to one that is predictable both in policy and implementation. We do not deny women and men of goodwill in Chinese government may at this very moment be working toward this goal. But we do believe that this challenge is monumental and unlikely to be met anytime soon.

Academic Implications

In a study of the history of China research in political science, Elizabeth Perry finds that the opening of China to the world from 1978 onward caused a seismic shift in the nature of works produced by China scholars. While most of the studies before the reform movement by necessity presented an outside and high-level view of the country, the postreform era has seen a proliferation of detailed studies of micro-level phenomena. This diligent work has afforded us many new insights, but it has also arguably resulted in an inability to see the forest for the trees. Perry's finding arguably also holds true in the related social sciences, including business. We know a lot about individual firms, about temple societies in remote villages, about informal finance, and about the obstacles to civil society. Rare is the attempt to put together all these various bits and pieces to present a holistic picture of the present shape and potential evolutionary path of the entire country. There are at least two good reasons for not doing so. First, it is difficult, because it requires the integration of a huge and constantly expanding body of knowledge. And it is academically risky, because the necessary high-level synthesis may invite criticism, accurate or not, of oversimplification and having left out important facts. The safe approach, therefore, is to study a small aspect of China in great detail and establish oneself as the world's foremost expert on it.

We accept these risks because a holistic analytical approach has distinct and overwhelming advantages. The principal one of these advantages is that the things being described are situated in their full context and not seen in deceptive isolation from it. There is little point, in our view, in drawing policy conclusions from a study of economic 'facts' if the societal and cultural surroundings are left out of the picture. How can one understand the apparently crazy diversification occurring in the private enterprises without understanding the traditions of insecurity and risk-hedging that rest on the society's distinct history? How can one explain the transaction cost efficiency of business networks without including the moralities of obligation exchange, the problem of finding reliable information, the surrounding insecurity?

Related to this is the connectedness of things across the society, and so the complexity and slowness of change. At the root of much economic behavior are attitudes to wealth and to cooperation that are connected invisibly deep below the surface of daily life. The labor market is subtly connected with the capital market and both with the political ideals. Education does not exist in its own space in isolation. Business behaves in ways the society wants it to behave, not in ways set by universal laws of mathematical tidiness.

To compare parts of business systems between societies is dangerous if the workings of those parts are assumed to follow universal rules. Life is not that simple. It is better to make the attempt to see a society as a complex adaptive system with its own built-in rules and to compare those whole systems, even though doing so demands some tolerance on the reader's part. We do not contend that certain universal rules do not apply, so the way markets behave, the way motivation works, the way prices react to influences are all—within limits—predictable. What we do say is that when business people go into the real world of China, they will find those guidelines to be of only limited value. Practitioners on the ground learn about the rest of the context by trial and error. We believe that the world of theory should acknowledge the sophistication with which the world of practice handles that challenge.

Our key conclusion is that the relative lack of institutionalized social capital is likely to have a seriously adverse impact on the future development of Chinese capitalism, in two concrete fashions. First, the absence of institutionalized social capital implies a relatively higher level of transaction costs in the economy, which reduces the number of transactions possible in the economy and thus has an adverse impact on economic performance. Network structures and the Internet may help reduce these transaction costs somewhat, but not as far as would be possible in the presence of genuine institutionalized trust.

Second, and more importantly, we have linked the absence of institutionalized social capital to organizational performance characteristics. Specifically, the absence of institutionalized trust inhibits the development of organizational forms capable of handling high levels of complexity in task performance and organizational structure. Goods and services requiring these levels of complexity are likely to remain beyond the capabilities of Chinese firms. In principle, being unable to produce certain goods and services is not unusual for an economy—as we have seen, societies specialize in what they are good at. The catch is that low complexity usually means low value-added. Specialization in low value-added activities is thus not a promising basis for China to grow rich. We believe that as a result of the implications of low institutionalized trust for the volume of transactions and the level of complexity firms are capable of handling, growth in China's per capita GDP is likely to level off a long time before it reaches levels in developed nations. While we cannot pinpoint the precise level at which this will occur, we surmise that it will be very difficult for China to attain a per capita GDP, at purchasing power parity exchange rates, in excess of two-thirds of levels seen in the United States.

Final Words

In conclusion, it bears repeating that we have deliberately limited our analysis to the impact of societal effects. The future evolution and success of Chinese capitalism is, of course, subject to a number of other issues. We have bracketed these issues from our analysis to keep complexity at a manageable level. By way of conclusion, we would like to give brief mention to three of the major ones, not least as a reminder that societal characteristics are not the only potential obstacles China faces in its economic development.

The first issue relates to the shape of the international political arena. While China is, at this stage, neither an economic nor a military super-power, it sees its reemergence to its erstwhile superpower status as a natural right. It is hard to argue with this logic. At the same time, unless China manages to play the diplomatic game extremely well and forgoes any major attempts to reshape the international political, institutional, and economic environment in its favor, it seems highly likely that the United States will increasingly feel threatened. For now, the prospect of economic gains from engaging China still seem to supersede defensive instincts, but history suggests that the emergence of a major power without conflict is a very rare event indeed. This does not necessarily imply that China and the United States will go to war. But it is a distinct possibility that the United States may take measures, overtly or covertly, to contain China's rise. This could occur, for instance, by limiting market access to Chinese goods and firms. There would be associated economic costs not only for China, but also the United States. Yet as the US security crackdown following 9/11 has demonstrated, national security concerns, whether real or imagined, almost always trump economic considerations.

A second major issue is demographic change in China itself. The one-child policy in effect in China since 1979 will have a dual effect on Chinese society. One is the virtual disappearance of large families, with profound implications for the concentric circles of interpersonal trust that we have discussed earlier. The second is that rapid societal ageing in China is a virtual certainty at this point. This demographic development is not unique; many European nations and Japan are bracing themselves for the costs associated with ever-fewer workers having to support ever more retirees. The challenge will be formidable, yet at least the European nations and Japan are already rich. China, by contrast, stands a real chance of growing old before it manages to grow rich. This will have an adverse impact on economic development, and it seems likely that the effects will begin to manifest themselves within the next ten to fifteen years. Rescinding the one-child policy may provide some long-term relief, yet at this point, there are no clear indications of government plans to this effect.

Last, but not least, there is the question of the future evolution of political governance in China. The possible (though not always likely) scenarios are endless, ranging from a breakup of the country over the reemergence of an imperial system to full-fledged liberal democracy. Our sense is that the CCP will prove highly adept at hanging on to power through a combination of oppression and reforms, though we are conscious of the fact that similar things were said about the Communist Party of the USSR in the 1980s. It is true that over time, the emerging middle class may demand more rights. However, as other Asian states have demonstrated, these may be granted without introducing Western-style democratic participation, and we consider the popular expectation of impending liberal democracy in China as very unlikely to materialize anytime soon. Regardless of which political scenario emerges in the end, the minimum requirements for further economic development are continued overall social order as well as stability in the general thrust of government economic policy. If whatever government emerges also succeeds in fostering high levels of institutionalized trust, the twenty-first century may indeed be China's. As has become abundantly clear, we remain skeptical about the prospect; at the same time we also know that when a complex adaptive system is capable of learning, it is also capable of yielding surprises.

Key References

Amsden, Alice H. 1992. *Asia's Next Giant: South Korea and Late Industrialization*. Oxford: Oxford University Press.

Gordon, David M. 1994. 'Chickens Home to Roost: From Prosperity to Stagnation in the Postwar U.S. Economy', in Michael A. Bernstein and David E. Adler (eds.),

Understanding American Economic Decline. Cambridge, UK: Cambridge University Press.

Perry, Elizabeth. 2005. 'Studying Chinese Politics: Farewell to Revolution?', *Fairbank Center for East Asian Research 50th Anniversary Conference*. Cambridge, MA.

Ralston, David A., James Pounder, Carlos W. H. Lo, Yim-Yu Wong, Carolyn P. Egri, and Joseph Stauffer. 2006. 'Stability and Change in Managerial Work Values: A Longitudinal Study of China, Hong Kong, and the U.S.', *Management and Organizational Review*, 2(1): 67–94.

Wilsdon, James, and James Keeley. 2007. *China: The Next Science Superpower?* London: Demos.

Witt, Michael A. 2003. 'From Last to Fast: Political and Economic Transformation in Korea, 1961', *INSEAD Case Study*. Singapore: INSEAD.

APPENDIX

1. Notes on Calculating the Contribution to the Trade Balance Measure of Comparative Advantage (Chapters 8–13)

In accordance with the methodology used by the OECD's *Science, Technology and Industry Scoreboard* (2003: 150), we compute this measure as follows:

$$(X_i - M_i) - (X - M)\frac{(X_i + M_i)}{(X + M)},$$

where $(X_i - M_i)$ is the observed trade balance in industry i and the remainder for the formula is the theoretical trade balance for this same industry i. To make the results comparable across countries, we express the results as a percentage of total trade.

Our data for computing these statistics for the United States, Japan, Germany, and South Korea come from the OECD STAN Bilateral Trade Database for manufacturing industries. Services trade data for 2003 were obtained by e-mail on 4 November 2005 in advance of their publication by the OECD in the database on Statistics on International Trade in Services. Our industry classifications follow those used by the OECD. According to the OECD, and as indicated in our figures showing the results, the manufacturing industries can be grouped by technology intensity into four broad categories: low, low–medium, medium–high, and high technology.

2. Comparative Advantage of Chinese Industries

We performed the same calculations outlined under point (1) of this Appendix for China. Since manufacturing trade data in the ISIC Rev. 3 classification used by the OECD are unavailable, we obtained data in Harmonized System (HS) classification from the United Nations Commodity Trade Statistics Database (Comtrade). We then used the OECD's methodology to map each HS category to an ISIC Rev. 3 category and sorted the result into the categories of industries used by the OECD and replicated in our comparative advantage calculations in Chapters 10–13. Services trade data were obtained from the UNCTAD *Handbook of Statistics* Online. In the services statistics, no breakdown is available for 'merchanting and other trade-related services,' 'operational leasing services,' and 'miscellaneous business, professional, and technical services.' These categories are combined under 'other business services.'

The results of these calculations are included in Figure 8.1 as a reference on p. 143.

3. List of Senior Executives Interviewed for Comparison of Executive Rationale

Countries and regions in alphabetical order, executives in alphabetical order by last names.

China

- Jessica Cai, General Manager, New Wish Light Industrial Co.
- Chen Wei Hui, President, Fujian Sanmu Group Co.
- Duan Zhuan Jian, Chairman, CuoZhen Corp.
- Guo Xiao Dong, Chief Partner, Xiamen Dadao Law Firm
- Huang Jinde, CEO, Xiamen Amber Fragrances Co.
- Huang Weinan, General Manager, China Tobacco Import Fujian
- Huang Xiao Dong, Vice President, Fujian Suimin Aluminium Sheet Co.
- Lin Kewei, General Manager, Xiamen Benma Industrial Co.
- Liang Tang, Chairman, YueCai
- Philip Lin, Deputy General Manager, Kaup Xiamen FLT Attachments Co.
- Liu Chuan Zhi, Chairman, Legend Holdings
- Lu Wei Dong, Director, Shenzen Shum Yip Equipment Co.
- Lu Yuebing, Managing Director, Climate Change Capital
- Luo Fangjun, Director, Xing Ye Industrial Securities Co.
- Jack Ma, Chairman & CEO, Alibaba
- Qi Qing, Chairwoman, Kery Bio-tech Inc.
- Shi Jian Xun, President, DaYa Tech
- Shi Wen Jun, CEO, Jiangsu Chia Tai Tianqing Pharmaceutical Co. Ltd.
- Wang Guo Zhan, General Manager, Quanzhou Haitian Textile Co.
- Wang Wenjing, Chairman & CEO, Usoft
- Wu Jin Xiang, Chairman, Xiamen Luyan Pharmaceutical Co.
- Wu Lai Chuan, General Manager, China Ocean Shipping Agency
- Xi Jin Song, Chairman, Shunye Steel Trading Co.
- Bill Yang, General Manager, Xiamen Innovation Metal Products Co.
- Yang Guiqing, Vice Chairwoman, Yili Corp.

- Yang Qing Quan, Vice General Manager, China Ocean Shipping Agency
- Scott C K Yang, Vice President, Vedan International Ltd.
- Zhang Qiming, Chairman, Panlong Investment Co.
- Jeanny Zhu, CEO, Guangzhou Zhong Che Railway Sales and Leasing Co., Guangzhou

A number of these interviews were conducted, using our interview schedule, by Professor Ming Zeng of the Cheung Kong Graduate School of Business in Beijing. We acknowledge his contribution with much gratitude.

Germany

- Dr. Uwe-Ernst Bufe, former CEO, Degussa
- Leonhard H. Fischer, executive board member, Allianz & Dresdner Bank
- Peter Fischl, CFO, Infineon
- Dr. Carl Hahn, former CEO, VW
- Dr. Wolf Klinz, executive board member, AGIV
- Hilmar Kopper, former CEO, Deutsche Bank
- Dr. Dietmar Kuhnt, CEO, RWE
- Dr. Ulrich Middelmann, Vice CEO, ThyssenKrupp
- Dr. Werner Schmidt, former CFO, VW
- Dr. Ronaldo Schmitz, former executive board member, Deutsche Bank
- Dr. Harald Schröder, former Vice CEO, Merck
- Dr. Henning Schulte-Noelle, CEO, Allianz
- Dr. Heinrich V. Pierer, CEO, Siemens
- Kurt F. Viermetz, Chairman of the Supervisory Board, HypoVereinsbank
- Dr. Herbert Wörner, former executive board member, Bosch; former CEO, Bosch Siemens Haushaltsgeraete
- Dr. Jürgen Zech, former CEO, Gerling
- Anonymous, CEO, DAX firm (one of Germany's thirty largest public firms)

The former executives on this list were generally not retired, but served on one or several supervisory boards. For instance, Hilmar Kopper was, among others, Chairman of the supervisory board of DaimlerChrysler, Dr. Herbert Wörner sat on the supervisory board of ThyssenKrupp, and so forth.

Hong Kong

- George K. Y. Chan, Chairman, Minstar Industrial Holdings Co., Hong Kong
- Ronnie Chan, President & CEO, Hang Lung Ltd.
- Philip Chen, CEO, Cathay Pacific
- Christopher Cheng, General Manager North Asia, Levi Strauss (Hong Kong) Ltd.
- Paul Chow, CEO, Hong Kong Stock Exchange

- Roger King, Member of the Board, Orient Overseas (Int.) Ltd.
- Peter T. C. Lee, Chairman, Hysan
- Michael K. H. Leung, Managing Director, Peoples Telephone Co. Ltd.
- Dr. David Li, Chairman & CEO, The Bank of East Asia Ltd.
- Dr. Helmut Sohmen, Chairman & President, World-Wide Shipping Group Ltd.
- Sir Gordon Wu, Chairman, Hopewell Holdings Ltd.
- William Ho, Managing Director, Growth Investments Ltd.

Most of these interviews were conducted by Emilio Manso-Salinas, a member of our research team exploring executive rationale. We acknowledge his contribution with much gratitude.

Japan

- Yoshikazu Hanawa, Chairman, Nissan
- Toru Hashimoto, former Chairman, Fuji Bank
- Terukazu Inoue, Special Auditor, Toyota
- Takeo Inokuchi, Chairman & President, Mitsui Sumitomo Insurance
- Masami Ito, President, Ito Ham
- Tetsuro Kawakami, former Chairman, Sumitomo Electric
- Yorihiko Kojima, Senior Executive Vice President, Mitsubishi Corp.
- Akira Uehara, President, Taisho Seiyaku
- Kaneichi Maehara, former board member, Sumitomo Life Insurance, Chairman, Sumitomo Life Research Institute
- Minoru Makihara, Chairman, Mitsubishi Corp.
- Hiroshi Nagata, Executive Vice President & board member, Mitsui & Co.
- Taizo Nishimuro, Chairman, Toshiba
- Akira Nishikawa, President & CEO, Mitsubishi Materials
- Koichi Ohmuro, Senior Managing Director & Senior Executive Officer, Mitsui Fudosan
- Masahiro Sakane, President, Komatsu Machinery
- Teruo Shimamura, President & COO, Nikon
- Yasuhiko Watanabe, former board member, Bank of Tokyo Mitsubishi, Senior Managing Director, Mitsubishi Estate

South Korea

- Moon-Seok Kang, President & CEO, Dong-A Pharmaceutical Co.
- Dr. Shin Ho Kang, Chairman, Dong-A Pharmaceutical Co.
- Chinhyun Kim, Advisor to the Chairman, Hyosung
- Dr. Dong-Jin Kim, President & CEO, Hyundai Motor Company
- Dong Yun Kim, Vice Chairman & CEO, Telson
- Dr. Joon Kim, Senior Managing Director, Kyungbang
- Milton S. Kim, Chairman, IT'S TV

- Syng J. Kim, Vice Chairman & CEO, SK Global
- Yongsung Kim, CEO, Neoplux Capital
- Dr. Chong S. Lee, Executive Vice President, LG Card
- Soo Young Lee, Chairman, DC Chemical
- Dr. Y. T. Lee, Chairman, TriGem Computer
- Yoon-Woo Lee, President & CEO, Samsung Electronics
- Chong Y. Pae, President & CEO, Samsung Corporation
- Yong Sung Park, Chairman, Doosan Heavy Industries & Construction
- Minsok Suh, Chairman & CEO, Dong-Il Corporation
- Anonymous, Chairman, small *chaebol*

United States

- Michael Alexander, President, The International Forum, former Director FASB, former Executive Partner, Touche Ross
- Robert Baylis, former Deputy Chairman, First Boston
- J. Frank Brown, former Global Advisory Services Leader, Pricewaterhouse Coopers
- Jon T. Elsasser, Director Corporate Relations, Timken
- Robert J. Herbold, former COO, Microsoft
- Victor J. Menezes, Director, Citigroup
- Joseph L. Rice III, Senior Partner, Clayton Dubillier & Rice
- Donald W. Blair, CFO & Vice President, Nike
- Doug Elix, Senior Vice President & Group Executive Sales and Distribution, IBM
- Richard Goodman, CFO, PepsiCo
- Arnold G. Langbo, former CEO & Chairman, Kellogg's
- James A. Lawrence, Vice Chairman & CFO, General Mills
- Leo F. Mullin, former CEO, Delta Airlines
- Mike A. Neal, Vice Chairman, GE, Chairman, GE Capital Services

Bibliography

Aldrich, Howard E., and Toshihiro Sasaki. 1995. 'R&D Consortia in the United States and Japan', *Research Policy*, 24: 301–16.

Allen, Franklin, Jun Qian, and Meijun Qian. 2004. 'Law, Finance, and Economic Growth in China', in *Wharton School Working Papers*.

Amsden, Alice H. 1989. *Asia's Next Giant: South Korea and Late Industrialization*. Oxford: Oxford University Press.

Baek, H. Young, and Lanying Huang. 2004. 'Taiwanese Investments in China: Foreign Direct Investment Scale and Performance', *Asia Pacific Journal of Economics and Business*, 8(2): 42–64.

Batjargal, Bat. 2005. 'Comparative Social Capital', in *William Davidson Institute Working Papers*. Michigan.

Berger, Peter L., and Thomas Luckmann. 1966. *The Social Construction of Reality*. London: Penguin.

Berger, Suzanne, and Ronald Philip Dore, eds. 1996. *National Diversity and Global Capitalism*. Ithaca, NY: Cornell University Press.

Biggart, Nicole Woolsey, and Rick Delbridge. 2004. 'Systems of Exchange', *Academy of Management Review*, 29(1): 28–49.

Boisot, Max. 1995. *Information Space*. London: Routledge.

—— and John Child. 1996. 'From Fiefs to Clans: Explaining China's Emerging Economic Order', *Administrative Science Quarterly*, 41(4): 600–28.

Bond, Michael Harris, Kwok Leung, et al. 2004. 'Culture-Level Dimensions of Social Axioms and Their Correlates across 41 Countries', *Journal of Cross-Cultural Psychology*, 35(5): 548–70.

Brodbeck, Felix C., Michael Frese, and Mansour Javidan. 2002. 'Leadership Made in Germany: Low on Compassion, High on Performance', *Academy of Management Executive*, 16(1): 13–15.

Calder, Kent E. 1993. *Strategic Capitalism: Private Business and Public Response in Japanese Industrial Finance*. Princeton, NJ: Princeton University Press.

Callon, Scott. 1995. *Divided Sun: Miti and the Breakdown of Japanese High-Tech Industrial Policy, 1975–1993*. Stanford, CA: Stanford University Press.

Cao, Yuanzheng, Yingyi Qian, and Barry R. Weingast. 1999. 'From Federalism, Chinese Style to Privatization, Chinese Style', *Economics of Transition*, 7(1): 103–31.

Carney, Michael, and Eric Gedajlovic. 2001. 'Corporate Governance and Firm Capabilities: A Comparison of Managerial, Alliance, and Personal Capitalisms', *Asia Pacific Journal of Management*, 18: 335–54.

—— —— 2002. 'The Co-Evolution of Institutional Environments and Organizational Strategies: The Rise of Family Business Groups in the Asean Region', *Organization Studies*, 23(1): 1–29.

Casimir, Gian, and Zhidong Li. 2005. 'Combinative Aspects of Leadership Style: A Comparison of Australian and Chinese Followers', *Asian Business and Management*, 4(3): 271–91.

Chandler, Alfred Dupont, Jr. 1977. *The Visible Hand: The Managerial Revolution in American Business*. Cambridge, MA: Harvard University Press.

Chang, Jung, and Jon Halliday. 2005. *Mao: The Unknown Story*. London: Jonathan Cape.

Chen, Feng. 2006. 'Privatization and Its Discontents in Chinese Factories', *The China Quarterly*, 185.

Chen, Ruiming. 1990. 'A Preliminary Analysis of the "Big Labour-Hiring Households"', in P. Nolan and F. Dong (eds.), *Market Forces in China: Competition and Small Business — the Wenzhou Debate*. London: Zed Books.

Chen, Xiao-Ping, and Chao C. Chen. 2004. 'On the Intricacies of the Chinese Guanxi: A Process Model of Guanxi Development', *Asia Pacific Journal of Management*, 21(3): 305–24.

Cheng, Bor-Shiuan, Li-Fang Chou, and Jiing-Lih Larry Farh. 2006. 'Do Employees' Authoritarian Values Matter? Effectiveness of People Vs. Task-Oriented Authoritarian Leadership in China and Taiwan Private Business', Paper read at International Association of Chinese Management Research, at Nanjing.

Child, John, and Alfred Kieser. 1979. 'Organization and Managerial Roles in British and West German Companies: An Examination of the Culture-Free Thesis', in C. J. Lammers and D. J. Hickson (eds.), *Organizations Alike and Unlike: International and Interinstitutional Studies in the Sociology of Organizations*. London: Routlege & Kegan Paul.

—— and Suzana B. Rodrigues. 2005. 'The Internationalization of Chinese Firms: A Case for Theoretical Extension', *Management and Organization Review*, 1(3): 381–410.

China State Council. 2005. 'China's Peaceful Development Road', in *Government White Paper*.

Chow, Irene Hau-Siu. 2004. 'Human Resource Management in China's Township and Village Enterprises: Change and Development During the Economic Reform Era', *Asia Pacific Journal of Human Resources*, 42(3): 318–35.

Coates, David, ed. 2002. *Models of Capitalism: Debating Strengths and Weaknesses*, 3 vols. Cheltenham, UK: Edward Elgar.

Crouch, Colin, and Wolfgang Streeck, eds. 1997. *Political Economy of Modern Capitalism: Mapping Convergence and Diversity*. London: Sage.

Curtis, Gerald L. 1988. *The Japanese Way of Politics*. New York: Columbia University Press.

_____ 1999. *The Logic of Japanese Politics: Leaders, Institutions, and the Limits of Change*. New York: Columbia University Press.

Cushman, Jennifer W. 1991. *Family and State: The Formation of a Sino-Thai Tin-Mining Dynasty*. Singapore: Oxford University Press.

Démurger, Sylvie. 2000. *Economic Opening and Growth in China*. Paris: OECD.

Desvaux, Georges, Michael Wang, and David Xu. 2004. 'Spurring Performance in China's State-Owned Enterprises', *McKinsey Quarterly*, Special edition: 96–106.

Diamant, Neil J., Stanley B. Lubman, and Kevin J. O'Brien, eds. 2005. *Engaging the Law in China*. Stanford, CA: Stanford University Press.

Dickson, Bruce J. 2003. *Red Capitalists in China: The Party, Private Entrepreneurs, and Prospects for Political Change*. New York: Cambridge University Press.

Ding, Daniel Z., and Malcolm Warner. 2001. 'China's Labour-Management System Reforms: Breaking the "Three Old Irons" (1978–1999)', *Asia Pacific Journal of Management*, 18(3): 315–34.

Ding, X. L. 2000a. 'Systemic Irregularity and Spontaneous Property Transformation in the Chinese Financial System', *The China Quarterly*, 163: 655–76.

_____ 2000b. 'The Illicit Asset Stripping of Chinese State Firms', *The China Journal*, 43 (Jan 2000): 1–28.

Djelic, Marie-Laure. 1998. *Exporting the American Model: The Postwar Transformation of European Business*. Oxford: Oxford University Press.

Dobbin, Frank. 1994. *Forging Industrial Policy: The United States, Britain, and France in the Railway Age*. Princeton, NJ: Princeton University Press.

Dolles, Harald. 2003. 'Evolution and Status of China's Private Entrepreneurship: An Economic Actors' Perspective', in Paper read at Euro-Asia Management Studies Association 20th Annual Conference, at Stockholm University School of Business.

Dong, Fureng. 1990. 'The Wenzhou Model for Developing the Rural Commodity Economy', in P. Nolan and F. Dong (eds.), *Market Forces in China: Competition and Small Business—the Wenzhou Debate*. London: Zed Books.

Dooley, Kevin J., and Andrew H. Van de Ven. 1999. 'Explaining Complex Organizational Dynamics', *Organization Science*, 10: 358–72.

Dore, Ronald Philip. 1973. *British Factory, Japanese Factory: The Origins of National Diversity in Industrial Relations*. Berkeley, CA: University of California Press.

_____ 1983. 'Goodwill and the Spirit of Market Capitalism', *The British Journal of Sociology*, 34: 459–82.

_____ 1986. *Flexible Rigidities: Industrial Policy and Structural Adjustment in the Japanese Economy, 1970–1980*. Stanford, CA: Stanford University Press.

_____ 2000. *Stock Market Capitalism: Welfare Capitalism: Japan and Germany Versus the Anglo-Saxons*. Oxford: Oxford University Press.

Dore, Ronald Philip, and Mari Sako. 1989. *How the Japanese Learn to Work*. London: Routledge.

Doz, Yves, J. Santos, and P. Williamson. 2001. *From Global to Metanational*. Cambridge, MA: Harvard Business School Press.

Dreyer, Edward L. 2007. *Zheng He: China and the Oceans in the Early Ming Dynasty 1404–1433*. London: Longman.

Dunning, John H., ed. 2003. *Making Globalization Good: The Moral Challenges of Global Capitalism*. Oxford: Oxford University Press.

Eckert, Carter J., Ki-baik Lee, Young Ick Lew, Michael Robinson, and Edward W. Wagner. 1990. *Korea Old and New: A History*. Cambridge, MA: Harvard University Press.

Eisenstadt, Shmuel N. 1968. 'The Protestant Ethic in an Analytical and Comparative Framework', in S. N. Eisenstadt (ed.), *The Protestant Ethic and Modernization: A Comparative View*. New York: Basic Books.

Elvin, Mark. 1973. *The Pattern of the Chinese Past*. Stanford, CA: Stanford University Press.

Elvis, P. J. 1999. 'The Strategy and Structure of the Large, Diversified, Ethnic Chinese Organizations of Southeast Asia', unpublished dectoral dissertation, University of Hong Kong, Hong Kong.

Fairbank, John K., Edwin O. Reischauer, and Albert M. Craig. 1965. *East Asia: The Modern Transformation*. Boston, MA: Houghton Mifflin.

Farrell, Diana, Ulrich A. Gersch, and Elizabeth Stevenson. 2006. 'The Value of China's Emerging Middle Class', *McKinsey Quarterly*, Special edition: 60–9.

Faure, David. 2006. *China and Capitalism*. Hong Kong: Hong Kong University Press.

Feng, Yunxia, and Edward F. McDonough. 2006. 'An Investigation of the Performance Appraisal Process in Chinese Companies Versus US Based MNCs', in Paper read at International Association for Chinese Management Research Annual Conference, June 15 2006, at Nanjing.

Feuchtwang, Stephen, ed. 2004. *Making Place: State Projects, Globalization and Local Responses in China*. London: UCL Press.

Feuerwerker, Albert. 1958. *China's Early Industrialization*. Cambridge, MA: Harvard University Press.

Fiss, Peer C., and Edward J. Zajac. 2004. 'The Diffusion of Ideas over Contested Terrain: The (Non)Adoption of a Shareholder Value Orientation among German Firms', *Administrative Science Quarterly*, 49: 501–34.

Fligstein, Neil. 1990. *The Transformation of Corporate Control*. Cambridge, MA: Harvard University Press.

—— 2001. *The Architecture of Markets*. Princeton, NJ: Princeton University Press.

Foster, George M. 1967. 'Peasant Society and the Image of Limited Good', in J. M. Potter, M. N. Diaz and G. M. Foster (eds.), *Peasant Society*. Boston, MA: Little, Brown.

Fruin, W. Mark. 1992. *The Japanese Enterprise System: Competitive Strategies and Cooperative Structures*. Oxford: Clarendon Press.

Fukuyama, Francis. 1995. *Trust: The Social Virtues and the Creation of Prosperity*. New York: The Free Press.

Garnaut, Ross, and Ligang Song, eds. 2003. *China: New Engine of World Growth*. Canberra, Australia: Asia Pacific Press.

Garnaut, Ross, Ligang Song, and Yang Yao. 2006. 'Impact and Significance of State-Owned Enterprise Restructuring in China', *The China Journal*, 55(Jan 2006): 35–63.

Geertz, Clifford. 1973. *The Interpretation of Cultures*. New York: Basic Books.

Gerlach, Michael L. 1992. *Alliance Capitalism: The Social Organization of Japanese Business*. Berkeley, CA: University of California Press.

Giddens, Anthony. 1984. *The Constitution of Society*. Berkeley, CA: University of California Press.

Gilboy, George J. 2004. 'The Myth Behind China's Miracle', *Foreign Affairs*, 83(4): 33–48.

Gold, Thomas, Doug Guthrie, and David Wank, eds. 2002. *Social Connections in China: Institutions, Culture, and the Changing Nature of Guanxi*. Cambridge: Cambridge University Press.

Goldman, Merle. 2005. *From Comrade to Citizen: The Struggle for Political Rights in China*. Cambridge, MA: Harvard University Press.

____ and Roderick MacFarquhar, eds. 1999. *The Paradox of China's Post-Mao Reforms*. Cambridge, MA: Harvard University Press.

Goodman, David S. G. 2006. 'Narratives of Change: Culture and Local Economic Development', Working papers, University of Technology, Sydney.

Grant, Wyn, William Paterson, and Colin Whitston. 1987. 'Government–Industry Relations in the Chemical Industry: An Anglo-German Comparison', in S. Wilks and M. Wright (eds.), *Comparative Government-Industry Relations: Western Europe, the United States, and Japan*. Oxford: Oxford University Press.

Greenwood, Royston, Roy Suddaby, and C. R. Hinings. 2002. 'Theorizing Change: The Role of Professional Associations in the Transformation of Institutionalized Fields', *Academy of Management Journal*, 45(1): 58–80.

Greif, Avner. 1993. 'Contract Enforceability and Economic Institutions in Early Trade: The Maghribi Traders' Coalition', *American Economic Review*, 83: 525–48.

____ 1994. 'Trading Institutions and the Commercial Revolution in Medieval Europe', in A. Abanbegyan, O. Bogomolov, and M. Kaser (eds.), *Economics in a Changing World*, Vol. 1: *System Transformation: Eastern and Western Assessments*. New York: St. Martin's Press.

____ 2006. *Institutions and the Path to the Modern Economy*. Cambridge: Cambridge University Press.

Guillén, Mauro F. 1994. *Models of Management: Work, Authority, and Organization in a Comparative Perspective*. Chicago, IL: University of Chicago Press.

____ 2001. *The Limits of Convergence*. Princeton, NJ: Princeton University Press.

Gulati, Ranjay. 1995. 'Does Familiarity Breed Trust? The Implications of Repeated Ties for Contractual Choice in Alliances', *Academy of Management Journal*, 38: 85–112.

Guo, Xiaoqin. 2003. *State and Society in China's Democratic Transition*. New York: Routledge.

Guthrie, Douglas. 1999. *Dragon in a Three-Piece Suit: The Emergence of Capitalism in China*. Princeton, NJ: Princeton University Press.

——— 2006. *China and Globalization*. New York: Routledge.

Hall, Peter A., and D. Soskice, eds. 2001. *Varieties of Capitalism*. Oxford: Oxford University Press.

Hamilton, Gary G. 1990. 'Patriarchy, Patrimonialism and Filial Piety: A Comparison of China and Western Europe', *British Journal of Sociology*, 41(1): 77–104.

Hane, Gerald. 1999. 'Comparing University–Industry Linkages in Japan and the United States', in L. M. Branscomb, F. Kodama, and R. Florida (eds.), *Industrializing Knowledge: University–Industry Linkages in Japan and the United States*. Cambridge, MA: MIT Press.

Harrison, Lawrence E. 1985. *Underdevelopment Is a State of Mind: The Latin American Case*. Cambridge, MA: Harvard University Centre for International Affairs.

Hayek, Friedrich Anton. 1945. 'The Use of Knowledge in Society', *American Economic Review*, 35: 519–30.

Heckman, James J. 2003. 'Flexibility and Job Creation: Lessons for Germany', in P. Aghion, R. Frydman, J. Stiglitz, and M. Woodford (eds.), *Knowledge, Information, and Expectations in Modern Macroeconomics: In Honor of Edmund S. Phelps*. Princeton, NJ: Princeton University Press.

Hendrischke, Hans. 2006. 'Networks as Business Networks', in B. Krug and H. Hendrischke (eds.), *China's Economy in the 21st Century: Enterprise and Business Behaviour*. London: Edward Elgar.

Himmelfarb, Gertrude. 2004. *The Roads to Modernity*. New York: Alfred A. Knopf.

Hirschmeier, Johannes, and Tsunehiko Yui. 1981. *The Development of Japanese Business, 1600–1980*. 2nd edn. London: Allen & Unwin.

Hofstede, Geert. 1980. *Culture's Consequences*. London: Sage.

——— 1991. *Cultures and Organizations: Software of the Mind*. London: McGraw-Hill.

Hollingsworth, J. Rogers, and Robert Boyer, eds. 1997. *Contemporary Capitalism: The Embeddedness of Institutions*. Cambridge: Cambridge University Press.

House, Robert J., P. J. Hanges, M. Javidan, P. W. Dorfman, and V. Gupta. 2004. *Culture, Leadership and Organizations: The Globe Study of 62 Societies*. Thousand Oaks, CA: Sage.

Huang, David D. H. 2004. 'Civil Society as an Analytic Lens for Contemporary China', *China: An International Journal*, 1–27.

Huang, Xu, Evert Van der Vliert, and Gerben Van der Vegt. 2005. 'Breaking the Silence Culture: Stimulation of Participation and Employee Opinion Withholding Cross-Nationally', *Management and Organization Review*, 1(3): 459–82.

Huang, Yasheng. 2003. *Selling China: Foreign Direct Investment During the Reform Era.* Cambridge: Cambridge University Press.

Huchet, Jean-Francois. 1999. 'Concentration and the Emergence of Corporate Groups in Chinese Industry', *China Perspectives*, 23 (May–June): 5–17.

IFC. 2000. *China's Emerging Private Enterprises: Prospects for the New Century.* Washington, DC: International Finance Corporation.

Imai, Ken'ichi. 1992. 'Japan's Corporate Networks', in S. Kumon and H. Rosovsky (eds.), *The Political Economy of Japan*, Vol. 3: *Cultural and Social Dynamics.* Stanford, CA: Stanford University Press.

Inagami, Takeshi, and D. Hugh Whittaker. 2005. *The New Community Firm: Employment, Governance and Management Reform in Japan.* Cambridge: Cambridge University Press.

Inglehart, Ronald. 1997. *Modernization and Postmodernization: Cultural, Economic and Political Change in 43 Societies.* Princeton, NJ: Princeton University Press.

____ 2000. 'Culture and Democracy', in L. E. Harrison and S. P. Huntington (eds.), *Culture Matters.* New York: Basic Books.

Inglehart, Ronald, and Christian Welzel. 2005. *Modernization, Cultural Change, and Democracy.* Cambridge: Cambridge University Press.

Inkpen, Andrew C., and Eric W. K. Tsang. 2005. 'Social Capital, Networks, and Knowledge Transfer', *Academy of Management Review*, 30(1): 146–65.

Jackson, Gregory. 2003. 'Corporate Governance in Germany and Japan: Liberalization Pressures and Responses During the 1990s', in K. Yamamura and W. Streeck (eds.), *The End of Diversity? Prospects for German and Japanese Capitalism.* Ithaca, NY: Cornell University Press.

Jackson, Gregory, and Hideaki Miyajima. 2004. 'Corporate Governance in Japan: Institutional Change and Organizational Diversity', Paper read at RIETI Symposium 'Corporate Governance in Japan: Converging to Any Particular New Model?' at United Nations University, Tokyo.

Jacobs, Norman. 1985. *The Korean Road to Modernization and Development.* Urbana, IL: University of Illinois Press.

Jenner, W. J. F. 1992. *The Tyranny of History.* London: Allen Lane.

Jia, Liangding, Junjun Zhang, Haiyan Qian, Rongjun Cui, and Yongxia Chen. 2006. 'A Study on the Similarities and Differences between the Cognitions of Western Theories and Chinese Enterprises on Motivations, Timing and Industrial Choice of Enterprises' Diversification', Paper read at International Association for Chinese Management Research Annual Conference, at Nanjing.

Johnson, Chalmers. 1982. *Miti and the Japanese Miracle: The Growth of Industrial Policy 1925–1975.* Stanford, CA: Stanford University Press.

Jones, Leroy P., and Il SaKong. 1980. *Government, Business, and Entrepreneurship in Economic Development: The Korean Case.* Cambridge, MA: Harvard University Press.

Kato, Takao. 2001. 'The End of Lifetime Employment in Japan? Evidence from National Surveys and Field Research', *Journal of the Japanese and International Economies*, 15: 489–514.

Kerr, Clark. 1983. *The Future of Industrial Societies*. Cambridge, MA: Harvard University Press.

Kerr, Clark, J. T. Dunlop, F. H. Harbison, and C. A. Myers. 1960. *Industrialism and Industrial Man*. Cambridge, MA: Harvard University Press.

Kogut, Bruce. 2003. 'Opening Address: Context in International Business Theory', Paper read at JIBS First Annual Conference on Emerging Research Frontiers, March 2003, at Duke University.

Kong, Siew-Huat. 2006. 'An Empirical Investigation of Mainland Chinese Organizational Ideology', *Asian Business and Management*, 5(3): 357–78.

Krug, Barbara, and Jeroen Kuilman. 2006. 'Whom Are We Dealing With? Shifting Organizational Forms in China's Business Sector', in B. Krug and H. Hendischke (eds.), *China's Economy in the 21st Century: Enterprise and Business Behaviour*. London: Edward Elgar.

Landes, David. 1998. *The Wealth and Poverty of Nations*. New York: Norton.

Lardy, Nicholas R. 1998. *China's Unfinished Economic Revolution*. Washington, DC: Brookings Institution Press.

Lazonick, William. 1991. *Business Organization and the Myth of the Market Economy*. Cambridge: Cambridge University Press.

Leung, Kwok, and Michael H. Bond. 2004. 'Social Axioms: A Model for Social Beliefs in Multi-Cultural Perspective', *Advances in Experimental Social Psychology*, 36: 119–97.

Lewin, Arie Y., and Jisung Kim. 2004. 'The Nation State and Culture as Influences on Organizational Change and Innovation', in M. S. Poole (ed.), *Handbook of Organizational Change and Development*. Oxford: Oxford University Press.

—— Chris P. Long, and Timothy N. Carroll. 1999. 'The Coevolution of New Organizational Forms', *Organization Science*, 10(5): 535–50.

—— Silvia Massini, Windfried Ruigrok, and Tsuyoshi Numagami. 2003. 'Convergence and Divergence of Organizing: The Moderating Effect of Nation State', in A. M. Pettigrew, R. Whittington, L. Melin, C. Sanchez-Runde, F. A. J. van den Bosch, W. Ruigrok and T. Numagami (eds.), *Innovative Forms of Organizing: International Perspectives*. London: Sage.

—— and Carroll U. Stephens. 1993. 'Designing Post-Industrial Organizations: Combining Theory and Practice', in G. P. Huber and W. H. Glick, (eds.), *Organizational Change and Redesign*. Oxford: Oxford University Press.

—— and Henk W. Volberda. 1999. 'Prolegomena on Coevolution: A Framework for Research on Strategy and New Organizational Forms', *Organization Science*, 10(5): 519–34.

Li, Peter Ping. 2005. 'The Puzzle of China's Township-Village Enterprises: The Paradox of Local Corporations in a Dual-Track Economic Transition', *Management and Organization Review*, 1(2): 197–224.

Li, Shaomin, Shuhe Li, and Weiying Zhang. 2000. 'The Road to Capitalism: Competition and Institutional Change in China', *Journal of Comparative Economics*, 28: 262–92.

Li, Shi. 1990. 'The Growth of Household Industry in Rural Wenzhou', in P. Nolan and F. Dong (eds.), *Market Forces in China: Competition and Small Business—the Wenzhou Debate*. London: Zed Books.

Lieberthal, Kenneth, and Geoffrey Lieberthal. 2003. 'The Great Transition', *Harvard Business Review*, October 2003: 3–14.

Lim, M. H. 1983. 'The Ownership and Control of Large Corporations in Malaysia: The Role of Chinese Businessman', in L. Y. C. Lim and P. Gosling (eds.), *The Chinese in Southeast Asia*. Singapore: Maruzen.

Lincoln, James R., and Michael L. Gerlach. 2004. *Japan's Network Economy: Structure, Persistence, and Change*. Cambridge: Cambridge University Press.

Liu, Yia-Ling. 1992. 'Reform from Below: The Private Economy and Local Politics in the Rural Industrialization of Wenzhou', *The China Quarterly*, 130: 293–316.

Lo, Vai Io, and Xiaowen Tian. 2005. *Law and Investment in China*. London: RoutledgeCurzon.

Lu, Le, and Ilan Alon. 2003. 'Changing Cultural and Economic Values of the Young and Educated in China', *Asia Pacific Journal of Economics and Business*, 7(2): 37–52.

Luo, Jar-Der. 2005. 'Particularistic Trust and General Trust: A Network Analysis in Chinese Organizations', *Management and Organization Review*, 1(3): 437–58.

MacFarquhar, Roderick, and Michael Schoenhals. 2007. *Mao's Last Revolution*. Cambridge, MA: Belknap Press.

Manow, Philip, and Eric Seils. 2000. 'Adjusting Badly: The German Welfare State, Structural Change, and the Open Economy', in F. W. Scharpf and V. A. Schmidt (eds.), *Welfare and Work in the Open Economy: Diverse Responses to Common Challenges*. Oxford: Oxford University Press.

Mathews, John A. 2006. 'Dragon Multinationals: New Players in 21st Century Globalization', *Asia Pacific Journal of Management*, 23(1): 5–27.

Maurice, Marc. 1989. 'Methode comparative et analyse societale', *Sociologie du Travail*, 2: 175–91.

Mayer, Michael C. J., and Richard Whittington. 1999. 'Strategy, Structure And "Systemness": National Institutions and Corporate Change in France, Germany and the UK, 1950–1993', *Organization Studies*, 20(6): 933–59.

Mertha, Andrew C. 2005. 'China's "Soft" Centralization: Shifting Tiao/Kuai Authority Relations', *The China Quarterly*, 184.

Meyer, Marshall, and Xiaohui Lu. 2005. 'Managing Indefinite Boundaries: The Strategy and Structure of a Chinese Business Firm', *Management and Organization Review*, 1(1): 57–86.

Naughton, Barry. 2007. *The Chinese Economy*. Cambridge, MA: MIT Press.

Nee, Victor. 1992. 'Organizational Dynamics of Market Transition: Hybrid Forms, Property Rights, and Mixed Economy in China', *Administrative Science Quarterly*, 37(1): 1–27.

—— and Cao Yang. 2005. 'Market Transition and the Firm: Change and Income Inequality in Urban China', *Management and Organization Review*, 1(1): 23–56.

Nolan, Peter. 2004*a*. *Transforming China: Globalization, Transition and Development.* London: Anthem Press.

—— 2004*b*. *China at the Crossroads.* Cambridge: Polity Press.

—— and Fureng Dong, eds. 1990. *Market Forces in China: Competition and Small Business—the Wenzhou Debate.* London: Zed Books.

Norris, Pippa, and Ronald Inglehart. 2004. *Sacred and Secular: Religion and Politics Worldwide.* Cambridge: Cambridge University Press.

North, Douglass Cecil. 1990. 'Institutions, Institutional Change and Economic Performance', in J. E. Alt and D. C. North (eds.), *Political Economy of Institutions and Decisions.* Cambridge: Cambridge University Press.

—— 1991. *Institutions, Institutional Change, and Economic Performance.* Cambridge: Cambridge University Press.

—— 1994. 'Economic Performance through Time', *American Economic Review*, 84(3): 359–68.

—— 2005. *Understanding the Process of Economic Change.* Princeton, NJ: Princeton University Press.

O'Sullivan, Mary. 2000. *Contests for Corporate Control: Corporate Governance and Economic Performance in the United States and Germany.* Oxford: Oxford University Press.

OECD. 2003. *OECD Science, Technology and Industry Scoreboard.* Paris: OECD.

—— 2005*a*. *OECD Economic Surveys: China.* Paris: OECD.

—— 2005*b*. *OECD Economic Surveys: Korea.* Paris: OECD.

Oi, Jean C. 1999. *Rural China Takes Off: Institutional Foundations of Economic Reform.* Berkeley, CA: University of California Press.

Okimoto, Daniel I. 1989. *Between Miti and the Market: Japanese Industrial Policy for High Technology.* Stanford, CA: Stanford University Press.

Ong, Lynette. 2006. 'The Political Economy of Township Government Debt, Township Enterprises and Rural Financial Institutions in China', *The China Quarterly*, 186.

Orrù, Marco. 1997. 'Institutional Cooperation in Japanese and German Capitalism', in M. Orrù, N. W. Biggart, and G. G. Hamilton (eds.), *The Economic Organization of East Asian Capitalism.* Thousand Oaks, CA: Sage.

Pac, Sung Moon. 1992. *Korea Leading Developing Nations: Economy, Democracy, & Welfare.* Lanham, ML: University Press of America.

Pearson, Margaret M. 1997. *China's New Business Elite: The Political Consequences of Economic Reform.* Berkeley, CA: University of California Press.

Pei, Minxin. 2006. *China's Trapped Transition: The Limits of Developmental Autocracy.* Cambridge, MA: Harvard University Press.

Pei, Xiaoge. 1990. 'Small Town Construction: An Alternative Path', in P. Nolan and F. Dong (eds.), *Market Forces in China: Competition and Small Business—the Wenzhou Debate*. London: Zed Books.

Pekkanen, Saadia M. 2003. *Picking Winners? From Technology Catch-up to the Space Race in Japan*. Stanford, CA: Stanford University Press.

Pomerantz, Kenneth. 2000. *The Great Divergence*. Princeton, NJ: Princeton University Press.

Porter, Michael E. 1990. *The Competitive Advantage of Nations*. New York: Free Press.

____ 2000. 'Attitudes, Values and Beliefs and the Microeconomics of Prosperity', in L. E. Harrison and S. P. Huntington (eds.), *Culture Matters*. New York: Basic Books.

____ and Rebecca E. Wayland. 1995. 'Global Competition and the Localization of Competitive Advantage', *Advances in Strategic Management*, 11(A): 63–105.

Putnam, Robert D. 2000. *Bowling Alone: The Collapse and Revival of American Community*. New York: Simon & Schuster.

Pye, Lucian. 1985. *Asian Power and Politics: The Cultural Dimensions of Authority*. Cambridge, MA: Belknap Press.

____ 1992. 'Social Science Theories in Search of Chinese Realities', *China Quarterly*, 132: 1161–70.

Ragin, Charles C. 1987. *The Comparative Method*. Berkeley, CA: University of California Press.

Ralston, David A., James Pounder, Carlos W. H. Lo, Yim-Yu Wong, Carolyn P. Egri, and Joseph Stauffer. 2006. 'Stability and Change in Managerial Work Values: A Longitudinal Study of China, Hong Kong, and the US', *Management and Organization Review*, 2(1): 67–94.

Rangan, Subramanian, and A. Drummond. 2002. 'Explaining Outcomes in Competition among Foreign Multinationals in a Focal Host Market', *INSEAD Working Paper*.

Rappai, M. V. 2006. 'From Market to Social Harmony', *China Report*, 42(3): 297–303.

Rawls, John. 1999. *Collected Papers*. Cambridge, MA: Harvard University Press.

Redding, Gordon. 1990. *The Spirit of Chinese Capitalism*. New York: de Gruyter.

____ 2005a. 'The Thick Description and Comparison of Societal Systems of Capitalism', *Journal of International Business Studies*, 36: 123–55.

____ 2005b. 'Principles of the Comparative Method in the Analysis of Societal Systems of Business: The Example of China', *Working Papers*. The Euro-Asia and Comparative Research Centre, INSEAD.

____ 2005. 'Feeling the Stones on the River Bed: prospects and implications for China's entry into the world of global competition', *Ivey Business Journal*, May–June 2005, 1–9.

Redding, Gordon, and Michael A. Witt. 2004. 'The Role of Executive Rationale in the Comparison of Capitalisms: Some Preliminary Findings', *INSEAD EAC Working Paper Series*. Fontainebleau, France.

Rosen, Daniel H. 2006. 'Comparative Disadvantage: What China Can't Do', *China Economic Quarterly*, Q3(2006): 45–51.

Rosen, Stanley. 2004. 'The Victory of Materialism: Aspirations to Join China's Urban Moneyed Classes and the Commercialization of Education', *The China Journal*, 51(Jan 2004): 27–51.

Rugman, Alan M., and Alain Verbeke. 2004. 'A Perspective on Regional and Global Strategies of Multinational Enterprises', *Journal of International Business Studies*, 35(1): 3–18.

Sato, Hiroshi. 2003. *The Growth of Market Relations in Post-Reform Rural China*. London: RoutledgeCurzon.

Schumpeter, Joseph A. 1976. *Capitalism, Socialism and Democracy*. London: Routledge. Original edition, 1942.

Schwartz, Frank J. 2003. 'What Is Civil Society?' in F. J. Schwartz and S. J. Pharr (eds.), *The State of Civil Society in Japan*. Cambridge: Cambridge University Press.

Schwartz, S. H. 1992. 'The Universal Content and Structure of Values: Theoretical Advances and Empirical Tests in 20 Countries', in M. P. Zanna (ed.), *Advances in Experimental Social Psychology*. New York: Academic Press.

—— 1994. 'Beyond Individualism/Collectivism: New Dimensions of Values', in U. Kim, H. C. Triandis, C. Kagitcibasi, S. C. Choi, and G. Yoon (eds.), *Individualism and Collectivism: Theory, Method and Applications*. Newbury Park, CA: Sage.

Siebert, Horst. 2005. *The German Economy: Beyond the Social Market*. Princeton, NJ: Princeton University Press.

Song, Byung-Nak. 2003. *The Rise of the Korean Economy*. Oxford: Oxford University Press.

Sorge, Arndt. 2005. *The Global and the Local: Understanding the Dialectics of Business Systems*. Oxford: Oxford University Press.

Spence, Jonathan D. 1990. *The Search for Modern China*. London: Hutchinson.

Stinchcombe, Arthur L. 1974. *Creating Efficient Industrial Administration*. New York: Academic Press.

Streeck, Wolfgang. 1996. 'Lean Production in the German Automobile Industry: A Test Case for Convergence Theory', in S. Berger and R. P. Dore (eds.), *National Diversity and Global Capitalism*. Ithaca, NY: Cornell University Press.

—— 1997a. 'Beneficial Constraints: On the Economic Limits of Rational Voluntarism', in J. R. Hollingsworth and R. Boyer (eds.), *Contemporary Capitalism*. Cambridge: Cambridge University Press.

—— 1997b. 'German Capitalism: Does It Exist? Can It Survive?', *New Political Economy*, 2(2): 237–56.

—— and Kozo Yamamura, eds. 2001. *The Origins of Nonliberal Capitalism: Germany and Japan in Comparison*. Ithaca, NY: Cornell University Press.

Studwell, Joe. 2002. *The China Dream*. London: Profile Books.

Sung, Yung-Wing. 2005. *The Emergence of Greater China*. New York: Palgrave Macmillan.

Takeuchi, Junko. 2003. 'Trade and Investment Liberalization and Industrial Restructuring in China', *RIM Pacific Business and Industries*, 111(8): 2–22.

Tam, Simon. 2001. 'The Nature of Entrepreneur-Environment Relations: A Participant Reconstruction Perspective', in *Hong Kong University School of Business Working Papers*, Hong Kong.

Tang, Jie, and Anthony Ward. 2003. *The Changing Face of Chinese Management.* London: Routledge.

Tenev, Stoyan. 2006. 'China's Ownership Transformation', *Far Eastern Economic Review*, 169(1): 22–5.

Thomas, L. G., III, and Geoffrey Waring. 1999. 'Competing Capitalisms: Capital Investment in American, German, and Japanese Firms', *Strategic Management Journal*, 20(8): 729–48.

Tsai, Kellee S. 2002. *Back-Alley Banking: Private Entrepreneurs in China.* Ithaca, NY: Cornell University Press.

Tsui, Anne S., Duanxu Wang, and Yichi Zhang. 2002. 'Employment Relationships with Chinese Middle Managers: Exploring Differences between State-Owned and Non State-Owned Firms', in A. S. Tsui and C.-M. Lau (eds.), *The Management of Enterprises in the People's Republic of China.* Boston: Kluwer Academic.

Volberda, Henk W., and Arie Y. Lewin. 2003. 'Co-Evolutionary Dynamics within and between Firms: From Evolution to Co-Evolution', *Journal of Management Studies*, 40(8): 2111–36.

Wang, Gungwu. 2003. *Ideas Won't Keep: The Struggle for China's Future.* Singapore: Eastern Universities Press.

Weber, Max. 1922. *Wirtschaft Und Gesellschaft (Economy and Society).* Tübingen, Germany: J. C. B. Mohr.

—— 1927. *General Economic History.* Translated by F. H. Knight. New York: Greenberg.

—— 1930. *The Protestant Ethic and the Spirit of Capitalism.* Translated by T. Parsons. London: Unwin. Original edition, 1904.

Wederman, Andrew. 2004. 'Great Disorder under Heaven: Endemic Corruption and Rapid Growth in Contemporary China', *The China Review*, 4(2): 1–32.

Westney, D. Eleanor. 1996. 'The Japanese Business System: Key Features and Prospects for Changes', *Journal of Asian Business*, 12(1): 21–50.

Whitley, Richard. 1992. *Business Systems in East Asia: Firms, Markets and Societies.* London: Sage.

—— 1999a. *Divergent Capitalisms: The Social Structuring and Change of Business Systems.* Oxford: Oxford University Press.

—— 1999b. 'Competing Logics and Units of Analysis in the Comparative Study of Economic Organization', *International Studies of Management and Organization*, 29(2): 113–26.

—— ed. 2002. *Competing Capitalisms: Institutions and Economies.* 2 vols. Cheltenham, UK: Edward Elgar.

Wilsdon, James, and James Keeley. 2007. *China: The Next Science Superpower?* London: Demos.

Bibliography

Witt, Michael A. 2001. 'Research Cooperatives', in A. Bird (ed.), *Encyclopedia of Japanese Business and Management*. London: Routledge.

—— 2003. 'From Last to Fast: Political and Economic Transformation in Korea, 1961', *INSEAD Case Study*. Singapore: INSEAD.

—— 2006. *Changing Japanese Capitalism: Societal Coordination and Institutional Adjustment*. Cambridge: Cambridge University Press.

—— and Arie Y. Lewin. 2007. 'Outward Foreign Direct Investment as Escape Response to Home Country Institutional Structures', 38(4): 579–94.

Wuthnow, Robert, J. D. Hunter, A. Bergesen, and E. Kurzweil. 1984. *Cultural Analysis*. London: Routledge & Kegan Paul.

Yang, Dali L. 1996. *Calamity and Reform in China: State, Rural Reform, and Institutional Change since the Great Leap Famine*. Stanford, CA: Stanford University Press.

—— 2004. *Remaking the Chinese Leviathan*. Stanford, CA: Stanford University Press.

Yeung, Henry W. C. 2006. 'Change and Continuity in Southeast Asian Ethnic Chinese Business', *Asia Pacific Journal of Management*, 23(3): 229–54.

Yu, Bonnie Bei, and Carolyn P. Egri. 2005. 'Human Resource Management Practices and Affective Organizational Commitment: A Comparison of Chinese Employees in a State-Owned Enterprise and a Joint Venture', *Asia Pacific Journal of Human Resources*, 43(3): 332–60.

Zhang, Lin. 1990. 'Developing the Commodity Economy in Rural Areas', in P. Nolan and F. Dong (eds.), *Market Forces in China: Competition and Small Business—the Wenzhou Debate*. London: Zed Books.

Zhang, Xueyuan, Patrick Reinmoller, and Barbara Krug. 2006. 'Foreign Firms in China: Success by Strategic Choices', Paper read at Netherlands Organization for Scientific Research Conference: Shift in Governance and the Emergence of a Chinese Business System, July 2006, at Hangzhou.

Zhou, Kate Xiao. 1996. *How the Farmers Changed China: Power of the People*. Boulder, CO: Westview Press.

Zhu, Cherrie J. 2005. *Human Resource Management in China*. London: Routledge.

Index

Acer 62, 130
adaptability:
  and China 166, 167
  and United States 162, 167
aerospace industry, and United States 164
agriculture 135
  and communes 104–5
allocative efficiency, and economic
    organization 19
American International 67
'Asian crisis' (1997–98) 70
Association of Southeast Asian Nations
    (ASEAN) 62
authority:
  and culture 22
  and future of Chinese capitalism 217–19
  and Germany 184
  and impact on middle management 216
  and Japan 170
  and local corporates 112–13
  and ownership 216
  and private sector 131
  and South Korea 198, 201
  and United States 155
automobile industry:
  and competitiveness of foreign firms 226,
    227
  and Germany 191
  and Japan 176, 177
  and South Korea 204–6

Bank of America 83
Bank of China 83
banking system:
  and allocation of capital 88, 89
  and control of 89
  and foreign banks 90
  and Germany 185, 188
  and Japan 171, 175
  and private sector 131, 134
  and South Korea 199, 202
Bao Steel 227

BASF 193
Bayer 193
BMW 191
Boisot, Max 104, 116
Broad Airconditioning 217
Buddhism 38, 39–40
bureaucratic capitalism 64–5
business organization, see local corporates;
    private sector; state-owned
    enterprises
business systems:
  and authority 22
  and common features 13
  and comparative advantage 151
  and connections within 33–4
  and coordination 22–4
  and diversity of 81, 231
  and embeddedness of 8
  and ersatz capitalism 73–4
  and explaining evolution of 16–17
  and external influences 24
  and historical context 23
  and identity 22
  and institutions and order 22, 26–7
  and management 23, 31–3, 56–7
  and meaning and order 25–6
  and national context 7–8
  and networks 23, 30–1
  and order 21–2, 26–7
  and meaning 25–6
  and ownership 23, 28–30
  and rationale 21
  and requirements of 16–17
    organizational 17–18
    societal institutions 18–21
  and role of the state 23–4
  and societal differences:
    culture 15–16
    interest groups 13
    role of government 14
    social development 14–15
    trust 15

business systems (*cont.*)
  see also collective sector; local corporates;
      private sector; state-owned enterprises

capital:
  and allocation of 88–90
    competition for 90
    foreign banks 90
    inefficiency of 89–90
    regional autonomy 88–9
    stock markets 89
  and economic life 22
  and Germany 185
  and Japan 171–2
  and local corporates 113–14
  and private sector 133–4
  and South Korea 199
  and United States 156–7, 161
  see also human capital; social capital
capitalism:
  and development of modern 4
  and requirements of 17
    organizational 17–18
    societal institutions 18–21
change 44
  and obstacles to 100–1
  and organizations 18
  and society 21
chemical industry, and Germany 191, 193
Cheung Kong 62, 72
Chiang Kai-shek 66
Child, John 104
China:
  and academic studies of 230
  and applicability of other capitalist
      systems 221, 222
    Germany 194–5
    Japan 180–1
    South Korea 207–9, 223–5
    United States 165–7
  and domestic market growth 2
  and economic modernization 3–4
    challenges of 6, 49
    embeddedness 7
    features of context 6–7
    path dependence 7
    political will to change 6
  and external influences 61
  and family 44–5, 54, 57–8
    Confucianism 38–9
    economic behavior 216
    entrepreneurship 58
    role of 127–9
    socialization within 91

  and future of capitalism in:
    authority 217–19
    demographic change 232–3
    foreign firms 226–9
    government 224–5
    ideological change 217
    innovation 219–20
    institutional trust 221–2, 224, 231–2
    international alliances 228
    international politics 232
    limits on transactions 222
    local government 225
    manufacturing 227–8
    multinational enterprises 222–3, 228–9
    political developments 233
    purpose of economic behavior 213–17
    trust 211–13
  and historical context 3, 36–7
    communes 49
    conservatism 45–6, 49
    early history 37–42
    economic organization 47
    effects of totalism 43
    ideal of the state 42–3
    Mao legacy 47–9
    philosophical schools 38–41
    role of family 44–5
    scientific failure 46–7
    state's supporting apparatus 44
  and historical legacy 51–2
    control by the state 52–3
    hierarchy 55–7
    mistrust 53–5
    technological dependence 59–60
  and models for economic evolution 8–11
    Chinese capitalism 9–10
    failure of state-control 9
  and private-sector revolution 2
  and reputation of 87
  and revolutions in 1–2
  and the state:
    control by 52–3
    effects of totalism 43
    ideal of 42–3
    limited reach of 224–5
    Mao's legacy 48–9
    Party dominance 48
    patrimonial state 86–7
    role of 86–7, 91, 110
    supporting apparatus 44
  and United States 223, 232
  see also local corporates; private sector;
      regional ethnic Chinese, and
      business; state-owned enterprises

'China Circle' 77–9
China International Marine Containers
    (CIMC) 118–19
Citigroup 83
civil society:
    and absence of 52, 110, 132, 213
    and development of 4
clan capitalism 10, 104
    and local corporates 111–12, 116–18,
        119–20, 212
coevolution 229
collective sector:
    and clan capitalism 104
    and geographical variations 103
    and history of 104–7
        communes 104–5
        decline of 107
        economic performance 105–6
        Great Leap Forward 105
        impact of market forces 106
        privatization 106–7
        productivity 106
        rural reforms 105
    and performance of 105–6, 120
    and privatization 106–7, 118
    and transformation of 103
    see also local corporates
commerce, and development of 4
communes 49, 104–5
Communist revolution 1–2
comparative advantage 149–52
    and business systems 151
    and Germany 191–4
    and Japan 176–80
    and measurement of 151
    and Porter's model of 150–1
    and social structure 151
    and South Korea 204–7
    and traditional explanation of 149–50
    and United States 162–4
comparative studies, and value of 147–8
competitiveness:
    and China 166–7
    and foreign firms 226–8
    and United States 160–1, 166
complementarities 33
Confucianism 38–9, 41, 42
    and South Korea 198
Confucius 37, 170
conservatism, and Chinese society 45–6, 49
coordination 181
    and business systems 22–4
    and future of Chinese capitalism 221–2
    and Germany 189

and information technology 78
and Japan 176
and management 31–3
and network capitalism 139
and networks 30–1
and ownership 28–30
and United States 161
    see also management; networks;
        ownership
corporate governance:
    and changes in 75
    and Germany 187
    and Japan 174
    and South Korea 120
corruption, and increase in 104
CP Group 62
Credit Suisse 83
crony capitalism, and ethnic Chinese 69
Cultural Revolution 2, 36, 105
    and effects of 87
culture:
    and business systems 15–16
    and Germany 182–4
    and Japan 168–70
    and shaping of institutions 25–6
    and South Korea 196–8
    and state sector 85–7
    and United States 153–5

Daewoo 203, 206
DaimlerChrysler 191, 223
demographic change, and impact of 232–3
Deng Xiaoping 2, 44, 53, 63, 78, 108, 113,
        131, 208, 210, 212
development:
    and economic organization 14–15
    and trust 15
developmental states 74
    and planning bureaucracy 93–4
'dragon multinationals' 71–3, 75–6
    and hybrid business forms 70–1, 75–7

economic behavior:
    and culture 15–16
    and national variations 8
    and purpose of 213–17
economic miracles 1, 210
economic organization:
    and culture 15–16
    and interest groups 13
    and obstacles to firm growth 119
    and role of government 14
    and social development 14–15
    and trust 15

economic organization (*cont.*)
  see also local corporates; private sector;
    state-owned enterprises
education:
  and expansion of 135–6
  and Germany 184, 185–6
  and investment in 115, 135
  and Japan 170, 171–2
  and knowledge acquisition
    129–30
  and primary level 136
  and quality of 136
  and South Korea 198
  and United States 155
efficiency, and organizations 17
Elvin, Mark 47, 124
embeddedness, and economic
    development 7
emigration, and regional ethnic
    Chinese 63–4, 65–6
  destinations 66
entrepreneurship:
  and family 58
  and regional ethnic Chinese 76
ersatz capitalism, and decline of 73–4
ethnic Chinese, *see* regional ethnic Chinese,
    and business
Evergreen 62

families 44–5, 54, 57–8
  as capital source 133
  and Chinese capitalism 9–10
  and Confucianism 38–9
  and economic behavior 216
  and entrepreneurship 58
  and private sector 129
  and role of 126–8
  and socialization within 91
  and United States 154–5
famine, and Great Leap Forward 105
feudalism, and early China 37
Feuerwerker, Albert 82
filial piety 38
firms, and growth of 140
  obstacles to 119
foreign direct investment (FDI) 61, 71, 75,
    88
  and sources of 78–9, 110
foreign firms, and China:
  alliances 228
  competitiveness 226–8
  multinational enterprises 228–9
Foster, George 91
Fujian 77

Gereffi, Gary 136
Germany:
  and applicability of system to
    China 194–5
  and authority 184
  and banking system 185, 188
  and capital 185
  and communitarian values 183–4
  and comparative advantage 191–4
  and coordination 189
  and corporate governance 187
  and culture 182–4
  and dual business structure 190–1
  and economic miracle 1
  and education 184, 185–6
  and government 184–5
  and human capital 185–6
  and identity 184
  and individualism 184
  and management 187–8
  and networks 186, 187
  and ownership 186–7
  and professions 190
  and shareholder value 182–3, 186–7
  and small and medium-sized enterprises
    190–1
  and social capital 186
  and stakeholder value 182–3, 188–9
  and structural inertia 189
  and trade unions 185
  and training 186, 190, 194
  and trust 186
Gilboy, George 95
globalization, and impact of 70
government:
  and business systems 14, 23–4
  and dilemma facing 132
  and economic organization 19
  and Germany 184–5
  and Japan 170–1
  and limited reach of 224–5
  and private sector 131–2
    supportive of 142–3
  and South Korea 198, 202–3
  and United States 155–6
  see also state, the
Great Leap Forward 2, 105
Guangdong 77
guanxi networks 54, 90, 92, 116
  and private sector 129
Guthrie, Doug 9, 83, 93, 117

Haier 217
He Qinglian 116

Heilbroner, Robert 212
hierarchy:
    and effects of 55–7
    and Japan 168, 171
    and management 96–7, 141
    and South Korea 198
high-technology industry:
    and China 219, 220
    and United States 164
Hitachi 177, 179
Hoechst 193
honesty, and Japan 5–6
Hong Kong 61
    and 'China Circle' 77
    and Chinese immigrants 66
    and company ownership 63
    as developmental state 74–5
    and expansion into China 77
    and government 223
    and industrialization 77–8
    and investment in China 79, 110
    and openness of 68
Hongkong and Shanghai Banking
        Corporation (HSBC) 67, 68, 71–2
Huchet, Jean-Philippe 95
human capital:
    and economic life 22
    and economic organization 19
    and education 135–6
    and Germany 185–6
    and Japan 171–2
    and local corporates 115
    and private sector 134–7
        training 136
    and South Korea 199
    and state-owned enterprises 90
    and trade unions 136–7
    and United States 156–7
    see also education; training
Hutchison Whampoa 71–3
hybridization, and conglomerate
        enterprises 70–1, 75–7
Hynix 206
Hyundai 202, 203, 205, 206, 207

ideals 8
    and economic behavior 129–31
    and search for new 217
identity:
    and clan relationships 111–12
    and culture 22
    and Germany 184
    and Japan 169–70
    and private sector 130

and South Korea 197–8, 201
    and United States 155
Ikea 226
Imperial Chemical Industries 67
individualism:
    and Germany 184
    and United States 154
individuals, and influence of 210
Indonesia, and ethnic Chinese 68
information:
    and economic organization 18
    and trust 54–5, 92
inheritance, and ownership 28–9
innovation:
    and economic organization 19
    and future of Chinese capitalism 219–20
    and Japan 179
    and organizational 229
    and United States 159–60, 162–4
institutions:
    and business systems 18–21, 26–7
    and cultural shaping of 25–6
    and order 22
    and trust 55, 92, 138, 211, 221–2
        barriers to developing 212–13
    and weakness of infrastructure of 126
interest groups, and business systems 13
international politics, and China 232
Internet, and influence of 61

Japan:
    and applicability of system to China
        180–1
    and authority 170
    and capital 171–2
    and collective identity 169–70
    and comparative advantage 176–80
    and coordination 176
    and corporate governance 174
    and culture 168–70
        purpose of firms 174
    and economic development 5–6
    and economic miracle 1
    and education 170, 171–2
    and employee-centric stakeholder value
        174–5
    and government 170–1
    and hierarchy 170, 173
    and human capital 171–2
    and innovation 179
    and management 173
        delegation 175
        employer-employee interdependence
        175

Japan (*cont.*)
  and networks 172, 173, 176
  and ownership 172–3, 174–5
  and planning bureaucracy 93–4
  and shareholders 174
  and social capital 172
  and structural inertia 176
  and trade unions 172
  and training 175–6
Jardine Matheson 67, 68
Jenner, W F 43, 126
Jiang Zemin 113, 210

Kia Motors Corporation 204
Kim Dae-jung 199, 203
Kim Woo-chong 203
Komatsu 177
Korea, *see* South Korea
Korean War 67

labor market:
  and labor supply 135
  and low-cost labor 134
Laozi 40
law:
  and economic organization 18
  and legal systems 29
learning:
  and organizations 17–18
  and private sector 129–30
Legalists 38, 40–1
Lenovo 223
Lever Brothers 67
LG Electronics 206
Li, Peter 107, 116
Li Ka Shing 71–2, 72–3
limited liability 29
local authorities:
  and competition between 88–9, 109, 110
  and future of Chinese capitalism 225
  and local corporates 107, 116–17
  and revenues raised by 88–9
  and state-owned enterprises 96
local corporates:
  and authority 112–13
  as business system in transition 107
  and capital 113–14
    sources of 114
  and characteristics of 81–2
  and clan capitalism 111–12, 116–18,
    119–20, 212
  and development of 215
  and human capital 117
  and management 120–1

and origins of 103, 107
  and ownership 118–19
  and rationale:
    borrowing of technology 110–11
    clan relationships 111
    improvement of local society 109
    local initiative 110
    national progress 108
    state control 110
    wealth-seeking 109, 217
  and social capital 115–18
    clan capitalism 116–18
    guanxi networks 116
    network capitalism 116
  and success of 217
  and variety of 107
London Tin 67

Macau 79
machinery and equipment industry:
  and competitiveness of foreign firms 227
  and Germany 191–3
  and Japan 176, 177
Malaysia, and ethnic Chinese 66, 68
MAN 191, 193
management:
  and business systems 23, 31–3, 56–7
  and different styles of 141
  and Germany 187–8
  and hierarchy 97, 141
  and impact of vertical order 217
  and increasing demand for skills of 115,
    165
  and Japan 173, 175
  and local corporates 120–1
  and management-worker relations
    218–19
  and private sector 141–2
  and professionalization 165
  and South Korea 201, 203
  and state-owned enterprises 96–7
  and style of 120
  and United States 159
    professionalization of 159
Manchu dynasty 1
manufacturing:
  and future of Chinese capitalism 227–8
  and growth of 2, 78
  and private sector 144–5
Mao Zedong 1, 128, 210
  and legacy of 47–9
Matsushita 177, 179
Matthews, John 75
McKinsey 226

meaning:
 and business systems 15–16
 and order 25–6
Mencius 37, 38
Mitsubishi Electric 179
Mitsubishi Heavy Industries 177
modernization:
 and commerce 4
 and trust 3–4
Mohists 38, 40
Mozi 40
multinational enterprises (MNEs):
 and Chinese capitalism 10–11
 and 'dragon multinationals' 71–3, 75–6
  hybrid business forms 70–1, 75–7
 and future of Chinese capitalism 222–3,
  228–9

nationalism, and economic policy 68–9
nation-state, and business systems 7–8
Naughton, Barry 77, 124
network capitalism:
 and competences of 143–4
 and coordination 138
 and local corporates 116
 and private sector 137–8
 and trust 211–12
 see also clan capitalism; networks
networks:
 and business systems 23, 30–1
 and changes in regional 75
 and Germany 186, 187
 and guanxi networks 54, 90, 92, 116, 129
 and Japan 172, 173, 176
 and local corporates 119–20
 and private sector 137–8, 140–1
 and South Korea 200
 and state-owned enterprises 94–6
 and trust 211
 and United States 157–8
 see also clan capitalism; network
  capitalism
Nolan, Peter 83, 98, 100
North Korea 201

office, accounting and computing
 machinery, and South Korea 204,
 206
order:
 and business systems 26–7
 and culture 21–2
 and institutions 22
 and meaning 25–6
 and trust 211

Organization for Economic Cooperation
 and Development (OECD) 84
organizations:
 and business systems 17–18
 and change 18
 and efficiency 17
 and learning 17–18
'Overseas Chinese', see regional ethnic
  Chinese, and business
ownership:
 and authority 218
 and business systems 23, 28–30
 and coordination 30
 and Germany 186–7
 and Japan 172–3, 174–5
 and local corporates 118–19
 and private sector 139–40
 and South Korea 200, 203
 and state-owned enterprises 92–4
 and United States 157

Park Chung-hee 198, 201, 202, 224
patents 219
 and registration of 166, 219–20
 and United States 162, 164
paternalism 131, 134, 217
path dependence, and economic
  development 7, 33
patrimonial state 86–7
patriotism, and South Korea 201
Perry, Elizabeth 230
Philippines, and ethnic Chinese 66, 68
Porsche 191
Porter, Michael E 149, 150
private sector 9–10
 and acceptance of 143
 and authority 131
 and capital 133–4
 and changes in 142–3
 and characteristics of 82
 and government influence 131–2
  political dilemma 132
  supporting role 142–3
 and historical tradition of 123–4
  fragmentation 124
  influence of 124–5
  inhibitions to growth 124
  ownership 124
 and human capital 134–7
  education 135–6
  trade unions 136–7
  training 136
 and identity 130
 and limits on organizational scale 139–40

private sector (*cont.*)
  and management 141–2
  and manufacturing 144–5
  and network capitalism 137–8
    competences of 143–4
  and networks 137–8, 140–1
  and ownership 139–40
  and productivity 139
  and rationale 126–30
    core ideals 128–9
    familism 129
    family wealth 126–8, 216
    guanxi networks 130
    learning 129–30
    national pride 128
    secrecy 130
    status 129
  and rebirth of 105
  and relations with outside world 132–3
  and social capital 137–9
    network capitalism 137–8
    trust 137–9
  and status of business owners 130
  and strength of 144
  and success of 142, 215
  and weakness of institutional
    infrastructure 125
privatization:
  and collective sector 118
  and town and village enterprises 106–7
productive efficiency, and economic
    organization 19
productivity:
  and collective sector 106, 120
  and private sector 139
professions, and development of 211, 212
property rights:
  and reform of 134–5, 143
  and weakness of 110

Qian, Alan J 114
Qian, M 114
Qin Shi Huang 40–1

radio, television and communications
    industry:
  and Japan 177–9
  and South Korea 204, 206
regional autonomy 87–8
  and regional competition 88–9
regional ethnic Chinese, and business:
  and access to developed markets 67
  and business organizations 62
  and contribution to China's growth 110

  and demand for products 67
  and economic significance of 66
  and emigrants from China 63–4, 65–6
    destinations 66
  and entrepreneurship 76
  and formative periods 62–3
  and historical influences:
    co-opting political support 69–70
    dealing with uncertainty 69
    Japanese occupation 69
  and influence of 61–2
  in modern era 70–6
    decline of ersatz capitalism 73–4
    'dragon multinationals' 71–3, 75–6
    globalization's impact 70
    Hutchison Whampoa 71–3
    hybrid business forms 70–1, 75–7
    multinational corporations 76
    small and medium enterprises 71
  and nationalist economic policies 68–9
  and restructuring of colonial companies
    67–8
  as traders in Southern Ocean:
    bureaucratic capitalism 64–5
    colonial era 63–4
    as middle men 64
    nationalist period 65
    post-colonial era 65
    tradition of 63
Rho Moo-hyun 199
Robert Bosch 193
Russia 1

Samsung 201, 202, 203, 206
Sanyo 178
savings rate 133
science:
  and China 46–7
    technological dependence 59–60
    weakness in applying 166
  and United States 159–60
  see also innovation; patents
secrecy, and private sector 130
service industries, and United States 162,
    164
shareholder value:
  and Germany 182–3, 186–7
  and Japan 174
  and South Korea 196–7
  and United States 153, 158
Sharp 179
Shih, Stan 130
shipbuilding industry, and South Korea 204,
    206

Siemens 193
Sime Darby 67
Singapore 61
    and Chinese immigrants 66
    and civil society 110
    as developmental state 74
    and government 225
    and investment in China 110
    and openness of 68
    and planning bureaucracy 93–4
small and medium-sized enterprises (SMEs):
    and China 9–10, 71, 195
        family wealth 216
        network capitalism 210–11
    and Germany 190–1
social capital 211
    and economic life 22
    and Germany 186
    and institutional 115–16
    and Japan 172
    and local corporates 115–18
        clan capitalism 116–18
        guanxi networks 116
        network capitalism 116
    and private sector 138–40
        network capitalism 138–9
    and South Korea 200
    and state sector 90–2
    and United States 157
    see also trust
social mobility, and economic
        organization 19
society:
    and change 21
    and culture:
        authority 22
        identity 22
        order 21–2
        rationale 21
    and external influences 24
    and institutional requirements 18–21
    and institutions and order 22
Sony 177–9
South Korea 1
    and applicability of system to
        China 207–9, 223–5
    and authority 198, 201
    and banking system 199, 202
    and capital 199
    and comparative advantage 204–7
    and corporate governance 200
    and culture 196–8
    and education 199
    and family control of *chaebol* 200, 203

    and government 198, 202–3
    and hierarchy 198
    and human capital 199
    and identity 197–8, 201
    and management 201, 203
    and multinational enterprises 223
    and networks 200
    and ownership 200, 203
    and patriotism 201
    and planning bureaucracy 93–4
    and shareholder value 196–7
    and social capital 200
    and stakeholder value 196
    and trade unions 199, 203–4
    and trust 200, 224
special economic zones (SEZs) 8, 131–2
stakeholder value:
    and Germany 182–3, 188–9
    and Japan 174–5
    and South Korea 196
Starbucks 99
state, the:
    and business systems 23–4
    and China:
        conservatism 45–6
        control by 52–3
        effects of totalism 43
        ideal of 42–3
        limited reach of 224–5
        Mao legacy 48–9
        Party dominance 48
        patrimonial state 86–7
        role of 86–7, 91, 110
        supporting apparatus 44
    and the developmental state 74–5
    see also collective sector; government;
        state-owned enterprises
state intervention, and business systems
        14
State-owned Assets Supervision and
        Administration Commission
        (SASAC) 83–4
state-owned enterprises (SOEs) 10–11
    and allocation of capital 88–90
        competition for 90
        foreign banks 90
        inefficiency of 89–90
        regional autonomy 88–9
        stock markets 89
    and corporate culture 96–7
    and decline of state sector 81, 82–3, 101,
        214–15
    and disconnection from market
        disciplines 83

state-owned enterprises (SOEs) (*cont.*)
  and historical influences:
    Cultural Revolution 87
    regional autonomy 87–8
  and human capital 90
  and leadership of 86–7
  and local authorities 96
  and management weaknesses 96–7
  and national champions 84, 96, 98,
    222–3
  and networks, absence of 94–6
  and ownership structure 92–4
  and Party connections 95
  and political control 93
  and reform of state sector 83–4, 99–100
    obstacles to organizational change
      100–1
  and return on assets 93
  and role of the state 85–7
  and segments of 84
  and social capital 90–2
  and State-owned Assets Supervision and
    Administration Commission 83–4
  and strategic industries 82, 83, 84, 96
  and strategy:
    bureaucratic weakness 94
    politicization of 93
  and trust 90–2
  and value added by 84
  and weakness of 97–8
status:
  and business owners 130
  and wealth 129
stock markets 89
strategy, and clan conglomerates 10
Sun Yat-sen 1, 43, 221
Swire group 67, 68
Syngman Rhee 202, 224

Taiwan 62
  and 'China Circle' 77
  and China-Taiwan relations 132–3
  and Chinese immigrants 66
  as developmental state 74
  and government 225
  and industrialization 77–8
  and investment in China 79, 110
  and planning bureaucracy 93–4
Taoism 38, 39, 40
taxation 88–9
technology:
  and China 46–7
    technological dependence 59–60
  and United States 164

Thailand, and ethnic Chinese 66, 68
ThyssenKrupp 193
Toshiba 179
town and village enterprises (TVEs) 105,
    106–7
  see also collective sector; local corporates
Toyota 177
trade unions:
  and Germany 186
  and irrelevance of 136–7
  and Japan 172
  and South Korea 199, 203–4
  and United States 155–7
training:
  and China 136, 194
  and Germany 186, 190, 194
  and Japan 175–6
  see also education
trust 53–5, 90–2
  and barriers to 212–13
  and economic development 15
  and future of Chinese capitalism 211–13,
    221–2, 224, 231–2
  and Germany 186
  and *guanxi* networks 54, 90, 92, 116
  and information 54–5, 92
  and institutional trust 55, 92, 138, 211,
    221–2, 224, 229–30
  and Japan 5–6, 172
  and modernization 3–4
  and network capitalism 211–12
  and private sector 129, 137–9
  and social capital 22
  and South Korea 200
  and United States 157
  see also social capital

Unilever 67
United Nations Conference on Trade and
    Development (UNCTAD) 88
United States:
  and adaptability 162, 167
  and authority 155
  and basis of economic behavior 215
  and business system 33–4
  and capital 156–7, 161
  and China 223, 232
    applicability of capitalist system
      165–7
  and comparative advantage 162–4
  and competitiveness 160–1, 166
  and coordination 161
  and culture 153–5
  and economic miracle 1

and education 156
and family 154–5
and government 155–6
and human capital 156–7
and individualism 154
and innovation 159–60, 162–4
and knowledge creation 162–4
and management 158
  professionalization of 158
and networks 157–8
and organization 161
and ownership 157
and science, application of
  159–60
and service industries 162,
  164
and shareholder value 153,
  158
and social capital 157
and technology 164
and trade unions 156–7

venture capital:
  and China 166
  and Japan 179
  and South Korea 207
  and United States 159, 160
Vietnam War 67
Volkswagen 191

Wadhwa, Vivek 136
Wal-Mart 225
Wayland, Rebecca E 149
welfare dependence 90
Whitley, Richard 92
World Trade Organization (WTO) 2

Yeung, Henry 73, 76
Yiwu 110

Zhao Ziyang 214
Zheng He 3, 45
Zhu Rongji 26, 81, 113, 210